"There is no shortage of books on bullying; finding one that makes a novel contribution is rare. Dr. Rigby's new book is such a contribution. It provides a unique approach – *multiperspectivity* – that brings together in one volume various lenses through which to examine bullying. The subjectivity of human experience is acknowledged, and *multiperspectivity* allows the reader to take the multiple interpretations of experience into account. Sprinkled with literary, philosophical, and historical allusions, Rigby provides a thoughtful and thorough narrative that exposes the limited ways in which each audience or position has considered the issue. He describes in detail the varied views of researchers, teachers, students, parents, and authorities in a highly readable style, drawing upon insights from psychology, sociology, philosophy, and history. I pride myself on be well-informed about bullying, but I must say I definitely learned a great deal from this fascinating and thought-provoking book. Taking these multiple perspectives into consideration promotes thinking more inclusively about how to tackle the problem."

Sheri Bauman, Professor of Counseling, University of Arizona, USA.

"This timely book from a pioneer of research into bullying takes account of different perspectives on bullying, and, crucially, enables the voice of the child to be heard. As Ken Rigby argues, one pair of eyes is not enough. More is needed to understand and deal with bullying and harassment in schools."

Helen Cowie, Emeritus Professor, University of Surrey, UK.

"Ken Rigby's latest book on school bullying highlights the differing perspectives on this important topic, from teachers, parents and pupils, as well as researchers. He brings a wealth of experience to his endeavour, and lightens the text with many illustrations and quotations. This is an immensely readable book, full of useful and thought-provoking observations, including on historical and cultural aspects. It will be a valuable contribution to the growing literature available to those concerned with reducing the prevalence of bullying, and making schools a happier place to work and study in."

Peter K. Smith, Emeritus Professor of Psychology, Goldsmiths University of London, UK.

"This book offers a most interesting perspective showing that bullying is both complex and value loaded, and consequently there will be different perspectives on both dynamics, prevention, and intervention. And moreover, that such different perspectives will be – to some degree – dependent on historical time, macro culture and position related to bullying; researchers, teachers, students, parents and so on. It provides the reader with a very broad overview of this complexity, based on research and other literature, which I liked very much."

Erling Roland, Professor of Educational Psychology University of Stavangar, Norway.

Multiperspectivity on School Bullying

Multiperspectivity on School Bullying is unique in providing a comprehensive account of school bullying from the perspectives of schools, teachers, parents, students and institutional authorities. It identifies diverse viewpoints and discusses their implications for addressing bullying and thereby improving the mental health and well-being of children.

Drawing on findings from studies conducted in a wide range of countries, including those undertaken by the author in his own country, Australia, this book examines experiences of bullying and debates around how bullying can be managed and discouraged. It outlines what is needed before an agreed understanding of the problem can be reached and more effective anti-bullying programs devised and implemented. The book examines both historical and cultural factors relating to bullying and violence; major theoretical and research perspectives on bullying; views of different social groups affected by bullying; and how different institutional authorities view school bullying. It highlights the need for a multiperspectivity approach to bullying, taking into account and evaluating a variety of viewpoints that are currently held.

This book will be of great interest to academics, researchers and students in the fields of bullying, wellbeing and mental health in schools. It will also be valuable reading for educational leaders around the globe.

Ken Rigby, OAM, is an Adjunct Professor at the University of South Australia.

The Mental Health and Well-being of Children and Adolescents

Series Editor: Garry Hornby (University of Plymouth)

Mental health disorders in children and young people are increasing, with one in four under-16s experiencing mental health difficulties that will disrupt relationships, education and work. In addition to this, one in ten under-16s suffers from a diagnosed disorder. Access to up-to-date research and appropriate interventions minimises the mental health challenges these children and adolescents face and reduces their potentially lifelong impact.

It has been internationally recognised that the scale of mental health research is low in relation to the burden of the disorder. This research-focused series will consist of titles that consider key issues affecting young people's mental health and well-being, exploring preventative measures, promoting positive behaviour, and sharing research to develop effective and efficient treatment.

Aimed primarily at researchers and postgraduate students, this series will also be of interest to practitioners in the mental health field, such as psychologists, and some in the field of education, such as counsellors, who would like to implement research-based findings in their clinical practice.

Please visit www.routledge.com/The-Mental-Health-and-Well-being-of-Children-and-Adolescents/book-series/MHWCA.

Books in the series include:

School Bullying and Mental Health
Risks, Intervention and Prevention
Helen Cowie and Carrie-Anne Myers

Mental Health and Academic Learning in Schools
Approaches for Facilitating the Wellbeing of Children and Young People.
Andrea Reupert

Multiperspectivity on School Bullying

One Pair of Eyes is Not Enough

Ken Rigby

Routledge
Taylor & Francis Group
LONDON AND NEW YORK

First published 2022
by Routledge
2 Park Square, Milton Park, Abingdon, Oxon OX14 4RN

and by Routledge
605 Third Avenue, New York, NY 10158

Routledge is an imprint of the Taylor & Francis Group, an informa business

British Library Cataloguing-in-Publication Data
A catalogue record for this book is available from the British Library

Library of Congress Cataloging-in-Publication Data
A catalog record has been requested for this book

ISBN: 978-1-138-21075-2 (hbk)
ISBN: 978-1-032-08106-9 (pbk)
ISBN: 978-1-315-45445-0 (ebk)

DOI: 10.4324/9781315454450

Typeset in Bembo
by MPS Limited, Dehradun

To My grandson, Lachlan Blake, for his continued interest and encouragement and to Garry Hornby for his kind and practical support in the writing of this book.

Contents

Figures

Tables

Series editor's introduction

This important and thought-provoking book is based on Ken Rigby's thirty years of involvement with research on bullying in schools. It draws on many research projects, a wide range of historical, cultural and literary sources, as well as the author's own experiences, to provide a comprehensive context for considering bullying, its prevention and management. It makes a unique contribution to the understanding of bullying and its impact on the mental health of children and young people.

It is now 20 years since the need for an increased focus on children's mental health in schools was addressed by publication of a landmark book providing information for teachers on a wide range of children's mental health concerns, including bullying (Atkinson & Hornby, 2002). In response to this issue, a book series was later created, dedicated to addressing the mental health and well-being of children and young people. The focus of books in this series is on presenting and evaluating the latest theory and research as well as disseminating innovative interventions and programs. The first book in the series focused on the impact of bullying in schools on children's mental health (Cowie & Myers, 2018), the second examined various approaches for promoting the mental health of children in schools and its impact on academic learning (Reupert, 2020), and the third focused on the use of mindfulness meditation for facilitating the wellbeing of children (Singh & Singh-Joy, 2021). This book, which provides an in-depth analysis of bullying in schools, is the fourth in that series.

The importance of this topic is brought home to most people by their own experiences at school. Reflecting on my own experiences of the bullying which went on at the grammar school I attended in England in the 1960s, I recalled a particular example of bullying. Many years after leaving the school, I found out that a boy in my class, who came across as effeminate and was regularly teased for being gay, later told another ex-classmate that he had been very hurt by this treatment, because he was not gay. I learned that, several years later, he had committed suicide. The lesson for me is that, although the impact of bullying may not be immediately obvious, the long-term consequences can still be devastating, so the responsibility for bystanders to intervene constructively and for teachers to be aware of and deal effectively with incidents of bullying, and to promote positive relationships between their students, was made clear to me.

During my time as a teacher in the 1970s, I was never sure what to do when cases of bullying came to light. Identifying the bullies and disciplining them seemed the only option, so that's what I did. Later, in my first job as a university lecturer, a student who did a brief counselling course with me, Sue Young, went on to use a counselling approach in her job as the anti-bullying coordinator for the Local Education Authority. Through her work with schools, she developed an intervention which she called the 'support group approach to bullying in schools.' This was evaluated and found to be very effective in the primary schools where she had implemented it (Young, 1998). Finding out about this sparked my interest in bullying, so as I taught teacher education students in the following years I always included a session on dealing with bullying, in which I presented several possible interventions that teachers could use. This led me to develop what I have called an ecological model of school interventions for preventing and managing bullying (Hornby, 2016). I was presenting this model for the first time internationally at a conference on bullying held in Australia at Surfers Paradise when I had the pleasure of meeting Ken Rigby. During our conversation, he introduced me to the Shared Concern approach to bullying and impressed me with his extensive knowledge of the topic. Since then I have read many of his books on bullying, so I was delighted when he agreed to write a new book on bullying to be part of the series on promoting the mental health and wellbeing of children and young people.

Rigby's book begins by citing reviews of research that found that interventions to prevent bullying are typically at best around 20% effective. Now, who would take a vaccine, or enrol their child in a reading program, that was only 20% effective? This low level of effectiveness provides part of the rationale for suggesting that there is no simple explanation for bullying or any silver bullet to deal with it.

Understanding school bullying is typically partial and fails to take into account the wide range of perspectives that are held by different researchers, teachers, students, parents and, often, crucially, what authorities say about bullying. Rigby argues that we need to listen to and understand what is being said by the different sources before effective action can be undertaken. That is, we need to appreciate alternative viewpoints and why they are held. This he refers to as 'multiperspectivity.' Only then are we likely to reach necessary agreement on what constructive methods are to be applied. At a time when unpopular or even alternative views on social issues and problems such as bullying are being ruthlessly cancelled, Rigby believes that this is a matter of the utmost importance.

This book is the first one of its kind to describe and evaluate a comprehensive range of perceptions of bullying and discuss what can be done about it, both historically and at the present time.

Garry Hornby (University of Plymouth)

References

Atkinson, M. & Hornby, G. (2002). *Mental Health Handbook for Schools*. London: Routledge-Falmer.

Cowie, H. & Myers, C.-A. (Eds.) (2018). *School Bullying and Mental Health: Risks, Intervention and Prevention*. London: Routledge.

Hornby, G. (2016). Bullying: An ecological approach to intervention in schools. *Preventing School Failure*, 60(3), 222–230.

Reupert, A. (2020). *Mental Health and Academic Learning in Schools: Approaches for Facilitating the Wellbeing of Children and Young People*. London: Routledge.

Singh, N.N., & Singh Joy, S.D. (2021). *Mindfulness-Based Interventions with Children and Adolescents: Research and Practice*. Abingdon, England: Routledge.

Young, S. (1998). The support group approach to bullying in schools. *Educational Psychology in Practice*, 14(1), 32–39.

Acknowledgements

The author wishes to thank the authors and publishers who have given permission to reproduce the following:

1. Mr Simon Kneebone for the drawings in Figure 2.1 and Figure 5.1
2. *Journal of Adolescent Health* for the inclusion of Figure 5.3

Chapter 1

Introduction

In the second half of the 20th century, there was a remarkable rise of interest in bullying; first bullying in schools, then in other places. Open today's newspaper and the chances are high that there will be news of bullying – among schoolchildren or among men and women in the workforce, or in the home, perhaps among politicians. It has become common to describe bullying as an epidemic, desperately needing a solution.

Research into bullying since 1990 has repeatedly confirmed that the prevalence of bullying in schools is unacceptably high. Drawing on all available survey results across 71 countries it has been estimated that approximately 32% of school children between the ages of 9 and 15 years were bullied for one or more days during the previous month (UNESCO, 2019). Further, research has shown that bullied children tend to experience emotional distress and in some cases mental health consequences that can last for a lifetime (Arseneault, 2018; Rigby, 2003).

Numerous anti-bullying policies and programs have been devised and applied in schools. Ttofi and Farrington (2011) identified 622 reports concerned with bullying prevention. Of these 44 provided data from which the effectiveness of program implementation could be calculated and on average a reduction in prevalence of being bullied between 17% and 20% was found. From these and other studies it can be inferred that well-conducted interventions in schools can have some positive effect, but the reported reductions in prevalence have been modest in size and some reported interventions had no positive effect. In some countries there have been reports of reductions in bullying prevalence over time (see Rigby & Smith, 2011); but in general, the reductions, though statistically significant, have been small. The problem of what to do to make substantial and enduring changes in bullying in schools remains much as it has been for generations and the grievous harm suffered by many victimised students at school continues.

Why is it then that despite the sustained attention to the problem of bullying in schools over the last 20 years or so, and the application of mandated anti-bullying policies and intervention strategies, we have made so little impact in promoting more positive interpersonal behaviour among students? The first

DOI: 10.4324/9781315454450-1

and most obvious reason is that bullying behaviour is deeply embedded in human nature and extremely resistant to change. This accords with the observation that aggressive and violent behaviour has for many centuries been a prominent feature of how humans have treated one another. Evolutionary psychologists insist that this tendency is inevitably present in varying degrees in everybody. It may be pointed out that serious violent behaviour between people in most countries has become less common with the increasing practice and acceptance of the rule of law (see Pinker, 2011). But legal remedies for non-criminal – and non-criminisable – forms of bullying, which make up the vast majority of acts of bullying in schools, are severely limited. Not surprisingly, many educationalists have turned for an answer to educational and non-confrontative methods of intervention.

A second reason for the relative failure of schools to address bullying effectively lies in the complexity of the problem and the difficulties that arise in seeking to appraise and take into account the range of possible explanations for acts of bullying and the suggestions and proposals on what to do. There is an understandable tendency for educators to look for a simple answer. Too often this results in the rejection and sometimes the denigration of perspectives that challenge the way one prefers to look at the problem. This results in not being exposed to points of view that others may hold and a reliance on people who support one's own point of view, such as colleagues or employers. The outcome is that one is only partially informed; one's prejudices are reinforced. Moreover, the opportunity to work together with stakeholders who see things differently is lost or jeopardised. The development of a truly agreed whole school approach and its implementation becomes uncertain or even impossible.

The thesis of this book is in fact simple. We must listen far more to what other people are saying and why they are saying it. The application of this proposition is not simple. We need to learn from history. We need to learn from research, also recognising that researchers do not, as a rule, speak as one; indeed, frequently disputing and contradicting one another. We need to identify differences within groups; for example, between children who are bullied at school and those who are not; and between parents of children who are bullied at school and parents for whom this is not the case.

What I am advocating is the adoption of what has been called multi-perspectivity. This may be roughly defined as the practice of seeing things as other persons or some groups see them. It will be suggested that in the last analysis this is impossible because our perceptions of other people's perceptions are always in a sense our own perceptions. Very well then. It is an ideal to which we can strive: in effect, a deliberate attempt to minimise subjectivity, to put ourselves (and our cherished disciplines) aside and attend non-judgementally to what others say.

This entails a much more broadminded approach to understanding bullying than has often been the case in the past. As Yoneyama (2015) has argued, the study of bullying has in recent years moved on from an extreme reliance on one source of information, for example, on inference from quantitative analyses generated mainly by social psychologists, important though this may be, especially in the testing of hypotheses. Horizons need to expand to accommodate insights from a range of disciplines, including theoretical sociology, cross-cultural studies, philosophy and history. This book provides a step in that direction.

In essence, I am asking the reader to accept the reality of the perceptions of others – as perceptions. Emphatically, it does not mean that they are necessarily right in the views they hold. Commonsense and moral judgement do not go out of the widow. What is claimed is that in engaging in this activity one may become aware of facts and viewpoints of which one would not otherwise have been aware; be led into considering a perspective one would not otherwise have sought to understand; and, often most importantly, enter into a relationship in which unforced cooperation is possible. Only then, I suggest, can we approach an optimum situation in which agreed and effective anti-bullying plans can be formulated and put into action.

This book is organised into two parts. The first is concerned with providing a background to what is understood by multiperspectivity, how bullying is commonly defined and how it may be understood, taking an historical and cultural perspective.

The second part examines the way bullying is viewed by people according to particular groupings. This includes first the researchers and scholars who have contributed through studies of bullying in schools. In addition, there are those who are closely connected with the process of acting and responding to what goes on in schools as far as bullying is concerned. These include teachers in schools as well as students and parents of children who are attending school. I have also included those who may be called authorities, those who influence how schools respond to bullying, either as institutional or other kinds of authorities. The last chapter consists of personal reflections.

The reader will observe that the content of much of this book is based on research undertaken, mostly in Australia, over the last thirty years, and also on personal observations as a schoolboy, ex-school teacher in England and Australia, and as a university researcher in the field of bullying. My own perspective is limited by these experiences, but in addition, it is limited by the selectivity of what I have chosen to examine and comment upon, not to mention the personal biases to which I am prone. I constantly remind myself that in this book I am trying to tell you how I think other people have viewed bullying and are now viewing bullying, in the hope that such awareness will contribute to a more comprehensive understanding and a greater determination to try to see and appraise the other person's point of view in order to work together.

In substance, the purpose of this book may be summed up in words attributed to Pablo Picasso: 'There is only one way to see things, until someone shows us how to look at them with different eyes.'

Part I

Multiperspectivity, bullying and history

Chapter 2

Multiperspectivity

> There is *only* a perspective seeing, *only* a perspective 'knowing'; the *more* affects we allow to speak about a thing, the *more* eyes, various eyes, we are able to use for the same thing, the more complete will be our 'concept' of the thing, our 'objectivity' Nietzsche (1887).

One year when I was in England, I went to see a cup tie between two fiercely competing soccer teams. By chance, I found myself in an enclosure reserved for the fans of the visiting team. Before long I was amazed at the observations that were being made around me. The game was, as expected, a rather brutal affair, with numerous stoppages for fouls and injuries committed or caused entirely (so it was claimed) by the members of the home team. Worse still, the referee was (so I was continually informed) in league with them, awarding numerous free kicks to the wrong team and stupidly admonishing members of the visiting team for serious fouls that they had not committed. It was an occasion on which I kept my opinions to myself.

Some years later, I discovered that two American social psychologists Hastorf and Cantril (1954) had documented a similar experience. Following a particularly heated football match between Dartmouth and Princeton in 1951, the researchers arranged for student supporters of the two teams to view a movie recording of the game and answer a questionnaire about what they saw happening. In particular, they were asked to say which side started the rough play. Among the Princetown supporters, 86% reported that the Dartmouth side started it. Only a minority of Dartmouth supporters saw it that way. The researchers concluded that 'it seems the "game" was actually many different games and that each version of the events that transpired was just as "real" to a particular person as other versions were to other people. In brief, the data here indicate that there is no such "thing" as a "game existing out there" in its own right which people merely "observe." The game "exists" for a person and is experienced by him (sic) only insofar as certain happenings have significances in term of his purposes' (Hastorf & Cantrill, 1954, p. 129).

DOI: 10.4324/9781315454450-2

Really, was there no game? Here I think subjectivism is pushed beyond its reasonable limit. But clearly, something had happened to the perceivers in order to account for the strikingly different perceptions. I reflected on whether I would have become aware of entirely different judgements if I had been standing in a different place, say in the enclosure for fans of the home team. How things may be perceived if you are standing in different places is cleverly portrayed below. Things can look different depending on where you are standing as in Figure 2.1.

I have called the gathering and interpreting of different perspectives multiperspectivity. We can never have ultimate knowledge of a 'thing in itself (Ding an sich)' as the philosopher Kant (1783) was at pains to point out. We can never know 'the truth, the whole truth and nothing but the truth.' Yet we can gain some understanding of a phenomenon by inquiring into how a thing is perceived. In other words, we can reduce, if not eliminate, the subjectivity of our perceptions and the related judgements we make.

For the most part, the term 'multiperspectivity' has been used in studies of historical events drawing upon multiple sources of information rather than relying upon a single account which may be at variance with others and therefore open to question and subject to bias. Multiperspectivity may also refer to a literary or dramatic device employed to deepen one's understanding of characters and events in a novel or play. In this book, multiperspectivity refers to the examination of multiple perceptions of a particular subject, namely bullying behaviour. There is nothing mysterious about it. We may do it – or fail to do it – every time somebody expresses a point of view on the subject. It does not

Figure 2.1 Different perceptions of the same things.

imply that we agree with the point of view being expressed. If we are wise-we listen carefully and seek to understand and appreciate it.

Psychologically, a perspective may be conceived as a distinctive way of regarding and considering things. It is a point of view held by a person or by a group. As is the case of a social attitude, a perspective is relatively enduring and tends to be resistant to change. It implies an interpretation, a belief or judgement. It is different from a fleeting impression or a reaction based upon a transitory mood. A person may be clearly aware of the perspective they are taking and able to articulate what it is. Alternatively, the perspective holder may not be aware or fully aware of the view being taken. There may be unconscious bias or prejudice, in which case the nature of the perspective may be inferred from behaviour rather than from overt self-disclosure. Beliefs underlying a perspective may be internalized and relate to strongly held values and well-considered evidence; otherwise, a perspective may be relatively shallow and derive from conformity to the largely unconsidered views of others.

In seeking to understand bullying and in addressing situations in which bullying occurs we must take into account the diverse points of view. By pooling information from such sources, a more comprehensive and more useful understanding can emerge. How knowledge of perceptions from different sources can contribute to a more comprehensive understanding of a phenomenon is suggested by the well-known story of the six blind boys and the elephant recorded in the ancient Jain literature (Figure 2.2).

One version of this story is as follows:

Figure 2.2 Six blind boys and the elephant.

> A group of blind boys heard that a strange animal, called an elephant, had been brought to the town, but none of them were aware of its shape and form. Out of curiosity, they said: 'We must inspect and know it by touch, of which we are capable.' So, they sought it out, and when they found it they groped about it. In the case of the first person, whose hand landed on the trunk, said 'This being is like a thick snake.' For another one whose hand reached its ear, it seemed like a kind of fan. As for another person, whose hand was upon its leg, said, the elephant is a pillar like a tree-trunk. The blind boy who placed his hand upon its side said, 'elephant is a wall.' Another who felt its tail, described it as a rope. The last felt its tusk, stating the elephant is that which is hard, smooth and like a spear.

In the happier version of the story, they listen to each other in good faith and work out together what this elephant-thing is really like. It has all the attributes that were reported. Each boy was telling the truth as he saw it. By putting the diverse impressions together they reach an acceptable view on the nature of an elephant.

The story however has an alternative ending. The sharing of the perceptions leads to disagreements. Each man concludes that the others are not telling the truth. They discover irreconcilable differences – and they come to blows!

Clearly, it is not enough to understand how people see a thing, whether it is a material object or a situation. Knowing what constitutes the diverse perceptions is often a necessary step but not a sufficient one. But equally clearly, we must take the first step, as ably as we can, before optimum knowledge can be applied.

As the story of the blind boys and the elephant suggests, a multi-perspective approach to understanding the nature of phenomena can result in the identification of aspects of a problem that would otherwise be hidden. The sharing of individual perspectives can result in a better understanding of a perplexing and complex issue – if stakeholders can be brought to appreciate the different perceptions that come to light!

Bullying and multiperspectivity

There are few if any areas in which opinions about a mode of behaviour are more diverse and conflicting, or more likely to generate heated argument, than in the study of bullying. Differences of opinion or viewpoint may be found among individuals and between groups. They relate to many aspects of bullying, for example,

- What constitutes bullying?
- How prevalent is it?

- How do you explain it?
- Who are the ones being targeted?
- Why do people bully?
- Is bullying wrong?
- Is it getting worse?
- What is to be done about it?

Gather a group of people together – academic researchers, schoolchildren, teachers, parents, researchers, media spokespeople, education department representatives, politicians – and (if they dare) they will express a range of different opinions, often dogmatically. The practical problem is how to gain a reliable picture of what they think; that is, what perspectives they actually hold. In some cases, as with researchers, there are copious accounts available, mainly through their publications. In other cases, we have to observe what they say and what can be inferred from what they do. It then becomes a task of helping people, especially those concerned with the social education of schoolchildren to understand where people and coming from and the reasons they have for taking the views they hold.

The acceptance of a multiperspectivity approach to bullying requires at least initially a high degree of tolerance. It is natural to want to close down the expression of opinions with which one disagrees, especially if their expression is thought likely to result in significant harm. The hard question is to decide when (if ever) tolerance becomes intolerable. Can one stand by and take no action when harm can be prevented? Multiperspectivity does not provide the ultimate answer. According to Goethe (1833/1999), tolerance should really only be a passing attitude: it should lead to appreciation. Appreciation is necessary if we are to gain the knowledge and understanding of where people stand and why they think as they do. Only then can we be in a position to address bullying in a reasonable manner and gain the cooperation that is needed. We are still a long way from getting thus far. Multiperspectivity is where we start.

Main points

1. Events as understood by one person or a group of persons can be biased as a consequence of the perspective or position from which they are viewed, both literally and figuratively.
2. Multiperspectivity describes a process by which multiple perspectives can be appreciated and evaluated.
3. Its application can have the effect of minimising subjectivity and providing knowledge and understanding that can be applied in addressing questions in which cooperation is needed.

4. Its value in the area of school bullying is paramount, given the large number of issues on which there are diverse points of view that need resolution.
5. Multiperspectivity should be regarded as a necessary starting point in addressing school bullying.

Chapter 3

Defining bullying

Given the diversity of opinion about bullying in recent years considerable effort has been devoted to providing a standard definition. In part, the motivation was to provide a means by which relevant research could be promoted, replications reported, and findings if possible confirmed. A standard definition was also seen as needed for the benefit of schools and workplaces. Only in this way, it was argued, could a collective understanding of bullying be ensured and appropriate steps taken to counter it.

The most prominent and most influential of the definers of bullying was a Swedish psychologist and researcher, the late, Dan Olweus.

He defined bullying as follows:

> A student is being bullied or victimized when he or she is exposed repeatedly and over time to negative actions on the part of one or more other students.

In this formulation, Olweus (1993) does not tell us what he means by negative actions. Later he was to expand:

We say a student is being bullied when another student or a group of students

- say mean and unpleasant things to make fun of him or her or call him or her mean and hurtful names
- completely ignore or exclude him or her from their group of friends or leave him or her out of things on purpose
- hit, kick push and shove around, or threaten him or her
- tell lies or false rumors about him or her or send mean notes and try to make other students dislike him or her

Olweus (1999, p. 31)

This way of seeing bullying caught on and was to be used in an ever-increasing number of studies of the phenomenon of school bullying. Multi-item scales were devised and shown to be reliable in the sense of being internally

DOI: 10.4324/9781315454450-3

consistent. Many schools were advised or even required to define bullying along similar lines.

Three features are generally seen as crucial.

> Bullying is intentional and deliberate
>
> It occurs in a situation in which there is an imbalance of power
>
> It is repeated over time

Not all researchers have accepted this formulation. For example, a report from the 2020 International Conference on School Bullying (United Nations Educational, Scientific and Cultural Organization, 2020) suggests that not all bullying is 'intentional.' This may lead one to conclude that bullying may be inferred from the feelings of the 'victim' or of witnesses, if any.

The definition of bullying provided by this international body is as follows:

> Bullying and cyberbullying involve power imbalance and occurs within a given network of school and community relationships, and is enabled or inhibited by the social and institutional context of schools and the education system.

This formulation reflects a growing awareness that social and environmental factors are related to bullying behaviour and that an extensive network of school and community relationships is involved. This is well established through much-published research (examined later). However, one may question whether it helps to smuggle into the definition an explanation of the phenomenon. One could for instance argue that a definition of 'stealing' as taking things from others without their permission is inadequate, because it doesn't allude to a network of relationships, such as one with a mentor like Fagin or a belief held by Proudhon and his revolutionary friends in the 1840s. that in a capitalistic society property is theft – so why not steal?

One intention of researchers behind the Olweus definition formulation was to distinguish between bullying and another form of aggression: fighting or quarrelling. In the former, an imbalance of power was assumed; in the latter, equality of power was assumed. Unfortunately, it was often a priori impossible to recognize an imbalance. One may be driven to infer the nature of the imbalance from the fact that the winner won

The difficulty inherent in seeing bullying as distinct from fighting is that these two theoretically distinct forms of bullying frequently occur together. Well known to the devotees and afficionados of boxing is the famous encounter in 1910 between Jack Johnson, the reigning black US champion, and the heavyweight contender, the great white hope, James J Jeffries, who had declared he was going into this fight 'for the sole purpose of proving that a white man is better than a Negro.' The fight was caught and well-preserved on film and shows Johnson continually overpowering and taunting Jeffries over 15 rounds of one-sided boxing, able at any time – so it was said – to 'put him away' by way of knockout. It was evidently more satisfying to insult and humiliate his adversary and demonstrate his superiority. So Jeffries was joyfully bullied, until quite unexpectedly the negro champion was knocked over, whereupon Johnson clinically knocked Jeffries out – and race rioting began.

Is this example of the relationship between fighting and bullying unrepresentative of what can and does happen in the schoolyard? I don't think so. The victim quite commonly fights back – or tries to – often pathetically, which suits the more sadistic kind of bully. Of course in extreme circumstances, it strikes the victim that discretion is the better part of valour – and he or she meekly submits. This may apply when the bullying is verbal as well as when it is physical. To be repeatedly crushed by a barrage of verbal abuse is not an uncommon experience, though not uncommonly the victim may struggle to give it back. It is the entirely supine victim who is exceptional.

Further, the notion that there is invariably a discernible imbalance of power when bullying occurs is hard to accept. For generations, Jewish and Christian believers have enjoyed the Biblical story of David (little David, the shepherd boy and king to be) and his encounter with the mighty Philistine, Goliath. No one was taking bets. The outcome of course was entirely unexpected, except, one might surmise, to the Lord; a stone from David's sling (luckily?) caught Goliath on the temple. But was it really unexpected? Perhaps not. According to an examination of the evidence regarding the supposed imbalance, Gladwell (2013) has argued that it may well have been that the lumbering giant was no match for the agile boy and may well have been intellectually disabled. He surmises further that given his grossly abnormal height Goliath probably suffered from acromegaly, a condition that is known to restrict one's vision. Recently there have been demonstrations that stones can be slung with devastating accuracy from the kind of sling that David was practised in using. What invariably constitutes an enduring balance of power is hard to imagine. The theory that wars can be avoided if a 'balance of power' between nations can be sustained has been invalidated time and time again – and also between kids in the playground (Figure 3.1).

A further concern was that the stipulation that bullying could not occur on one occasion, it had to repeat. Some critics objected. Being subjected to abusive behaviour on one occasion would normally count as being bullied. Telling a child that he or she should come back if it has recurred may under some circumstances be insufferable.

For some teachers and parents, it was the underlying motive of the bully that got their attention. It was enough that there was a reprehensible intent. Hence the popularity of a definition proposed by the Welsh educators, Delwyn Tattum and Eva Tattum (1992, p. 147). According to them:

Figure 3.1 Goliath and David.

> Bullying is a wilful conscious desire to hurt another person and put that him/her under stress.

Many schools in the United Kingdom adopted this definition and incorporated it in their anti-bullying policy. The Department of Education in Scotland promoted it in their schools. Again critics spoke up. Was it really bullying if someone had the desire to hurt but took no action, perhaps thinking better of it? What if the possible victim was unharmed? Behaviourists were particularly hostile to this formulation and took exception to what they saw as an unnecessary, invisible and unmeasurable construct such as nebulous desire. Yet if we are concerned with how some people are inclined to perceive bullying or report on bullying, this view cannot be dismissed.

If I may add a personal observation, I have on a number of occasions conducted a sort of experiment in workshops I have provided for teachers. In discussing forms of bullying, I present a slide with an array of pictures depicting what most people readily recognize as bullying. I ask them to look closely at each one and say what they have in common. The answer I get is that somebody is wanting to hurt somebody! I do not think that this is a completely adequate way of defining bullying, but many people do (see Rigby, 2012a). There are limitations to this view. It has been pointed out that not all bullying is motivated by the desire to hurt. Not all bullying is considered malign. Some, it is suggested, is simply a means of getting what one wants, such as dominant status or higher approval from others, without necessarily hurting anyone.

Around the same time as the Tattums were insisting upon 'desire to hurt' as a basic element in bullying, a group of researchers in Sheffield, England, led by Professor Peter Smith formulated another influential definition.

> Bullying is the systematic abuse of power Smith and Sharp (1994, p. 2).

Admirably succinct, this definition is broad-ranging and makes explicit what many see as basic in thinking about bullying. It is first of all wrongful behaviour. Often in the drive to examine social questions in a value-free way we miss the obvious; at least what most people see as obvious, the immoral or unethical core of bullying. But this definition of Smith and Sharp does more than that. It draws our attention to what is seen as the legitimate role in the exercise of power – that which is not an abuse. It leads us into deep ethical water

How we may decide on whether an action is ethically justified became a source of much controversy in the last century following the publication of 'Situation Ethics: The New Morality' by Joseph Fletcher (1966). In it, he argued that there are no absolute rules or principles that can determine whether an action is unethical. What is right depends on the situation. We must take into account the actual circumstances, what is practical and what is pragmatically justified. Moral decision-making, he asserted, is contextual and dependent on circumstances. Here is an example of what may apply in appraising a possible bullying incident. A woman is seen repeatedly admonishing a child, using threatening and violent language. She is physically restraining the child who is crying. Big imbalance of power + intentional aggression + repetition (looks systematic) + evident hurtfulness. Taking a longer look at this, we may notice that the child is recklessly running into a busy road at great risk of serious injury. Verdict: not bullying.

'Situation ethics' caused a storm because it seemed to suggest that there are no rules, only commonsense conjecture that can be changed – whenever it suits! Fletcher's answer, as behoves a theologian (later he said he was an atheist) was to grant that there was one absolute. Love, he declared is the only absolute (it is intrinsically good). His critics were not readily convinced that such an 'absolute' was capable of application. Nevertheless, his scepticism regarding the rules we seek to apply and the definitions we propose are relevant to how bullying is often seen today.

Regardless of the difficulty of deciding what may or may not constitute an abuse of power, the way bullying is officially defined in Australian schools draws on the proposal made by Smith and Sharp, at the same time recognizing or acknowledging the general context in which bullying takes place, namely in the area interpersonal relations. Here is the definition of bullying that schools in Australia are expected to adopt, as provided by the Australian Government Department of Education and Training (2016).

> Bullying is an ongoing and deliberate misuse of power in *relationships* through repeated verbal, physical and/or social behavior that intends to cause physical, social and/or psychological harm

As we have seen, definitions vary and are in some respects inconsistent. They are useful when they provoke thought and even in some cases dissent, but may be counter-productive if they are imposed as the 'truth.' This becomes apparent when researchers deny the validity of points of view expressed by non-researchers, such as teachers, students and parents. They are prone to lay down the law – and insist that the ignoramuses need to be educated.

One is reminded of the exchange between Humpty Dumpty and Alice in 'Through the Looking Glass' (Carroll, 1865/1982, p. 184).

> 'When *I* use a word,' Humpty Dumpty said in rather a scornful tone, 'it means just what I choose it to mean – neither more nor less.' 'The question is,' said Alice, 'whether you *can* make words mean so many different things.' 'The question is,' said Humpty Dumpty, 'which is to be master that's all.'

No, that's not all. Definitions can serve useful purposes. The Olweus formulation of bullying, in particular, has generated much useful research, some of which has been replicated and findings confirmed. But from the point of view of helping us to think about how people think about bullying behaviour, that is perspectives on bullying, it has its limitations, and can – I will argue – at times be counterproductive. As Edward de Bono has argued, words are encyclopedias of ignorance because they freeze perceptions at one moment in history and then insist we continue to use these frozen perceptions when we should be doing better. I think we can understand bullying better, if we allow ourselves to listen carefully to how people are using the word, without declaring their ignorance.

Summary points

1. The study of bullying in recent years has led to the development and promotion of a diversity of definitions, each of which reflects the purposes for which it was devised and the perspective of the author(s).
2. Principally as an aid to research in the area, the definition of bullying proposed by Olweus in 1993 has continued to be highly influential. It has been adopted or adapted by many educators concerned with schools. As such, bullying is commonly seen as involving repeated intentionally

aggressive behaviour in which there is an imbalance of power and is distinct from fighting.

3. Alternative or complementary definitions have included some other criteria in describing bullying, including the desire to hurt or put under pressure those who are targeted; the wrongfulness of bullying behaviour in constituting an abuse of misuse of power; and the embeddedness of bullying in situational contexts.
4. Whilst each of these definitions may be seen as helpful in addressing school bullying in one way or another, they each reflect a perspective on bullying that is not beyond criticism.
5. Rigid adherence to particular formulations can have the effect of delegitimizing other perspectives and hinder progress in understanding how bullying may be viewed and addressed.

Chapter 4

Historical and cultural perspectives

Bullying is commonly seen as a modern phenomenon. When Koo (2007) provided a major review of the history of bullying he drew upon documents only from the mid-1800s. The omission of earlier evidence of bullying and associated perspectives on bullying may be due to changes in the meaning of the word 'bullying.' According to the online etymological dictionary (https://www.etymonline.com/word/), the word 'bully' came into the English language at the end of the Middle Ages, probably from Middle Dutch 'boele' meaning 'lover.' It was used as a term of endearment applied to either sex, but later became a familiar form of address to a male friend. Nothing, it seems, could be further removed from how the word is used in English today.

We find this old usage in Shakespeare's Henry V first performed in 1599. In it, the flamboyant soldier, Pistol, declares his deep admiration for his warrior king.

> The king's a bawcock, and a heart of gold,
> A lad of life, an imp of fame,
> Of parents good, of fist most valiant.
> I kiss his dirty shoe, and from heartstring
> I love the lovely bully.

By the mid-19th century, the term had acquired negative connotations. Charles Dickens (1839, 2003) in his novel, Oliver Twist presents a portrait of the beadle, Mr Bumble, the tormentor of young Oliver.

> He had a decided propensity for bullying: derived no inconsiderable pleasure from the exercise of petty cruelty; and, consequently, was (it is needless to say) a coward.

From this, we might infer that over a period of two or three hundred years people in England had changed their minds about bullying. From a joyous appreciation of the lovely bully, they had come to see him (and perhaps her) as a miserable and deplorable specimen of humanity. But not so. In another

DOI: 10.4324/9781315454450-4

play by Shakespeare, 'Measure for Measure,' performed in 1604, Isabella rebukes her bother as a petty tyrant

> O! it is excellent
>
> To have a giant's strength, but it is tyrannous to use it like a giant.

Here we see an excellent illustration of what is meant by the modern definition of bullying as the systematic abuse of power. It is the word 'bully' that changed not the concept. The questions we may ask concern whether the kinds of behaviour that we call bullying were essentially different from those that were generally regarded as reprehensible, especially by victims, in the past for the same reason, that is, because they constituted a systematic abuse of power.

Perhaps the closest equivalent in ancient times to what is understood as bullying today is to be found recorded in some parts of the Psalms in the Old Testament. There are in this text written around 3000 years ago numerous examples of how people were being maltreated by others more powerful than themselves. What the victims of bullying had to say about their experiences has been reported and discussed at some length in my book, *New Perspectives on Bullying* (Rigby, 1998). Here I provide some examples to illustrate the point that how some people were bullied thousands of years ago and how they felt about it was hardly different from how victims feel today.

> All day long my enemies insult me; those who mock me use my name in cursing.
>
> They tell lies about me and say evil things about me, attacking me for no reason.
>
> They are around me now; wherever I turn watching for a chance to pull me down.
> All who see me make fun of me; they stick out their tongues and shake their heads
> My enemies make trouble for me all day long; they are always thinking up some way to hurt me. They gather in hiding places and watch everything I do.
> They plan to hurt and destroy me.
> All my enemies and especially my neighbours treat me with contempt; those who know me are afraid of me – of being seen with me. When they see me in the street they run away.
> When I look beside me I see there is no one to help me. No-one cares for me
> Even my best friend, the one I trusted most, the one who shared my food has turned against me.

The reported reactions to such experiences remind one of bullied children reflecting on their misery.

> Everyone has forgotten me, as though I were dead.
> I am always in disgrace. I am covered with shame from hearing the sneers and insult s of my enemies who choose to hate me.
> Insults have broken my heart and I am in despair. I had hoped for sympathy but there was none; for comfort, but I found none
> My strength has gone like water spilled on the ground
> I am like a dumb man and cannot speak.

A further feature evident in the statements reported by victims in the Psalms is the extreme anger that is felt towards those who bully them

> May my enemies die before their time; may they go down alive into the world of the dead
> May they disappear like water draining away; may they be crushed like weeds in a path.
> May they be like snails dissolve into slime; may they be like a baby born that never sees the light.

Here for comparison is a sample of student comments on how they have been treated and they have been affected by bullying at school, from a survey of schoolchildren Australia reported by Rigby and Johnson (2016)

> They kick me and I get hurt a lot
> Annoyed because they follow you around
> Nobody cared for me and nobody wanted me to be alive
> I felt like I am not a person to anyone else
> Want to move school and never come back
> Angry, furious, wanting to bash them
> Pissed off with them and wanting to punch them in the face
> Terrified, I felt like leaving the school and just kept crying
> Nauseous all the time and probably suicidal
> Can't trust these people any more
> Mad and scared
> Nobody would play with me
> Like I had no purpose
> Felt like a drop of water on the ground

The mode of bullying then as now included a perception of being systematically abused taking the form of physical and verbal abuse, name calling, hostile gestures, ridicule, rumour-spreading, exclusion and ostracism. The bullies often acted in groups. There was in many cases a sense of hopelessness, isolation and despair and occasionally bursts of anger and desire for revenge.

Then as now we may detect agonized self-pity and a cry for justice. In the Jewish culture of the time we hear a desperate plea to God to put things right:

> Listen to my cry for help for I am sunk in despair. Save me from my enemies; they are too strong for me.
>
> Punish them for what they have done, for the evil they have committed.
>
> My God, my God, why has thou forsaken me?

Shorn of their religious connotations we might conclude that the experiences and responses of people who were bullied across a span of 3000 years or so were much the same, at least among the Jewish people described in the Psalms, and children bullied in schools today.

Estimating bullying prevalence

Recent research has drawn upon the now extensive results from the administration of measures of bullying prevalence administered through questionnaires completed at intervals of several years by school children in a number of countries. Findings from such research was not available prior to the 1990s. Hence any variations in bullying prevalence at different times and in different places must be inferred through an examination of relevant historical and archaeological sources. Further, as we have seen, 'bullying' is a term that has only been used in its present sense in the last 200 years. One must therefore look for evidence that is consistent with a concept of bullying discussed earlier; that is, the systematic abuse of power.

One suggestion is that the prevalence of bullying can be estimated roughly by reported levels of violence. It may reasonably be objected that violence is not the same thing as bullying. Some bullying does not involve violence, as that term is generally understood – that is, as the use of extreme physical force. Further, there can be violence without there being bullying, as when people of about equal power engage in a physical fight. The relationship between aggression, bullying and violence is indicated in a Venn diagram in Figure 4.1.

Can we assume that estimates of violence in a community can be used as an approximate marker of levels of bullying Some recent research into the relationship between the prevalence with which individual children are bullied in different ways suggests that we can. Children who report being bullied relatively often physically, i.e., violently, as in being hit or kicked by other students, commonly report being bullied relatively often in non-physical ways, as in being verbally abused and cyberbullied (Johansson & Englund, 2020;

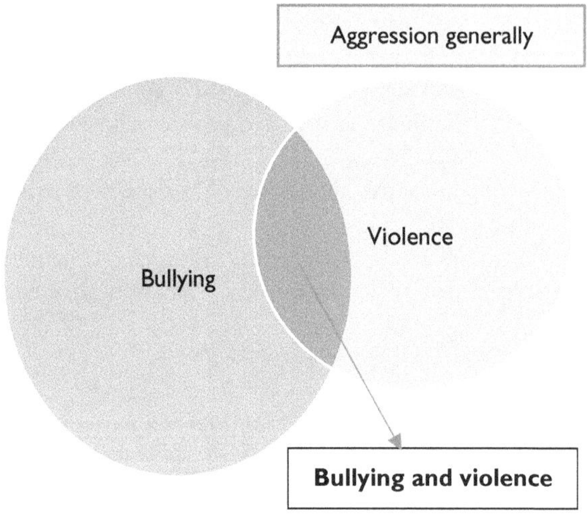

Figure 4.1 The relationship between aggression bullying and violence.

Rigby, 1998; Rigby & Johnson, 2016). It is suggested that any changes over time in the prevalence of violence in a community may reflect changes in the prevalence of bullying, especially violent bullying. But can we now access adequate historical, anthropological and archaeological evidence to draw conclusions about levels of violence at different times and in different places?

Violence and aggression in time and place

It has been evident from the early research of anthropologists that societies differ substantially in the rate of aggressive behaviour among its people. For instance, Margaret Mead (1935) identified two contrasting primitive societies in the Pacific: the Mundugamor where violent behaviour was very common, and the Arapesh noted for the gentle and cooperative interpersonal behaviour. A more recent study by Fry (2017) has reported differences between 90 societies on a 12-point scale on a continuum of peacefulness to aggressiveness. At one extreme were the Lepcha of the Himalayas described as follows

> Overt conflicts are relatively few and not very severe. Quarreling is so strongly disapproved of that it is the responsibility of all to make every effort to prevent disputes or stop them once they have broken out (p. 4)

At the other extreme, there was the Jivaro of Ecuador

> Concerns about conflict and violence affect most aspects of daily life. There is little institutional cooperation and little interpersonal trust. As a

> result individuals with some assistance from kin and occasional friends and individuals seek achievements and the establishment of a reputation for aggressiveness (p. 4).

Fry quotes a saying of the Jivao: 'I was born to die.'

Not unlike the Jivaro of Ecuador were the inhabitants of Sparta in the 4th Century BC. In their society, ruthless and aggressive behaviour was encouraged to such a degree that compassion for victims of bullying behaviour was hardly possible. In Sparta babies identified at birth as weak were killed; boys who showed signs of being irresolute were targeted for harsher treatment. Mothers treated their sons with contempt if they showed signs of fear. A Spartan woman is reputed to have handed her son his shield before he left for battle saying, 'Son, come back either with it or on it!' Another mother, seeing her son who had run away during a battle, asked, 'Where did you plan to escape?' Lifting up her dress she inquired 'Do you plan to crawl back in here from where you were born!?' The complaints of the Jews as recorded in the Psalms would have been dismissed as the bleatings of cowards and deserving of further ill-treatment (see https://my.uopeople.edu/pluginfile.php/57436/mod_book/chapter/38899/HIST1421.U1.Athens.Sparta.pdf). Such aggressiveness and violence – and their opposite – in the examples cited above, refer to conditions that may permeate a whole society. Virtually everyone is involved. One might say that being violent or peaceful is a community norm.

A great deal of violence can be attributed to individuals or organized groups. Examples at different times in history and in different places are prolific. Between the 8th and 14th centuries the Vikings were responsible for much of the violence perpetrated in Western Europe. In the 11th century, the invasion of England by William the Conqueror led to widespread devastation. The Mongol ruler, Genghis Khan, ravaged in Asia in the 12th and 13th centuries. He is quoted as saying:

> The greatest joy a man can know is to conquer his enemies and drive them before him. To ride their horses and take away their possessions, to see the faces of those who were dear to them bedewed with tears, and to clasp their wives and daughters in his arms (Cited from Gat, 2006, p. 147).

Such violence can sometimes be attributed to a psychotic or quasi-psychotic personality, or what is now sometimes called moral disengagement (the term 'evil' being virtually out of circulation, at least in social science). Much violence however has been justified in 'moral' terms – and from *that* perspective cannot be considered as an abuse of power; therefore not bullying. From a modern perspective, we would see the actions described above as an extreme form of bullying, that is, an egregious, systematic abuse of power.

The use of violence by the rulers has been justified in many places as consistent with religious belief. Hence in Roman times, emperors claimed godlike status: their word was law. In the late Middle Ages in Europe rulers claimed a divine right to govern and to pass on this right to their children. This was supported by political philosopher, Robert Filmer (1680) for whom the monarch could do no wrong. Henry VIII could, for instance, decree what sort of clothes or costumes could be worn by his people according to their social status, and punish the non-conformers. Such bullying was seen by many as entirely justifiable. This dispensation came to an abrupt end with the execution of the English king Charles 1st in the 17th century; Louis XVI during the French Revolution of the late 18th century; and Tsar of Nicholas 11 of Russia in the early 20th century. Yet something that is clearly akin to the theory of divine right lingers on in some popular attributions to State constitutions. In the year 2020, the President of the United States can pardon whomsoever he (or she) will, regardless of the culpability of their crime. In justification of the legitimacy of this power, constitutional lawyers, Shenkin and Levine (2019, p. 17) assert that 'Americans rightly view the constitution as a *sacred* document' (my italics).

Justifications for certain categories of people to be treated as inferior or undesirable have been widely accepted in some countries and at some times. Perhaps most conspicuous has been the practice of slavery, that is forcing people of lower status to do things for you, a practice ended in most (not all) countries in the 19th century. A form of slavery, known as 'fagging' persisted until most recent times in private schools in England and Australia. It seemed quite reasonable to many teachers and students that older boys should be privileged and force younger boys to serve them or receive punishment for failing to do so. Another 'acceptable' target for abuse was gayness or being thought to be gay. Homosexual behaviour was legally punishable in many countries until the late 1960s and remains so in some countries today.

In terms of the numbers of people who have been the objects of violent attack, one must recognize the immense contribution of war, both between territories or countries and within countries in the case of civil wars. Although one may speak of powerful countries bullying less powerful countries (see Rigby, 2006) the motivation for attacks on persons during war tends to be different from what we normally see when an individual is bullying someone. The persons taking action, as in dropping an atomic bomb on civilians, may be seen as just following orders; not unlike the subjects in the famous Milgram experiment, some of whom greatly disliked and protested about what they were told to do, but still obeyed (Milgram, 1965).

Any examination of cultural differences relating to violence should include the rejection of heretics, that is, people who do not conform to the orthodox view on what to think and what to do. In some countries and at some times this rejection has entailed the most violent and brutal treatment. In the 16th and 17th centuries in Europe, it included people who held unorthodox views about religion or religious practices. Calvin has provided the classic statement on the justification of violence directed at heretics like Servetus, who questioned the validity of the Trinity and was accordingly burnt alive in Geneva in 1553.

> Some say that because a crime consists only of words there is no cause for such severe punishment. But we muzzle dogs; shall we leave men free to open their mouths and say what they please. God makes it plain that the false prophet is to be stoned without mercy. We are to crush beneath our heels all natural affections when honor is at stake, the father should not spare his child, nor the husband his wife, nor the friend his friend who is dearer to him than life (Cited in Pinker, 2011, p. 171).

The 'muzzling of dogs,' that is the silencing as far as possible of people with unorthodox opinions, such as Socrates and Galileo, has been a recurring historical theme, sometimes with lethal consequences; sometimes, as in recent times, less severely through what is called 'cancelling,' whereby careers are blighted rather than lives terminated.

Has bullying got worse over time?

For many people, it is almost self-evident that bullying has become more prevalent. In part, this appears to be due to attention being focused very much on the here and now as reflected by media reports, which are written to gain attention and sell. The view that things were so much better years ago is encouraged by some religious beliefs. In 2017 a Gallop poll in the United States claimed that 24% believed that everything recorded in the Bible was literally true, including the account of the Garden of Eden, a paradise in which humans were first thought to live. Following an act of disobedience to God, it is said, evil came into the world. Cain killed Abel. More and more violence was to follow. A similar perspective was offered by the French philosopher, Rousseau (1772) who believed that primitive man lived at peace with Nature and with fellow humans, that is, until he was devastated and demoralized by 'civilization.' By contrast, the British philosopher Thomas Hobbes (1651) opined that in primitive times life was almost unendurable, being 'solitary, poor, nasty, brutish and short.' Only recently have some researchers sought empirical evidence to provide answers to this question.

It must be acknowledged that the task of determining empirically whether there has been a general trend towards the lessening in bullying is beset with considerable difficulties, even if we accept the view that bullying prevalence can be indexed by estimates of violence at different times. As suggested above, in this brief account of human violence differences in time and place have been profound with periods of relative peace alternating with periods of extreme violence.

The most persuasive claim that violence has been reducing over time, especially since the Middle Ages in Europe has been made by the eminent

American psychologist, Steven Pinker (2011), in his book, *The Better Angels of Our Nature: a History of Violence and Humanity*. Given the title, it seems to imply that humans have become in a sense more 'angelic.' In fact, his thesis is that humans have learnt to behave themselves better largely under the increasing demand by governments for law and order.

In his book, Pinker has drawn on a mountain of research findings that may provide an indication of the prevalence of violence over time. In order to obtain estimates of violence in prehistoric times, he describes what has been reported by archaeologists who have examined burial sites from which it is possible to infer cause of injury leading to death. Drawing on reports from 21 prehistoric burial sites examined in different parts of the world Pinker reports that approximately 15% of the bodies died as a result of violent assaults (p. 39). He notes that this figure is similar to that based on estimates from contemporary or recent hunter-gatherer communities. This vastly exceeds figures for modern societies, where the homicide rate is less than 0.01%, even in countries that experience relatively high levels of violence. His conclusion is that indeed life in prehistoric times was, as Hobbes had opined, 'nasty, brutish and short.'

Historically, Pinker is able to draw upon a good deal of documentary evidence. The data to which his analyses apply are wide ranging and include homicide, physical assault, wars, lynchings, torture, cruel punishment, criminal executions, slavery and terrorism. The conclusion he draws is that across many forms of violence there has been a consistent reduction in prevalence in each of these areas.

As an example, Pinker refers to the work of Eisner (2001) which includes estimates of homicides per 100,000 people per year in a number of European countries since 1500. Some of the findings are shown in Figure 4.2.

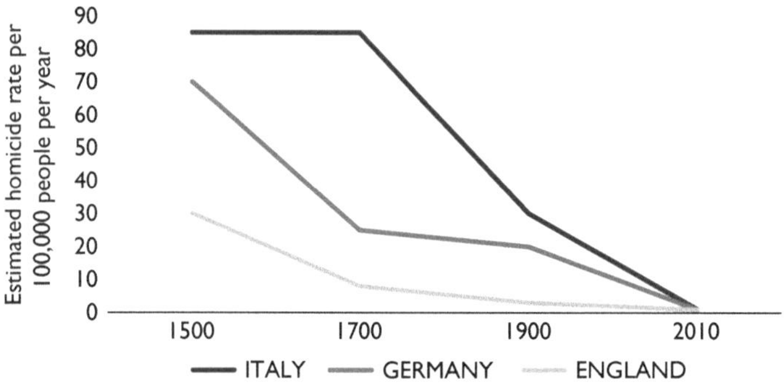

Figure 4.2 Homicide rates in three Western European regions, 1850 to 2000.

Homicide rates varied between regions until recently, with Italy much the highest. Since 1500 there has been a reduction in homicide in all three regions. By the beginning of the 21st century cases of homicide were similarly very low, estimated at 0.1%?

Pinker also examined the numbers of deaths occasioned by war as a percentage of population at different points in time and claims that despite the carnage of the world wars of the 20th century the trend has been downward. It should be emphasized that such events were less a product of individual or personal aggressiveness than a consequence of international politics. Conscripted soldiers have at times been found to be lacking in animosity towards the 'enemy.' In the classic film, 'All Quiet on the Western Front,' a German soldier is depicted as emotionally distressed at having killed, intentionally, in trench warfare, a French soldier who had tried to kill him. He searches for the wallet of the dead man so that he can write to the man's family, to assuage his guilt.

Further statistics cited by Pinker do however strongly suggest that people have over time become less inclined to take part on acts of violence. Based on trend analyses he claims that this applies to acts of terrorism, parents slapping children, mobs lynching targeted individuals, men raping women and the tyranny of domestic violence. Consistent with such behavioural changes over time, community attitudes appear to have become less aggressive and more humane. Pinker traces reductions over time in support for slavery, the death penalty for offenders, and the persecution of homosexuals.

Why have these changes taken place? Pinker attributes these changes to the emergence of states with power to apply some measure of control over violent interpersonal behaviour and diminish lawlessness. His thesis is supported through comparisons that can be made using indices of violence applied to communities which live in the States and those that have little or no governmental structures. The explanation for the role States have taken in seeking to manage violence need not be seen as necessarily humanitarian or public spirited. As Harari (2014) has suggested, the motivation of those who assumed power could have been to institute a lucrative 'protection racket' paid for through taxation. Thus people could feel safer physically, if not financially more secure.

Other writers have advanced the suggestion that the transition from hunter gatherer mode of life to one in which agriculture was the common mode contributed in the short run to greater violence. The hunter gatherers could usually move on if they were being attacked. There were usually many other places where they could hunt and collect food. The agriculturalists stayed put as long as they could to protect all they had. This transition increased the motivation for people to accept State control, with the result that over time the power of the State grew ever greater. Occasional large scale wars between States mostly replaced skirmishes between tribes and deadly altercations between individuals. Over time, Pinker claims that the transition from non-State to State has produced not another Eden but a much welcome safer existence.

A further explanation for diminishing interpersonal violence has been advanced; namely that people have on average become more intelligent and therefore more enlightened over the years. Pinker supports his view with empirical data, drawing on the findings reported by Flynn (2007) who claimed that average IQ scores obtained in the 1950s were substantially higher – by approximately 15 points than those obtained from people tested some 40 years previously. The assumption here appears to be that moral or enlightened behaviour is related to intelligence. This may be disputed. Nazi war criminals at the Nuremberg trial recorded an average IQ of 128. Arguably the most celebrated criminal of all, Hermann Wilhelm Goering, had an IQ in the gifted range at 138. However, recent research has documented a significant decline in IQ in some countries (Dutton, Van der Linden & Lynn, 2016).

A further possibility is that the decline in violence is related to a decline in religious fanaticism so prevalent in 16th and 17th centuries in Europe. Over time religious fanaticism has mostly died down as far as Christianity is concerned, but religious belief can still serve as an inducement for some people to act violently towards non-believers, as the recent history of terrorism shows. With the rise of science in the 18th century, rational explanations for events began to overturn religious convictions, and increasingly to question abuses of power that have been supported by some religious beliefs.

In generalizing about the effects of religious beliefs on bullying behaviour, it should be recognized that at times and through the efforts of exceptional people religious belief has served as an antidote to violence and oppression. The English politician and evangelical Christian, William Wilberforce (1797), the English politician is remembered for his tenacious and successful campaigning against the slave trade in the 19th century. In a speech delivered in the English House of Commons in 1791 he said:

> Never, never will we desist till we have wiped away this scandal from the Christian name, released ourselves from the load of guilt, under which we at present labour, and extinguished every trace of this bloody traffic, of which our posterity, looking back to the history of these enlightened times, will scarce believe that it has been suffered to exist so long a disgrace and dishonour to this country.

His proposed bill was heavily defeated, but led to his further more successful attempts to stop the slave trade and eventually to the abolition of Slavery in the British colonies in 1833.

Evidence of a decline in school-based bullying in recent years

Based largely on the persuasive work of Pinker, it may be claimed that the prevalence of violence has declined substantially since prehistoric times and that it is likely that this decline has been accompanied by a reduction in bullying conceived as a systematic abuse of power. Data on the prevalence of bullying covers a period roughly from the mid-1990s to the present time. Has there been a continuation of the trend as far as school bullying is concerned? The popular answer judging by media reports and commentary is that bullying in schools is increasing. Bullying is typically described as an epidemic or even pandemic. In the context of Covid-19, this appears to be an excessive claim.

In fact, repeated longitudinal surveys conducted in many countries using self-report measures of whether students have experienced being bullied and/or have bullied others indicate significant reductions over time. The earliest study examining possible changes over time in bullying prevalence in schools was reported by Molcho et al. (2009). They obtained data from schoolchildren in 27 countries between 1993 and 2006. Averaging out results on self-reports of being bullied they concluded that 'chronic bullying' had reduced over a 12 year period from 19.3% to 10.6% – a reduction of 45%. Similar findings were reported by Cosma et al. (2020) who note that reductions were occurring more among boys than among girls. A study by Rigby and Smith (2011) examined results from additional data sets from the USA, Finland, Lithuania, England and Wales and provided further results supporting the claim that bullying prevalence was declining, albeit modestly. In the USA a very large scale study by Waasdorp et al. (2017) based on self-reports of 246,306 students attending 109 schools in Maryland has reported significant reductions over a 10 year period in being bullied, bullying others and witnessing students being bullied (see Figure 4.3). In addition, an increasing tendency to feel safe at school was reported. There is now persuasive evidence of a modest decline in bullying in schools in many, but not all countries.

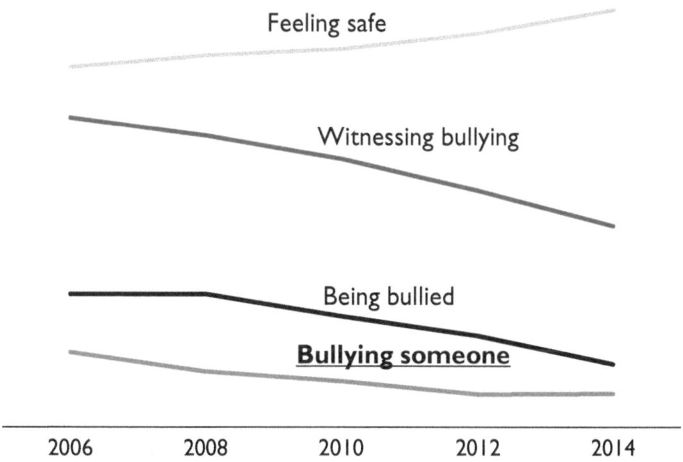

Figure 4.3 Trends relating to student reports of bullying in US school.

Despite these encouraging results not all countries have reported reductions in bullying prevalence. A UNESCO (2019) study reports that of the 71 countries and territories with trend data on the prevalence of bullying in the period 2002 to 2017, 35 have seen a decrease, 23 no significant change and 23 a worsening in prevalence (see https://en.unesco.org/themes/school-violence-and-bullying).

Bullying per se in schools now appears to be decreasing in prevalence in many countries. It may be seen as continuing the gradual decrease in bullying inferred from studies of overall changes in violent behaviour reported by Pinker and others. Whether the decrease in school bullying continues and in time extends to all countries remains to be seen.

Perspectives on school bullying, then and now

We have seen how people in different times and different places have viewed violent and aggressive behaviour, with some deploring it, others promoting and justifying it and some accepting it as part of life to which one must adjust. It is only relatively recently that perspectives on bullying as distinct from attitudes to violence have been given much attention.

A starting point in such an examination is to be found in the public reactions to a novel by Thomas Hughes (1857, 1968) called '*Tom Brown's Schooldays.*' This book described the lives of schoolchildren attending an English boarding school in the mid 19th century. It was modelled on the experiences of its author who had himself attended such a school. Central to this story is the bullying of Tom Brown by an older boy, the notorious Flashman, who was responsible for a series of brutal assaults upon Tom Brown and his friend. The book was a popular success. Of particular interest is the sixth edition of the book in which the author included a preface containing comments or, as he calls them, Reviews, based on correspondence he received. To these Hughes adds his own responses. For a further discussion of the issues raised by this publication (see Rigby 1997).

The view expressed by the one reviewer captures the feelings that the book generally evoked in Victorian England at this time.

> It fills me with grief and misery to think what weak and nervous children go through at school – how their health and character for life are destroyed by rough and brutal treatment.

The reviewer notes that there were some people at the time who were deluded into believing that fear and nervousness could be cured by violence, and that 'knocking about will turn a timid boy into a bold one.' 'Every medical man,' he adds, 'knows the fatal effects of terror, or agitation, or excitement, to nerves that are oversensitive.'

Reflecting on the fictionalized bullying of Tom Brown, he describes the plight of many students attending public schools as one of horrendous suffering.

> 'The fact is, that the life of a small boy at a large school is one of peculiar hardship and suffering. He is entirely at the mercy of proverbially the roughest things in the universe – great school boys; and he is deprived of the protection which the weak have in civilized society; for he may not complain; if he does, he is an outlaw – he has no protector but public opinion, and that an opinion of the very lowest grade, the opinion of rude and ignorant boys.'

He contrasts the concern shown towards adults who are assaulted with the indifference shown towards victims of school bullying.

> 'One of our judges not long ago refused to extend the protection of the law to a child who had been ill treated at school. If a party of navies had given him (sic) a licking, and he had brought the case before a magistrate what would he have thought if the magistrate had refused to protect him on the ground that if such cases were brought before him he might have fifty a-day from one town only.'

The solution? Implicitly the reviewer is arguing for a rule of law to be applied to regulate or take action with regard to bullying behaviour in schools and the necessary provision of adequate supervision, but not, he emphasizes that of a 'magisterial' kind. To reduce or eliminate the need for such action, the reviewer proposes that students be schooled in centres set up for different age groups. The assumption being that bullying is due to older, more powerful boys bullying the younger and more vulnerable. Later research was to show that bullying takes place most commonly between students of approximately the same age and is of a mostly non-physical kind.

The second reviewer took a somewhat different line. He dismisses the view that grouping students according to age is the answer, pointing out, rather proudly it seems, that his little girl, 'who looks like an angel' and is attending a nursery, was bullying another girl twice today! Here we have the recognition, unusual for its time' that school bullying is not all about boys' behaviour. Also, one might add, is all bullying deplorable – not seemingly if it is practiced by one's angelic daughter. Unlike many of his contemporaries, he disparages the use of older students (the so-called 'sixth') to maintain order and justice. Rather he sees it as necessary to get the 'lower fellows' to scorn it, thereby 'eradicating mercilessly the incorrigible.' How students are to be guided or persuaded to act in this way is not made clear.

Teachers (or masters as they were called) were seen as being able to stop the bullying, if they are motivated to do so.

> 'A master who really cares for his fellows is pretty sure to know instinctively who in his house are likely to be bullied, and knowing a fellow to be really victimized and harassed, I am sure he can stop it if he is resolved.'

Somewhat inconsistent with what has been said earlier about 'eradicating the incorrigible,' this reviewer concludes with what may be seen as voicing a more modern view of inculcating positive relations in students through an educational process.

> Bullying should be fought, like all school evils, but more than any by dynamics rather than by mechanics, by getting the fellows to respect themselves and one another, rather than by hitting by them with a thick stick.

As in much of what was said in response to the issue raised by the novel, the comments are rich in rhetoric but sparse in detail and practicality.

In commenting upon the reviewers' views, Thomas Hughes appears to damn with faint praise. He won't say that the Reviewers do not have 'a certain plausible ground for their dicta.' But he opines they limit their observations to the early part of their lives at school, not acknowledging that at least at Rugby school, where the redoubtable Mathew Arnold was headmaster, students emerged towards the end of their schooling as exemplary young men for whom 'the thoughtful life' had become habitual.

The larger part of the author's rejoinders concerns the criticism he had received to the effect that the book contained too much preaching. He declares that he disdains the very idea of a book that merely entertains and that the whole purpose of his writing is in fact to preach. He illustrates this perspective with a story of a black soldier, in a West Indian regiment, tied up to receive a lashing for drunkenness crying out to his captain who was exhorting to him to sobriety in future

> 'Cap'n if you preachee, preachee; and if floggee, floggee; but no preachee and floggee, too: to which his captain might have replied. 'No Pompey, I must preach whenever I see a chance of being listened to, which I never did before; so now you must have it all together; and I hope you may remember some of it.'

Thomas Hughes knew his audience well and produced an enduring best seller. Muscular Christianity of which he was a great proponent appealed to many in Victorian England; but as evidenced from the two Reviewers whose comments Hughes selected for inclusion in this preface to a late edition of his book there were intimations of a growing discontent with the neglect of a serious problem; but also, it should be said, from Hughes a determined effort, in the name of moral earnestness, to whitewash the authorities responsible for the schooling of children.

What is most striking looking back to a time 150 years ago are the similarities in the perspectives taken by the readers of this 19th century classic and perspectives held by many people today. These range from extremes of righteous indignation that bullying should be rife in schools to an acceptance that stoically enduring the torment could 'make a man' of a boy. As is the case today, opinion about how to deal with the problem, if any actions was divided between those who favoured punishment as the answer or, as we would say, zero tolerance, and an educational approach – 'getting the fellows to respect themselves and others.' How this was to be done was unclear. A new perspective was to emerge in more recent times which sought to suggest ways about how it could be done.

Recent history

Recent history has been marked by a vast acceleration of attention being paid to the problem of bullying in schools. Such attention has involved activity of different kinds. Some has been focused on defining and promoting human rights as they apply to relations between people. A second related activity has focused upon research into bullying behaviour and ways in which bullying can be prevented and addressed.

Human rights

The assertion of human rights has a long history going back thousands of years and at times involving legal and quasi declarations, enshrined in documents such as the Hammurabi code of laws, in 1754 BC; the Magna Carta in 1215; and the Declaration of the Rights of Man at the start of the French revolution in 1789. However, it is only in the years following the Second World War that human rights were accorded high prominence internationally through the agency of the United Nations by its Universal Declaration of Human Rights in 1948. Subsequently, more and more attention was given to identifying situations and circumstances in which people were being treated unfairly and unequally. These included discrimination and abusive treatment on the basis of race or ethnicity, disability, religions, gender, age, sexual orientation; more recently the list has been extended by including rights of animals.

This increased attention and sensitivity to harm that is unfairly directed in the community has led to the encouragement of action to promote the right of children in schools not to be bullied. In 2008 a group of anti-bullying activists met in Switzerland and formulated the Kandersteg Declaration Against Bullying in Children and Youth. Among its resolutions it contained this statement:

> Every child and youth has the right to be respected and safe. Bullying is a violation of this basic human right.

This belief is now being endorsed in the Anti-Bullying policies of schools in many parts of the world.

Recent research into bullying

Prior to the 1990s, there were hardly any publications in academic journals on school bullying. Over the last 30 years or so there has been a steady increase of papers and books dealing with the subject. Figure 4.4 charts the increase in such publications.

Peer reviewed publications on bullying in schools, as reported in the data base, psychinfo, began in 1991 and – after a slow start – the rate increased rapidly before flattening out over the last few years. Publications on cyber bullying began in 2006, shortly after the phenomenon was recognized, and have increased year after year, more recently at an accelerating rate. What has emerged from the contribution of research into bullying is discussed in Chapter 5. Here we may simply note that this research has generated a wide range of perspectives on bullying and the evaluation and application of methods of addressing the problem.

According to Smith (2014), the history of research into bullying can be seen as involving in four waves. The first wave (1970s to 1988) consisted of studies undertaken in Scandinavia, largely by the late Dan Olweus who examined questionnaire data based upon large samples of schoolchildren in Norway and provided estimates of the prevalence of bullying, its relationship with a range

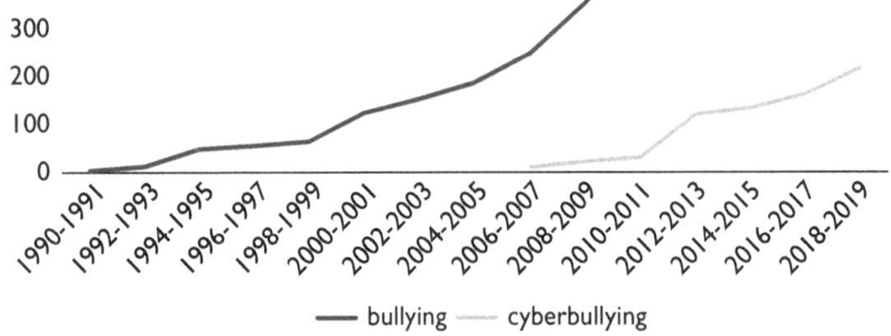

Figure 4.4 Publications on bullying and cyberbullying in schools 1990–2019.

of social variables, and the effects of an intervention to reduce bullying in schools. The work of Olweus inspired researchers in other countries to undertake similar work.

Between 1989 and the mid-1990s further studies were undertaken in other countries, including Australia (Rigby and Slee, 1991); England (Smith and Sharp, 1994) and Canada (Pepler and Craig, 1995). Notably, during this second phase, the concept of bullying was broadened to include indirect and relational bullying such as rumour spreading and social exclusion. Also, during this time period research was undertaken in Japan focusing on group bullying known as 'ijime' (Toda, 2016).

The third wave (mid-1990s to 2004) saw a rapid expansion of research in a many countries, including Finland (Salmivalli et al., 1996) and the United States (Graham and Juvonen, 2001). During this period interest developed in Finland in participant roles in bullying, thus extending earlier work by Pepler and Craig in Canada.

The fourth wave from 2004 continued the trend towards increased attention to issues relating to bullying in more and more countries. It included for the first time cyberbullying (Shariff, 2008), which was seen as an increasingly serious form of interpersonal aggression. During this period much attention was being directed in research towards developing models that described the complex interaction of factors that led to bullying behaviour (Espelage et al., 2015) and also the devising and evaluating of proactive ways that could prevent bullying from occurring in schools, for example through the development in children of social and emotional competence (Low et al., 2015).

Summary and conclusions

1. Although the term 'bullying' in English has changed its meaning since the Middle Ages in Europe, there is documentary evidence that some behaviour that we would now call bullying occurred in some, if not all, cultures throughout history.
2. Assuming a close relationship between bullying and interpersonal violence, there have been substantial differences between cultures in the prevalence of bullying behaviour.
3. Bullying behaviour, understood as the abuse of power, has been attributed at different times to various factors, including the norms relating to how people are expected to behave; the violence of powerful leaders; beliefs about the rights of authorities (secular and/ or religious) to impose their will forcefully on others; and the acceptance that certain categories of persons, such as ethnic minorities, identified heretics and homosexuals, warranted abusive treatment.
4. Archaeological and historically documented evidence points to a trend towards a general reduction of violent behaviour – and, by inference, to a corresponding reduction in bullying behaviour.

5. Explanations for this reduction in aggressive behaviour include (i) the increasing application of the Law to regulate and control behaviour that is harmful to others, and (ii) the increasing recognition that individuals and groups have basic human rights that include being safe from being bullied.
6. Only recently has bullying per se become a subject for systematic research, expanding and deepening each year as new topics or foci are included in a growing number of studies. To date, applications of the knowledge have achieved modest success in some but not all countries in reducing the prevalence of bullying.

Part II

Diverse perceptions of school bullying

In this part of the book, we examine the perspectives on bullying held by people according to their group membership. It is not suggested that the perspectives are the same for all group members but rather that there is a tendency for groups to see bullying in much the same way and make similar judgements. It is further recognized that individuals may be influenced by their membership of more than one group. For example, a person may be a teacher, a parent of a schoolchild and a researcher. Personal experiences related to involvement in bullying may also play a part.

The groups chosen are those that have a particular interest in bullying in schools either because they have engaged in systematic research in the field and/or have role in society that results in them having a particular perspective on bullying. These include, first, those who carry out research in the area and have perspectives on bullying that can generally be inferred from their publications. Next, are groups who are closely involved in schools as teachers, counsellors, students and parents of school children. Within the group of schoolchildren can be distinguished subgroups that may be identified according to whether they engage in bullying or are bullied, or are both bullies and victims. Another relevant subgroup is student bystanders. These are students who are present when bullying occurs and witness what is happening. Parents of schoolchildren are included as a group and are further distinguished according to their children's engagement in bullying at school. A final group comprises those who are regarded in some degree as community authorities insofar as they may influence how bullying is regarded and acted upon. They include those that have institutional authority, as do Departments of Education and the Law, and also those that may be seen as relevant authorities without having any coercive power, as in the case of the media in its various manifestations and also those whose authority (if any) is derived from having relevant and perceived expertise in the field, as for example in Australia, the National Centre Against Bullying (NCAB).

DOI: 10.4324/9781315454450-101

Chapter 5

Theory and research perspectives

Before I began my undergraduate studies in psychology at the University of Adelaide, I would pass over lightly such phrases as 'Psychologists believe that ...' 'According to Psychologists' and 'From a psychological point of view ...' And believed them. As more and more theories, research findings and schools of thought were brought to my attention my innocence crumbled. I was on my way to being a cynic. Now I constantly hear from the experts doing the rounds at teacher conferences that what they say and what is acceptable is only that which is 'evidence-based.' But this may mean different things to different people. So, I tell myself that it is good to hear what they say, however much they may contradict each other. I ask: what does it mean looking at bullying like that?

It may be the case that research into any area can be 'pure' in the sense' of providing facts and relationships between selected variables, without any evident intention to improve things. But in the area of bullying, it is hard to find any study that is not to some degree concerned with addressing the question of how bullying and its harmful effects can be eliminated or reduced. In short, it is not a value-free area of research. With few (rather a few, perverse exceptions) they agree that bullying is bad. Secondly, despite the very large amount of research that has been published, even that which has been peer-reviewed, there are numerous claims that either contradict each other or place greatly different emphases on perspectives that are promoted by some other researchers.

On what do they actually agree? Unsurprisingly, they agree that evidence-based findings are preferable to 'findings' that are based upon intuition and/or tradition. They may dispute which research methods are likely to provide more valid outcomes; for example, whether quantitative, qualitative or mixed methods are more acceptable and useful. They may differ over what methods of data analysis are appropriate. However, on the whole, there is general agreement that evidence-based conclusions trump all others.

Examining in detail the ever-expanding corpus of research contributions to the study of bullying is beyond the scope of this book. Hence the selection will, almost inevitably, exclude some views or perspectives based on research,

DOI: 10.4324/9781315454450-5

perhaps at times misguidedly through my own ignorance or bias. I should point out first that I am not implying that the perspectives being described are such that their proponents invariably fail to recognize the relevance of other views. For the most part, researchers make contributions that they see as complementary to what other researchers are making. However, their perspectives are ones that they see as consistent with research findings (often their own) and the ones they feel should be emphasized.

Ancestral influence

'The view that bullying in school can, at least in part, be explained by reference to ancestral influence is a recurring proposition in research into the causes of bullying. The earliest research publication on bullying by Frederic Burk (1897) sought to explain the bullying behaviour of children in this way. It begins with brief case studies of bullying and cruel teasing among children from over a thousand accounts derived from direct observations, reminiscences and hearsay. Here is an example.

> I saw a boy (aged 10) rush at a boy (aged 7) punch him along the pavement, throw him down and sit on his head. Every moment or so the larger boy would pinch the other's ear and demand, 'Beg to get up?' Each time the victim would screw up his face in pain and shout 'No.' At last the tormentor grew tired and with a parting kick left his victim to get up as best as he could.'

Whenever he could, Burk asked the bullies to explain why he or she had acted as he or she did. They were, he writes, unable to provide an explanation. He concluded that the motivation was unconscious and the behaviour should be interpreted as consistent with the popular Recapitulation Theory (Haeckel, 1866), as applied to childhood development. He opined that bullying behaviour among children is affected by how their remote ancestors acted in circumstances in which there was a desperate struggle to survive. They are, he argued, primed to repeatedly engage in aggressive behaviour, especially in pursuing others, throwing them down, striking, and hurling stones at them. From the standpoint of consciousness, he suggests that 'such actions may derive from broken neurological fragments that are parts of a chain involved in the pursuit, combat, capture, torture and killing of men and women' (p. 368).

Burk's proposed explanation for bullying lacks support from modern psychology. The Lamarckian theory that qualities developed through activities practiced in a life-time can affect the behaviour of offspring, let alone future generations to come, has found little support based on credible evidence, though some writers, including the playwright, Bernard Shaw and the novelist, Arthur Koestler, have thought it plausible. It nevertheless has some appeal to those who view young people as prone to barbaric acts – if left to their own devices, as described in 'The Lord of The Flies' (Golding, 1955). Lacking in solid evidence, the perspective that the bullying of children can be traced to primitive savagery not yet outgrown, is nevertheless the way some still people look at bullying. This perspective is suggested by the indignant observation sometimes made when children behave in a grossly uncivilized way. 'They are just little savages!'

Evolutionary perspective

More recently some researchers have sought to explain bullying behaviour drawing upon evolutionary theory. It has been proposed that bullying behaviour is an evolutionary adaptation that has made possible the survival of organisms that are genetically predisposed and able to dominate others. According to prominent psychologists, Volk et al. (2012), this includes adolescents, especially male adolescents, whose bullying behaviour is adaptive to the school environment. In support of their contention, they note that bullying behaviour is prevalent in schools in all countries in which it has been researched. Culture they argue, makes little difference. Far from being maladaptive, as some have argued, those who bully at school tend to be physically healthier than others, enjoy above average self-esteem and are admired by many or most other students. They are also able to make accurate assessments of the motives of others and to get what they want. Volk et al. concede that some students who bully are also bullied themselves (so-called 'bully-victims') and have relatively poor mental health. It is the 'pure bullies' they mainly have in mind.

Given that some students are predisposed to bully, what implications are there for those who wish to see bullying reduced? According to Volk et al., there must be an emphasis upon making rewarding outcomes for bullying less achievable through the imposition of tough disciplinary policies. They also acknowledge that the rewards sought by bullies may be achieved by encouraging them to achieve success through non-hurtful actions, as in promoting the well-being of others. This perspective on bullying is sometimes seen as divorced from moral considerations and akin to the philosophy endorsed by the 19th century philosopher Herbert Spenser who coined the term 'the survival of the fittest.' At a popular level, the conception of humans as no more that 'naked apes,' as suggested by Desmond Morris (1967) has been seen by many as consistent with this perspective on bullying and unfortunately can be construed as unchangeable, or even by some as desirable.

Opposing this view is the opinion expressed by John Stuart Mill, the 19th century philosopher, cited by Wright (1994, p. 341).

> If there are any marks at all of special design in creation, one of the things most evidently designed is that a large proportion of animals should pass their existence in tormenting and devouring other animals… If Nature

> and Man are both works of a Being of perfect goodness, that Being intended Nature as a scheme to be amended, not imitated by Man.'

Whilst the evolutionary perspective on animal and human development is widely held by specialists in the field, its application as an explanation for bullying is much disputed, especially as a total explanation. Some have maintained that altruism that is unconnected with prioritizing personal survival or care for one's progeny or the persistence of one's genes does in fact occur and appears to be incompatible with orthodox evolutionary theory (Carter, 2005).

Genetic influence

Related to the evolutionary perspective on bullying, many recent studies have examined links between genetic factors and the involvement of children in bullying, either as a bully, a victim or and bully-victim; for example studies by Ball et al. (2008) and Veldkamp, Boomsma and De Zeeuw (2019). These studies included large samples of identical or monozygotic twins, that is, having the same genetic makeup, and large samples of fraternal or dizygotic twins that do not. It has been reported that the former are much more alike as far as bullying is concerned, even when the identical twins are reared apart. For example, if one identical twin engages in bullying the other twin will have a strong tendency to do so. It has been concluded that a child's behaviour, as a bully or as a victim, is significantly affected by his or her genetic inheritance. These findings do not deny that the child's environment may play a part, sometimes through an interaction with the genetic influence

Conscious of the danger of their study being misunderstood Veldkamp, Boomsma and Zeeuw wisely concluded:

> It must be stressed that it is certainly not someone's fate to be a bully or victim (or both), but some children are more vulnerable to these social roles, and individual differences in this vulnerability are substantially due to genetic differences. Thus, becoming a victim, bully or bully-victim is not fixed beforehand, but is not randomly determined either (p. 339).

This perspective on bullying is nevertheless often unacceptable to educationalists who may fear that its acceptance would justify the belief that trying to change the behaviour of those involved in school bullying is a hopeless cause.

The role of personality

A perspective held by many people is that bullying and being bullied is due to personality differences such that one person is inclined and able to dominate those who are less able to resist. Some psychologists have sought to identify characteristics that are relatively stable and help to explain cases of bullying.

One may distinguish between physical characteristics such as build and physique and psychological characteristics of the kind that may be identified through personality tests.

Physical characteristics

Probably the most ambitious and intensively researched physical typing of individuals was proposed in the 1940s by a US psychologist William Sheldon (1940). He claimed that physical build could be measured according to the degree to which individuals conformed to three extreme types: the ectomorph, the mesomorph and the endomorph, as caricatured below in Figure 5.1.

He further suggested that individuals who conformed most to these physical categories tended to have certain psychological characteristics. The extreme ectomorph was described as cerebrotonic, that is, self-conscious, socially anxious, artistic, thoughtful, quiet and private; the extreme mesomorph was adventurous, assertive, competitive, and fearless; and the extreme endomorph was relaxed, sociable tolerant and peaceful. Given these extremes the mesomorph was thought to be most likely to engage in bullying, being typically aggressive and liable to engage in petty crime. No prize for guessing who the victim was.

Figure 5.1 Sheldon's types of physique in boys.

Plausible though this typology may seem (it was enthusiastically adopted and promoted by Aldous Huxley in 1946) few, if any, researchers have tested and demonstrated its validity. It is generally regarded as unreasonable stereotyping. It nevertheless may apply to some extent as far as physical bullying is concerned, given the obvious imbalance of power between most mesomorphs and most ectomorphs, and be consistent with a perspective on bullying which suggests that differences in physical build may allow one to say who is the bully when children are in conflict. As more and more bullying is seen to be non-physical Sheldon's typology may now be considered to be less convincing.

Psychological characteristics

Explaining behaviour as a consequence of the personalities of individuals has a long history, dating at least as far back as Greek physician Hippocrates (c. 460–c.370 BC) who attributed basic individual differences to their possession in a different measure of four bodily fluids, these being blood, yellow bile, black bile, and phlegm. Galen (129 AD- 200 AD) subsequently proposed that types of person could be identified as predominantly sanguine, melancholic, choleric or phlegmatic, a typology accepted widely for nearly 2000 years. In the 1960s this old formulation was adapted by the English psychologists, Eysenck and Eysenck (1975) to produce a measure of dimensions of personality assessed by the Eysenck Personality Inventory (EPI) which reported scores for extraversion, neuroticism and psychoticism. This test was found to be psychometrically reliable and included measures that were related to reported engagement in bullying and being bullied at school. In one study male primary school students rated by their teachers as prone to bully their peers were found to score significantly higher than others on extraversion, whereas victims of school bullying were found to score significantly lower than average on this (Slee & Rigby, 1993). Children identified as bullies were also found to score higher than average on psychoticism, which indicated a low regard for the feelings of others. Subsequently, Mynard and Joseph (1997) reported that bully/victims (students who bully others and are themselves bullied) were significantly higher on neuroticism than other students; a finding confirmed in other studies.

Subsequently, many personality correlates of bullying behaviour and being victimized have been reported. Of particular interest has been the relationship between involvement in bullying behaviour and self-esteem. There is general agreement that children who are often bullied at school have low self-esteem as indicated by psychological testing. This may be seen as a consequence of being bullied or an explanation of why they are bullied. It may be that both processes occur, that is having low self-esteem 'invites' bullying and bullying lowers it further. This was claimed by Egan and Perry (1998) on the basis of a longitudinal study of primary school children who had experienced being bullied at school.

There are different claims concerning the self-esteem of students who bully others. In Ireland, O'Moore and Kirkham (2001) assessed children identified as bullies and others and found that bullies were below average on a measure of self-esteem. However, when in another study, bully-victims were excluded from data analyses it became clear that the remaining 'pure bullies' thought highly of themselves (see Polastri et al., 2010). It has been further claimed that their inflated opinion of themselves could perhaps best be called narcissism. In any case, the perception of a bully as a person who needs to have his or her self-esteem raised to get him or her to stop bullying is questionable.

This research has implications for how educators may view bullying. A perspective on bullying that leads teachers to recognize that low self-esteem on the part of some targeted students may be a factor that induces bullying may lead teachers to help victims to increase their self-esteem, for example through achieving success – ideally through developing better social skills. The research suggesting that helping children who bully (and are not bullied) to raise their self-esteem may encourage a counterproductive strategy. Such a perspective on why children bully is unlikely to be successful in many cases, according to the research, as 'pure bullies' typically have high self-esteem, perhaps sustained by successful bullying!

A number of studies have focused on the relationship between bullying others and the possession of highly undesirable characteristics, for instance, low levels of agreeableness, machiavellianism, narcissism, psychopathy and sadism (see VanGeel et al., 2017). Whilst this research can encourage educators to recognize the existence of pathological conditions that may lead some students to engage in bullying, it can also reinforce a view that bullying is generally a highly unnatural form of behaviour that requires the attention of psychiatrically trained professionals.

Finally, under the heading of 'personality' one may include views expressed in psychoanalytical theory of which there are many variants. They have in common the view that an individual is motivated more by unseen forces than by conscious and the rational thought. Theorizing by Freud (1901/2018) suggested that the primary driving force in humans is the id (basic instinct), which may or may not be restrained by the superego (or conscience), and is oftentimes controlled by the ego, a perception of 'reality,' which makes one aware of possible negative consequences of an action. A saying attributed to Freud is that 'man is as bad as he dare to be.'

Various mechanisms have been suggested to account for the choice of victim by perpetrators, including 'projection' as in attributing undesirable characteristics one views oneself of having (perhaps unconsciously), to other people, and thereby justifying hurting them. Another example is 'displacement,' that may occur when a person is targeted as a safer alternative to attack than the person who is the antagonizer. This process being known as 'scapegoating.' Whilst such ideas have plausibility and enter into perspectives on understanding bullying, practical implications for addressing school bullying are often unclear and the psychoanalytical approach is commonly considered only appropriate for work with pathological cases by trained psychotherapists.

Taken as a whole. the perspective based on studies of personality suggests that children who are likely to be involved in bullying behaviour in one way or another can be identified through personality assessments or explained through personality or psychodynamic theory. Arguably, such knowledge may enable a teacher to identify students who are more vulnerable or at risk and need special attention. For some educators, however, this view is seen as liable to promote the stereotyping of bullies and victims and lead to mistaken and harmful action.

Reinforcement theory

Reinforcement theory provides a different perspective on bullying. It suggests that in explaining bullying and addressing bullying there is no need to postulate and seek to assess hypothetical internal states of the kind examined by personality theorists. According to this perspective, the variables relevant to addressing bullying are to be found outside the person.

The focus here is upon what effects bullying has on the subsequent behaviour of the perpetrator. If an act of bullying has positive outcomes for the perpetrator it is likely to be repeated. Such outcomes may include the desired submission of others and being admired for being dominant. Preventing recurrence requires changes in the contingencies of reinforcement, such as rewarding actions that are considered socially desirable and incompatible with harming others, or, as far as possible, getting bystanders to withhold any support for aggressors. In line with earlier research on operant conditioning, the use of punishment is generally not recommended, as its effects are seen as temporary at best (Skinner, 1953).

This perspective on bullying has been incorporated in an approach to addressing bullying known as Positive Behavior Support (Ross & Horner, 2009) and adopted in some schools. It involves close monitoring of the behaviour of selected individuals who bully, followed immediately by the delivery of appropriate reinforcement. This is difficult to apply in schools as most bullying takes place out of the sight of teachers. Recognizing this difficulty, the proponents of this approach propose that time be spent by teachers in class with children before they go out at breaks into the playground, reminding them of the kind of behaviour that is unacceptable and how they should behave. In so doing, the pure principles of behaviourism are set aside. Students are to be guided in their behaviour by an understanding of what the teachers expect of them.

This general perspective is attractive to some educators in that it avoids making judgements (seen as stereotyping) about the personalities of individual students. The emphasis upon non-punitive interventions is also appealing to some teachers. The practical problem of being able to treat students who bully as cases in a clinical sense by arranging appropriate and systematic reinforcement for individual students in situ is however quite daunting and often impractical, especially given teacher workloads.

Social competence

Social competence may be defined as the ability to interact with another person and thereby achieve desired goals. These goals may be seen from the outside as positive or negative. As applied to the study of bullying, one may view the bully as 'competent' in one sense if he or she is able to dominate another person; the potential victim is competent if he or she prevents this from happening. An alternative formulation is that 'competence' refers to the ability to interact in a socially desirable way with another person or persons that is in such a way that both or all parties find satisfactory. This is to view 'competence' in a positive sense.

It is thought that a basic element in being able to interact in a socially competent manner is the ability to discern what the other person is thinking or feeling. This has been assessed in 'theory of mind' experiments' in which cues are provided that can lead a person to correctly identify another person's thoughts or intentions. One such test involves looking at pictures of people's eyes and drawing conclusions about how they are feeling, eg., happy or angry (Baron-Cohen, 2009). Research has shown that children who frequently bully others generally possess this quality, sometimes called cognitive empathy (see Sutton, Swettenham & Smith, 1999). It may in fact serve as an asset that facilitates subtle, manipulative and machiavellian forms of bullying. What is likely to be lacking in children who bully is emotional empathy: the capacity to feel and respond positively to what the other is feeling, as in sympathising with another's sorrow or misfortune (Jolliffe & Farrington, 2006).

Social bias theory

Within sociology and social psychology it is held that much bullying results from social bias against members of selected social groups. These commonly include racial or ethnic minority groups, homosexuals, people with disabilities, especially intellectual disabilities, those with unusual physical appearance, obese people, and those with non-mainstream religious affiliations. There is considerable variation between cultures in those who are mainly targeted and the frequency with which they are bullied. Explanation for bias-based bullying draw upon both historical and psychological analyses.

One influential social theory suggests that negative attitudes towards specific groups of people may occur for different reasons. Kelman (1961) proposed that biased attitudes may arise according to different processes. In some cases the biased attitude may be superficial and due to compliance. It may be held because it seems to pay to think and act in a particular way so that other people think well of you. Alternatively, a biased attitude may be adopted because it promotes a sense of identity. This involves a process of identification with a group or cause that has the potential to help a person to feel significant. Finally, an attitude may be held because it is thought to be consistent with one's (fallible) knowledge and basic beliefs. Kelman's analysis suggests that there is no single reason why a bias may be held. Viewing prejudiced thinking in this way can lead to a better understanding of why an individual may hold a particular perspective

Gender and bullying

Do boys and girls differ in their involvement and perceptions of bullying? The research evidence suggests that they generally do. It has been reported in countless studies that regardless of culture boys engage in bullying more often girls, although the differences are particularly striking in the area of physical bullying. Whether girls are bullied more often is less clear and does appear to be dependent on cultural factors. In the recent survey in Australia by Rigby and Johnson (2016), the results indicated that girls reported being bullied more often; in the study undertaken in the United Arab Emirates by Rigby, Haroun and Ali (2019a) boys reported being bullied more often. By and large, reports indicate that bullying takes place within gender groups, that is boys bully boys and girls bully girls. However, where cross gender bullying occurs, boys are much more likely to be the perpetrators (Rigby, 1998; Rigby & Johnson, 2016) at least in Australia, and probably elsewhere. Finally, research supports the contention that girls are generally more supportive of victims than are boys (Rigby & Johnson, 2006). In the light of these findings, one would expect boys and girls in schools to have somewhat different perspectives on bullying.

The issue that has rightly occupied most attention in relation to gender and bullying has been the bullying of females by males, evident in many social contexts, most notably recently in Australia in the area politics and government. Whether the supposed greater desire on the part of males to achieve dominance is related to evolutionary and biological forces or more to social structures and prejudices that have a long history is hard to determine. There is, however, with few exceptions among scholars and educators a belief that the bullying of females by men is a serious social and moral problem involving an abuse of power that is evident in schools and can have important consequences for subsequent behaviour in the workplace and in homes.

Positive psychology in schools

The term positive psychology can be used as a slogan, but is also promoted as a scientific, evidence-based theory (Seligman, 2002). Its appeal lies primarily in its encouragement to be resolute, cheerful and optimistic as opposed to being uncertain, depressive and pessimistic. Under the general heading of positive psychology, there have been some programs applied in schools that have claimed success in reducing bullying. These have emphasized psychological strengths, actual or potential, of students in bringing about positive behaviours that can be further cultivated by educational means employed by teachers.

Various attempts have been made to identify key strengths, for example by Ryff and Keyes (1995). They listed the following: autonomy; environmental mastery; personal growth; positive relations with others; purpose in life, and self-acceptance. In applying interventions in schools based upon the principles of positive psychology schools have made use of lessons delivered by teachers focusing on various positive qualities. For example, Richard, Rivers and Akhurst (1995) engaged secondary school students in England in a series of exercises and discussions designed to induce positive ways of thinking and pro-social attitudes. These were intended to promote altruism, optimism, empathy, being good-natured or amiable; social acceptance, patience, fairness and the ability to work with others on group tasks or towards a collective goal. The researchers reported a reduction in bullying relative to a control school, and a marginal improvement in wellbeing but no change in mental health. A similar intervention involving a series of lessons focusing on understanding and countering bullying plus the development of appropriate social skills was undertaken in schools in the United Arab Emirates, resulting in reductions in the prevalence of being bullied among girls but not boys (Rigby, Haroun & Ali, 2019b).

Closely allied to the positive psychology movement is what has been termed social and emotional learning (SEL), vigorously promoted since 1994 by the Collaborative for Academic, Social, and Emotional Learning (CASEL). CASEL have defined SEL as the processes through which children and adults understand and manage emotions, set and achieve positive goals, feel and show empathy for others, establish and maintain positive relationships, and make responsible decisions (Weissberg et al., 2015). The importance of SEL has been recognized in many countries. In the United States, for instance, 18 States have required K-12 schools to educate children to attain acceptable levels of social as well as academic competence (Shriver & Weissberg, 2020). Other countries such as England and Australia have followed suit. A leading advocate of this approach in England has described the delivery of SEL programs in classrooms as the 'dominant orthodoxy in education systems across the world' (Humphrey, 2013, p. 136). The specific content of programs has varied widely, with some including the promotion of positive mindsets, creativity and restorative justice. This has led to some critics to describe SEL as an exceedingly 'fuzzy' concept (Hess, 2017) and as a panacea for all that ails schools, both academic and behavioural (Zhao, 2018).

The most popular version of SEL has been provided by Second Step (Committee for Children, 2012). This has a clear rationale that makes it particularly relevant to bullying in schools. Lessons have focused on four qualities: empathy, emotional control, problem-solving capacity and assertiveness:

1. **Empathy**, especially affective or sympathetic empathy, such that any hurt experienced by another person will elicit support or at least the cessation of any intentional hurtful behaviour.
2. **Emotional control**, especially of emotions such as rage that may motivate one to attack another person or to go to pieces if attacked and thus be unable to cope.
3. **Problem solving capacity**, especially in responding calmly and effectively when confronted with interpersonal difficulties.
4. **Assertiveness**, especially in situations in which standing up for oneself is important and justified.

According to this model, described in Figure 5.2 SEL can be developed in students through classroom instruction and related activities that enhance personal qualities of empathy, emotional control, problem-solving capability

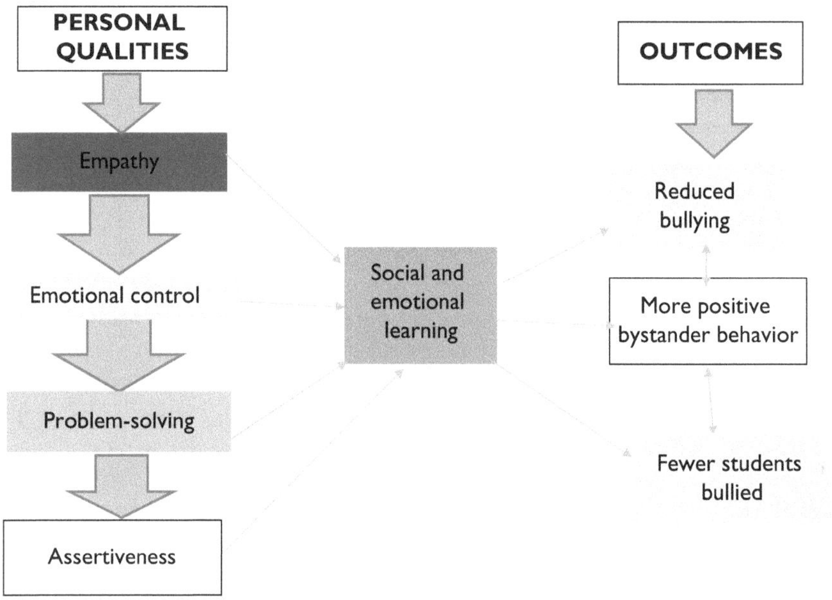

Figure 5.2 The relationship between personal qualities of students and hypothesized outcomes to bullying and pro-social behaviour.

and assertiveness, leading to a reduction in bullying, more positive bystander behaviour and fewer students being bullied.

Given the claims made in relation to SEL and its adoption by many schools, it is important to appraise this approach rigorously by considering the available evidence. Some studies of the use of this approach have reported positive results in reducing bullying (see Smith & Low, 2013). In others, no improvements have been recorded. As reported in Rigby and Griffiths (2018) at least three studies have examined possible links between SEL and bullying as distinct from anti-social behaviour or delinquency. A randomized control trial of the effects of a SEL program was undertaken with 1,296 students attending 33 elementary schools in the United States (Brown et al., 2011). There were significant reductions in physical bullying perpetration; however, no changes were found for non-physical bullying perpetration, or for being victimized. A similar outcome was reported by Espelage et al. (2015a) following a SEL program applied to 47 middle school students with disabilities; that is, bullying perpetration reduced but victimization did not. A further relevant study has been reported by Espelage et al. (2015) in an evaluation of the Second Step program. This was undertaken in 36 schools drawing on results of an intervention with 3658 students in Years 6 and 7. Over a 3-year period no direct effects on either bullying perpetration or being victimized were found. There was, however, a reported reduction in delinquent behaviour, which in turn was related to reduced bullying. This suggests that SEL programs can have some significant effect on bullying behaviour, especially of a delinquent kind, which makes up a significant though relatively small proportion of bullying. In the UK, evaluations of the SEAL program (a British adaptation of SEL) in secondary schools undertaken by Humphrey, Lendrim and Wiggleworth (2010), one of the assessed outcomes was 'behaviour problems.' On this broad category of behaviour, which included bullying, no significant effect was found. Explanations have been suggested for the limited success of SEL in its impact on bullying. These include: inadequate involvement on the part of school leadership, a failure to employ programs with content best suited the local context, an absence of whole school planning and a lack of appropriate training for teachers (Durlak et al., 2011; Polanin et al., 2012; Humphrey, 2013).

Currently, opinion among researchers is divided as to the benefits of SEL. Given, the limited success of SEL programs in reducing bullying, it appears that more work is needed to ensure reliable outcomes, especially in providing content that is most relevant to bullying and interpersonal aggression and the means by which programs are implemented.

Views on the philosophy of positive psychology

As noted earlier, positive psychology is attractive because it encourages personal optimism. It is worth noting, however, that optimism taken to an extreme has encountered strong criticism, some dating back to the 18th century satirical novel of Voltaire called 'Candide,' in which the hero of this book steadfastly continues to assert the message of his director, Dr. Pangloss, that this is, 'the best of all possible worlds,' despite the most calamitous things that are happening to him and those around him. More recently. Barbara Ehrenreich (2009) has sounded a similar note in her book, 'Smile or Die'; a bitter commentary on unbridled optimism that denies objective reality and cynically attributes responsibility to the victims of abuse rather than to circumstances that need to be remedied. A more academic commentary from a philosopher, Dienstag (2006), suggests that through the ages important contributions from writers have justified pessimism as a philosophy, though not as a personal characteristic (see for example the writings of Nietzsche, Schopenhauer and Freud). At a commonsense level, Dienstag opines that a realistic assessment of a difficult situation can serve as a protection against severe and unexpected disappointment.

Resilience

One perspective on bullying focuses primarily on the contribution of low levels of resilience on the effects of being bullied. Resilience is seen as that which determines positive outcomes over time despite facing significant adversity. Given the frequently reported negative effects of being bullied on many children, experiencing being bullied must be regarded as a significant adversity. Resilience is generally viewed as both a personality trait and as a protective influence derived from supportive relationships with others, such as family members and peers. Like many personality traits, it has been found to be related to genetic factors (Wu et al., 2013) and has been regarded as consistent with evolutionary theory (Moore and Woodcock, 2017). Parenting styles have also been related to resilience, with warm, supportive families reported as more likely to have resilient children. Resilience has been inferred from student reports, for example agreeing with the statement, 'I can deal with whatever comes my way.' Students endorsing this have been reported unsurprisingly with being less severely affected by being bullied (Hinduja & Patchin, 2010).

Opinion is divided as to how resilience can best be promoted. One of Australia's best-loved poet, or writer of doggerel, C.J. Dennis (1913) had one answer:

> Get a ------- move on
> Have some -------sense
> Learn the ------- art of
> Self de ------ fence.

Some researchers seem to have agreed. Twemlow et al. (2008) evaluated a martial arts-based program in three elementary schools as part of a Gentle Warrior Program and reported subsequent significant reductions among boys (but not girls) in aggressive behaviour and also in increasing helpful bystander behaviour. Similar outcomes have been reported as occurring after a course of training in Karate was undertaken by Italian secondary school children (Greco, Cataldi & Fischetti, 1919). These students were found to have increased their scores on measures of resilience and self-efficacy. The authors commend the training as a means of reducing bullying in schools. My own experience is that some (but not all) Departments of Education in Australia are averse to recommending such programs on the grounds that the acquired skills may be employed to hurt others. Rather more acceptable are anti-bullying initiatives that promote self-discipline through the use of yoga, which has been reported as building resilience and fortitude (Pandya, 2020), and mindfulness which, it is claimed, can promote greater tolerance as well as self-control (Brown, Ryan & Creswell, 2007; Foody & Samara, 2018).

Moral disengagement

Moral disengagement is a concept developed by an American psychologist, Bandura (1999) to explain how persons sometimes convince themselves that ethical standards do not apply to them in a given context. Subsequently, researchers including Hymel and Bonanno (2014) and Thornberg et al. (2019) have applied the concept to account for bullying and have shown that measures of moral disengagement are positively related to bullying behaviour.

Various mechanisms have been identified as underlying moral disengagement. According to Pozzoli et al. (2012), there are four: (1) cognitive restructuring, as in believing that, 'stealing someone's bicycle without their permission is just borrowing it'; (2) minimizing one's agentive role, as in believing that, 'kids can't be blamed for using bad words if all their friends do it' (3) disregarding and distorting the consequences, as in believing that, 'teasing someone does not really hurt them' and (4) blaming and dehumanizing the victim, as in, 'kids who get mistreated usually do things that deserve it.'

Drawing on data from a sample of 38 elementary school classes in Italy, Pizzoli et al. distinguished between the mechanisms that are significantly related to individual bullying behaviour, that is, cognitive restructuring; and those that can be attributed to the combined views of students in their classes, namely minimizing one's agentic role, disregarding and distorting the (harmful) consequences, and blaming and dehumanizing the victim. They concluded that bullying due to group membership or influence tends to be more common in schools and varies between classes. The perceived harmfulness of group bullying has been reported by victimized students as significantly greater than that caused by bullying undertaken by individuals (Rigby, 2020).

Various suggestions been made as to how moral disengagement can be overcome. Some involve teachers promoting pro-social values such as considerateness and doing so in such a way that the values become internalized and not adopted simply through compliance to please the teacher or to avoid punishment. According to Israeli researchers, Roth, Kanat-Maymon and Bibi (2010) students who recognize that their teachers support their autonomy in deciding how to behave are significantly less likely to experience moral disengagement and bully their classmates. There is evidence, reported by Georgiou, Charalambous and Stavrinides (2020) that among secondary school adolescents in Cyprus the practice of mindfulness, defined as the ability to pay full, undistracted attention to present events, can reduce moral disengagement in schoolchildren. In some schools, techniques to induce mindfulness have been applied by trained teachers to help develop this capacity in children (Crane et al., 2010). Interventions with pre-adolescent students employing a spiritual education program, promoting mindfulness have been reported as successful in increasing pro-social behaviour in a study conducted internationally across 15 countries (Pandya, 2017).

Surprisingly, there has been little research examining the effectiveness of reducing moral disengagement as a means of countering bullying using traditional religious instruction. An exception is a largescale study in Australia using data based on parent reports from approximately 13,000 households (Wilkins, 2016). Comparisons were made between reported bullying prevalence in Catholic schools which promote Christian beliefs and related moral values and State schools that do not. Estimated prevalence of bullying in State schools was reported as approximately 50% higher than in the Catholic schools. However, given differences in the nature of the student intakes in the two kinds of schools, with State schools catering for a wider diversity of children, interpretations of the reported difference have been questioned.

Environmental influences on bullying

Among researchers, there is a general acceptance that environment plays a part in increasing the likelihood of bullying. Increasingly the term 'ecological' has been used to describe aspects of the broader environment that are thought to be relevant to human interactions and bullying in particular (Bronfenbrenner, 2009; Hornby, 2015). This has meant excluding some physical aspects of the environment, such as the stars (to the protests of astrologers) and trees (to the dismay of animists). Typical of the elements that are included are the family, the local community, the school and the country. According to social ecological theory, such sources of influence interact with each other and affect the behaviour of individuals or groups involved in the bullying as perpetrators, victims, bully-victims and bystanders.

A basic distinction is made between environmental factors that have left their mark primarily through past experiences, for example, family functioning or dysfunction in early childhood, as well as those factors that are at work contemporaneously, as in the case of the classroom climate and peer group pressure at school.

Family influences

Following the seminal text by John Bowlby (1969), emphasis is often placed upon the role of attachment or bonding in the early years of infancy as the primary factor in determining the capacity of individuals to relate positively to each other. The failure to establish a close emotional relationship with a caregiver as a baby appears to have serious implications for relationships with others later in life, including the likelihood of bullying others and being victimized in the school environment (Williams & Kennedy, 2012). Styles of parenting have also been shown to be related to the bullying behaviour of children. Extreme forms of parenting, as in being highly authoritarian and controlling, or laisser-faire and non-controlling, have each been reported as associated with children bullying at school. Parent overprotection has been found to be related to their children being bullied at school (Lereya, Samara & Wolke, 2013). Arguably, overprotection involves serious limitations on the development of social skills needed to cope with those who might seek to bully them. A perspective on bullying encouraged by such findings may result in parents being held responsible for their child or children being involved in bullying at school, sometimes unjustifiably so.

Community influence

The ethos of the community in which children grow up has been found to affect whether they become involved in bullying. One study conducted in Italy has reported that the low socio-economic status of the community in which a student lives has an effect on bullying behaviour that is independent of the effect that derives from the socio-economic status of a child's family (Jansen et al., 2012). The neighbourhood where a child lives may help to determine whether he or she is involved in bullying at school. It is thought that children from relatively deprived areas may hold attitudes and practice behaviours that lead to them being bullied or to engage in bullying others school.

National differences

There is evidence that there are substantial differences between the prevalence of bullying in different counties; for instance, in Sweden, the prevalence of bullying, as reported by students claiming to have been bullied 'sometimes' over the last 12 months has been estimated at 5.6.%, whilst that in Lithuania as 40.0% (Due et al., 2005). Many factors may account for such differences, including ethnic mix, historical events resulting in continuing hostility between groups, and unresolved antagonisms related to religious or ideological differences. Economic inequality appears to be one of many factors.

It is clear from various studies that bullying tends to be greater in countries where there is greater socio-economic inequality. Such inequality has been assessed using the so-called the Gini index, according to which '0' indicates complete equality of income and '1' complete inequality, that is the wealth is in all in the hands of one person. One study reported by Elgar et al. (2009) was concerned with the relationship between economic inequality in 37 countries and the extent to which students aged approximately 11 years reported that they bullied other students. As indicated in Figure 5.3 a moderately strong positive relationship was found. In countries like Turkey economic inequality is about 1.7 times greater than that of Sweden and bullying others about 6 times higher. Similar relationships have been reported in a study that examined the relationship between reportedly being bullied at school and economic inequality. It has been shown that it is not the overall or average economic level of income in a country that has been found to influence the level of reported bullying but rather economic disadvantage.

Socio-economic status or affluence does appear to make an important difference to the prevalence of bullying in many countries. Where the economic inequality is particularly low, bullying is generally low; where the

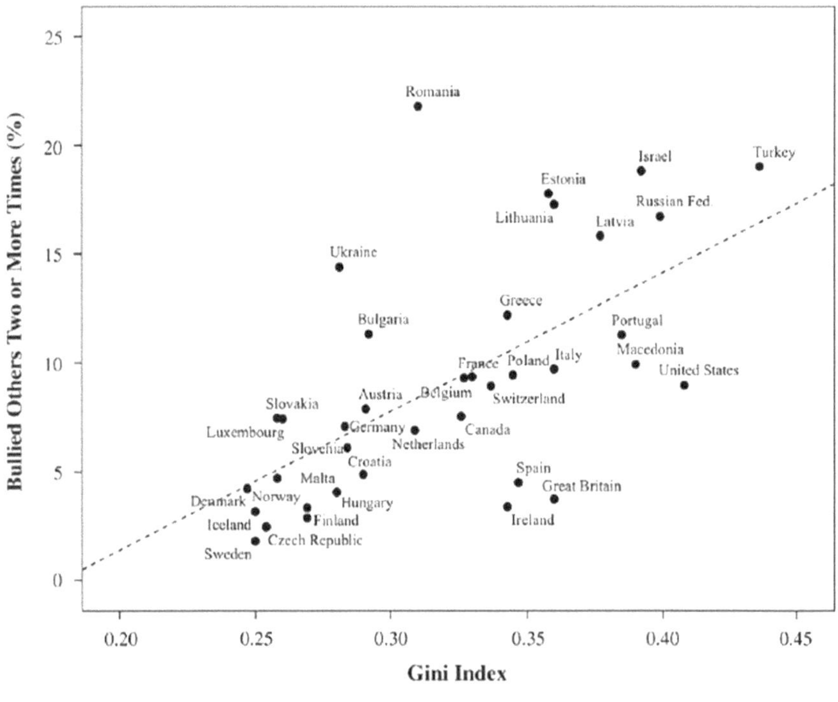

Figure 5.3 The relationship between economic equality within a country and reported bullying at school.

prevalence is high bullying tends to be high. In countries with great inequality the competition for resources is strongest; in extreme cases, survival or at least a tolerable existence may depend on not being dominated by others – in short, not being bullied. This may be avoided by bullying others. Further, highly lucrative outcomes and financial security may result from successful bullying. Not surprisingly, in countries where there is a great deal of inequality the overall level of bullying is relatively high. By contrast, the incentive to dominate others is lower in countries where there is greater economic equality.

Physical climate

Reference to climatic difference as a factor in bullying behaviour will strike the reader as odd, as in a seemingly absurd proposal that was made by Montesquieu in the 18th century. He speculated that the tendency to act aggressively was stronger in hot countries. He pointed out that strict discipline and draconian laws were found to be necessary in Arab countries because the people tended to become overheated, passionate and dangerous – and therefore more inclined to bully!

A recent study suggests that climate may in fact have a significant effect on interpersonal behaviour. It has been claimed that variations in the ambient temperature of an area may in fact be associated with personality differences that relate to bullying (Wei et al., 2017). For their study, two countries were selected: the United States and China. In areas where the temperature was on average less 'clement,' that is varied most from an ideal temperature for humans of 22 degrees Celcius, after controlling for age, gender, education and socio-economic status, respondents were found to be significantly less agreeable and conscientious and more emotionally unstable – characteristics (noted earlier) that have been found among students who tend to be involved in bullying in schools. A further suggestion has been made that extremes of cold or very hot weather may result in people being confined more often to their homes and are thus deprived of opportunities for developing social skills needed to interact optimally with others.

School and classroom climate

Whatever the case may be regarding physical climate, there is considerable agreement that the social climate to which children are exposed at school can contribute to bullying behaviour. Defining what is meant by school climate has led to formulations that are perhaps more notable for their rhetoric than for their objectivity, for instance, school climate has been described as, 'the heart and soul of school life.' Distinctions have been made between various aspects of the climate. It can be seen as relating especially to that which is conducive to learning and academic excellence, or as the quality of interpersonal relationships between members of the school community, or as the norms and values that are inculcated and endorsed by the school. Attempts to relate school climate to bullying have focused on particular aspects As an example, Petrie (2014) assessed perceptions of the school climate by students in Australia using reliable measures of (i) student-teacher relationships (ii) peer relations (iii) a sense of belonging to the school and (iv) a perception of safety at school. It was reported that students involved in bullying at school had more negative assessments on each of these measures. Other studies have claimed that relatively high levels of bullying prevalence are found in schools at which the climate of the classroom and/or the climate of the school in general is perceived by students negatively (Thapa et al., 2013).

Peer group pressure

Peer pressure has been seen as particularly important in explaining bullying behaviour. Hence some research into bullying has focused on group processes and how students are affected by their relationship with groups of peers and by the norms and values they share (Salmivalli, 2010). As a consequence, many students may engage in bullying as a group or bully someone under pressure from their friendship group. They may place a greater store on loyalty to their mates than on other sources, such as what the school expects of them. Alternatively, they may feel that it is in their interest to act as they think their peers expect them to act – and thereby retain their much valued support. Thus bullying has come to be seen as part of a group process, rather than due to the independent volition of individual children (Garandeau & Cillessen, 2006). This view of bullying negates or minimizes the role that individual personality or character may play in explaining bullying behaviour.

It should not be presumed that peer group pressure is essentially negative. Considerable research has been undertaken, for instance by Pepler in Canada and Salmivalli in Finland to identify the contribution of positive bystander behaviour in discouraging or stopping bullying from continuing. A corollary of this general view of bullying is that interventions are needed at the group level, that is with the students who are influencing each other to act in ways that lead to bullying and also with students who can take action against bullying through positive bystander behaviour.

Interventions

Schools typically take action, either proactive or reactive or both, thereby changing the environment within a school, hopefully, to reduce the prevalence of bullying. Earlier we examined actions undertaken by some schools in promoting SEL. Here we may note features of reactive interventions and

Table 5.1 Confronting, non-confronting and mixed forms of intervention

Confronting	*Non-confronting*	*Mixed*
Direct Sanctions/ Traditional Disciplinary Approach	Mediation	Restorative Practices
School Tribunals/Bully Courts	Support Group Method	Strengthening the Victim
	Method of Shared Concern	

their rationale as examined by researchers. (A more extended discussion of reactive interventions is given in Rigby (2012b).

Forms of intervention have been diverse and currently there is no generally accepted classification or typology. A simple dichotomy has been proposed according to which interventions may be described as confronting or non-confronting (Garandeau, Poskiparta & Salmivalli, 2014); that is, confronting the bully or bullies or seeking to explore with those involved in the bullying how the bullying can best be resolved. Some interventions may involve elements of confronting and non-confronting as in Restorative Practice in which identified 'bullies' are required to accept responsibility for the bullying, but are then led to discuss with the practitioner (teacher or counsellor) and the 'victim' what further action may be needed. Victimized students may be asked directly to consider how they can change their behaviour in seeking to cope more adequately with bullying, to discuss options and voluntarily undertake training to develop appropriate social skills. Table 5.1 suggests a trichotomy of reactive intervention methods.

These methods of intervention are examined further in the following chapter on the Perspectives of Teachers together with descriptions of their application and reported outcomes in addressing bullying. There is considerable disagreement among researchers as to which are the most effective and appropriate methods of intervention and under what circumstances they are likely to be successful. For instance, Ttofi and Farrington (2011) rate interventions through the use of direct sanctions or punishment for bullying behaviour as the most effective. Some other researchers have provided reports that are highly supportive of alternative methods of intervention, such as Restorative Practice (Wong, Cheng & Ngan, 2004); the Support Group Method (Smith, Howard & Thompson, 2007; Young, 1998); or the Method of Shared Concern (Rigby & Griffiths, 2011).

Putting it all together

Researchers in the field of bullying almost always see themselves as intent on providing evidence for an approach to countering bullying which accords best with the findings derived from their own investigations and/or those of others. In short, they tend to be 'applied researchers' promoting a distinctive view on what can and should be done to counter bullying. Increasingly many have come to recognize that the problem of school bullying is highly complex and many interacting factors contribute to its happening. Models of bullying have become increasingly complex as they seek to take into account multiple factors and multiple intervention strategies. The recognition of such complexity has led to the increasing promotion of what is called the social ecological model as a means of understanding bullying and what can be done about it

The basic idea underlying this perspective on bullying, however, is not new. It may be encapsulated in a simple formula suggested by the American social psychologist, Kurt Lewin (1936). He proposed that all behaviour could be viewed as a consequence of an interaction between a person and that person's environment. This he expressed in the well-known formula, B = f (P.E), where B is behaviour, f stands for function, P stands for Person and E for the Environment. This formulation was seen as theoretically capable of shedding light on all forms of social and interpersonal behaviour, from drug addiction and committing suicide to playing football and getting married. It was a matter of identifying what constituted the relevant factors that influenced the behaviour and how they interacted with each other. Attempts were made to generalize about the nature and kinds of factors that needed to be taken into account. A general ecological model was suggested by Bronfenbrenner in 1977 and his formulation has led some researchers to theorize about the complex web of factors that relate to bullying behaviour. Typically they include peer influence, home and family background, community attitudes, school and classroom climate, relations with teachers, and relations between the school and parents (Espelage & Swearer, 2010; Espelage, 2014).

The question of what is the 'P' with which aspects of the environment interact is rarely asked. An American contemporary of Lewin, Gordon Allport (1968), gave an interesting answer. Everybody he claimed is in some respects:

Like no other person

Like some other persons

Like all other persons

In the search for generalisations about how person and environment interact to bring about bullying behaviour to produce bullying behaviour some researchers have adopted the second view of what a person is, that is, like some other persons and not like others, and identifiable by reference to personality dimensions.

In the1960s and 1970s the English psychologist, Eysenck (1997) elaborated a plausible account of how differences in three basic dimensions of personality might interact with environmental factors. As noted earlier, these dimensions were extraversion-introversion; high and low neuroticism and high and low psychoticism, each related to reported behaviour of children involved in bullying either as bullies or victims or as both.

Eysenck claimed that children were affected by some aspects of the environment in different ways, according to whether they were relatively introverted and/or inclined towards neuroticism. He suggested that introverted people were more conditionable and cited the experimental work of Franks (1957) which reported that introverts acquired conditioned responses with fewer trials than extroverts. Arguably they were more amenable to control by authorities such as teachers. With them, strong disciplinary treatment was considered unnecessary. Children high on neuroticism were prone to react to negative events with high levels of anxiety and to find it hard to control their behaviour. Children high on psychoticism were thought to lack empathy and need more help in forming positive relationships. Hence it seemed to follow that bullying behaviour, how victims were affected and how they needed to be treated depended on both personality factors and the environment, past and present. This line of thinking has led some psychologists to view aspects of the environment as affecting individual students differently and justifying different approaches depending on a student's personality type. However, this perspective on how bullying behaviour may be treated may not be acceptable to some teachers who hold the view that students who commit similar offences must, as a matter of justice, be treated in the same way.

A more comprehensive analysis of the interaction between the nature of the person and the environment has been suggested by Rigby (2014) following the view expressed by Tattum and Tattum (1992) that central to the explanation for bullying behaviour is a desire to hurt and dominate another person or persons. The strength of that desire is held to be determined by various interacting factors, including genetic endowment, child rearing practices, the community ethos, negative peer group pressure, and the occurrence of personally frustrating events. Figure 5.4 illustrates this suggested process.

Whether an individual takes a particular course of action is seen as depending on a decision-making process that takes into account perceived advantages in doing so, such as material gains or losses and changes of social status. In some cases, the impulse to act aggressively dissipates or is suppressed, especially if it is relatively weak and something positive occurs to change the motivation. In other cases, the desire to hurt or dominate may lead to a fight in which the conflict is between persons of about the same strength or power. The third possibility is to engage in bullying, that is to act aggressively towards a person or group that can offer little or no resistance. Here specific prejudices may determine the choice of target, together with judgements as to what will be achieved; for example, an increase in social status and greater acceptance by one's friendship group Choice of the means of bullying may be influenced by what is seen as likely to be effective in the

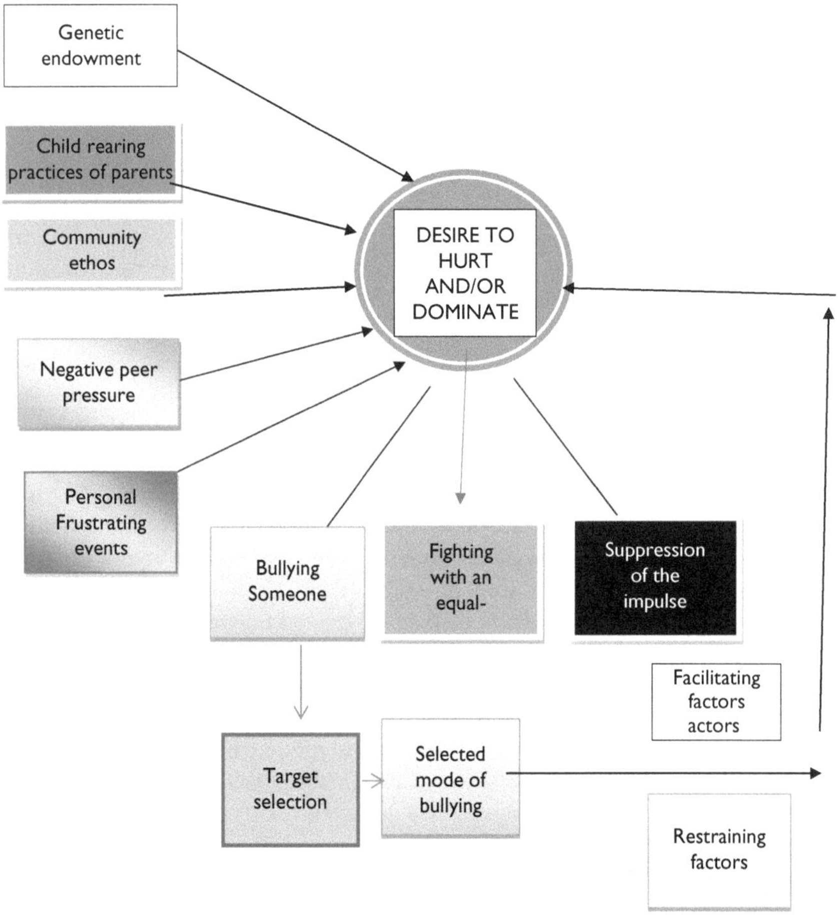

Figure 5.4 Theoretical model linking desire to hurt with contributory factors and bullying behaviour.

particular case and what is pragmatically justified. Cruel teasing or cyberbullying may seem to involve less risk than employing physical assault. Having decided what might be done, the actual circumstances present when the action may begin are likely to influence what happens next. The bullying may be encouraged and facilitated by supportive or by passive bystanders and by the absence of teacher supervision. On the other hand, bystanders may discourage and restrain the bullying. Anticipation of action that may be taken subsequently by the school may inhibit the potential aggressor. If the action brings about positive outcomes for the 'bully' such as a rise in status one might expect the bullying to continue and the cycle becomes difficult to stop.

This model suggests that the conditions that give rise to the desire to hurt should be addressed, where possible, for example, through schools providing a warm supportive climate and minimizing frustration. How students handle frustration and control their anger also needs to be addressed, for example through the implementation of SEL or similar programs, and the encouragement of positive bystander behaviour. The model recognizes the important part that can be played through school policies and practices that monitor and restrain bullying behaviour. In placing the desire to hurt and dominate others as a central feature of bullying, it identifies, as some models do not, the importance of addressing a basic cause (not the only one) of bullying behaviour through psychological and moral education.

One critique of this framework for understanding and addressing bullying suggests that not all bullying is driven by a desire to hurt. For some children who bully, it argued, the primary motive is to achieve higher status as part of a pecking order. In some cases of bullying the desire to hurt may be lacking or of secondary importance: the primary goal is to enhance or protect one's personal status. In other cases, the goal is simply to hurt and enjoy hurting another person, as in sadistic bullying. In some cases, we may find both the desire to hurt and a desire for greater status at the expense of someone else.

Another way of looking at bullying is that devised by researchers Ajzen and Fishbein (1980) in their Theory of Reasoned Action, elaborated further by Ajzen (1991) in the Theory of Planned Behavior (see Figure 5.5). In this

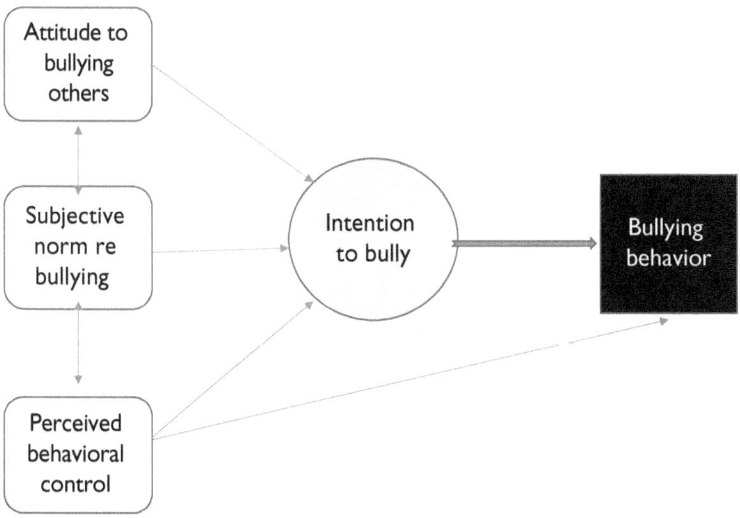

Application of the Model of Planned Behavior to bullying, based on Azjen (1991)

Figure 5.5 The theory of planned behaviour.

formulation 'person factors' included (i) personal attitudes towards a specified kind of action or action, are derived from an evaluation of expected outcomes; and (ii) believing one has the capacity to carry out the bullying act or acts, that is, perceived behavioural control. The environmental contribution is seen as coming from what other people (especially members of one's friendship group) are believed to think about one carrying out an action, that is, the perceived group norm. This is seen as constituting a pressure to undertake a particular act or refrain from doing so. Taken together these factors are thought to predict intention to act. Ajzen claims that the intention to act is closely correlated with actually doing so.

This theory has not often been used in research into bullying-in-general, although some studies have examined its utility in predicting cyberbullying among schoolchildren in Belgium (Heirman & Walruve, 2012; Pabian & Vandebosch, 2014).

One study in Australia sought to apply the theory in predicting *intention* to bully others attending coeducational secondary schools (Rigby, 1997). Reliable multi-measures of attitudes to bullying, perceived capacity to bully others, and normative pressure to bully at school were each found to be independently predictive of an intention to bully. The combination of all these factors increased predictability. The results suggested that the personal characteristics or beliefs of students, as inferred from their attitudes to bullying and perceived capacity to bully, together with knowledge of perceived social norms, could explain a great deal of bullying behaviour.

As is common with psychological models, there is no explicit recognition that personal moral considerations enter into whether a child bullies someone. It does however provide a simple framework that focuses attention on the role of social norms, what a child believes are the likely outcomes of bullying someone and the capacity of children to bully or resist being bullied.

Conclusions

As this chapter illustrates, points of view on bullying among theorists and researchers are exceedingly diverse, sometimes contradictory, and at times complementary. Generally, research contributions emphasize one way of looking at bullying and/or intervening to tackle it. In so doing they encourage some perspectives on bullying and discourage others. 'Truth' has been defined by the philosopher, Pierce (1878/1986) as 'the opinion which is fated to be ultimately agreed to by all who investigate.' If this is so, the prospects of arriving at the truth about bullying is likely to be distant. Currently what research into bullying has provided are plausible grounds, theoretical and empirical, for holding certain beliefs about its causes and consequences, with some related suggestions as to how it may be addressed. How the theoretical formulations and empirical findings can best be integrated and form an agreed way of understanding and addressing the problem is a 'work in progress' we hope.

It is natural to feel some disappointment and even dismay if you happen to be an administrator or teacher, to find such diversity and controversy among theorists and researchers when you desperately want to know what to do to counter bullying. Yet it would be unfair to liken the places where controversies about bullying among researchers are found to Babel. Not all voices of researchers shut out other voices. There are signs that some views are well supported and complementary. I am personally persuaded by the simple but very powerful suggestion made 80 years ago by Kurt Lewin that all behaviour is the function of the interaction of person and environment. How this can be better elaborated, understood and applied in countering bullying is the current challenge.

Chapter 6

Perspectives of teachers

Whatever the perspectives of researchers may be, it is the perspectives of teachers that matter more in the everyday task of countering bullying in schools. Like researchers, they have their agreements and disagreements; but on one thing they are agreed – there is a pressing and practical need to have a collective approach to what they are trying to achieve. I have yet to meet any bunch of teachers who do not believe in a 'whole school approach'; indeed it is a basic article of faith. Researchers may hypothesize and disagree, but teachers have a job to get on with. This is not to say that all teachers have the same views on the nature of bullying and the best way to deal with it. In this chapter, we will examine what differences in views there are among teachers and also between teachers and most researchers, as well as where teachers tend to see things in much the same way.

As I have tried to show, there have been substantial changes over the course of history on how bullying has been perceived, as well as substantial differences from place to place. The same is true of teacher perceptions of bullying. As far as I can discover, there has been no documented history of how teachers have changed in the way they perceive bullying. I must therefore draw upon my own impressions between 1937 when I first attended primary school in England to the present day in Australia, drawing on impressions in my various roles as a school teacher from 1958 to 1968 and as a researcher, since 1990, mainly in Australian schools.

As with everybody I have talked with over the years bullying was a feature of school life as they have remembered it. My own experience as a schoolboy was not exceptional. We knew who the bullies were and who their victims were – and most of us tried to steer clear of them. Yet, surprisingly, in retrospect it is hard to recall any teachers who expressed any concern about what was happening. Before 1990 or thereabouts it was virtually a non-issue – at least in England, as far as teachers were concerned. It is true that a succession of books, biographical or in some cases autobiographical, had been written by literary luminaries, such as Aldous Huxley, Graham Greene, John Betjeman, C.S Lewis and George Orwell, drawing on their own school experiences, but teachers, it seemed, were not buying any of this. As a teacher in primary and

DOI: 10.4324/9781315454450-6

secondary schools for ten years in six different schools, there was never a staff meeting that I attended at which the issue of bullying received any attention.

By 1990 the climate had changed. As a university researcher into bullying, I got to visit many schools in Australia and some overseas and talked to hundreds of teachers and read all I could about the newly discovered problem. Most schools were beginning to recognize that it was a serious issue. Governmental bodies began to insist that schools took notice of it. Having a school anti-bullying policy was mandated. Yet resistance continued in some schools. I recall being invited to one school around 1990 to discuss the issue with the Principal, who seemingly had forgotten about the invitation and its purpose. He agreed to talk – and invited his deputy to join us. I explained that we were meeting to talk about bullying. The Principal looked alarmed and sought support from his deputy. 'There is no bullying here,' he declared. The deputy nodded dutifully in agreement. 'Perhaps,' I suggested diplomatically, 'occasional harassment?' Being a softer name for much the same thing, this was acceptable. The Departments of Education were also resistant. Yes, I was told by a Departmental representative in South Australia in the early 1990s, that student behaviour was sometimes 'inappropriate,' but that each school resolved any such difficulties through Behavior Management. Gradually, under increasing pressure from government policy makers, community leaders, media reports and parental outcries, nearly all schools 'toed the line.' Nearly all. I still hear from some principals that bullying never occurs at their school. But the transformation of schoolteacher attitudes towards bullying over the last 30 years has been truly remarkable.

How teachers define bullying

Here is the approved definition of bullying that teachers are given in Australia, where I live:

> Bullying is an ongoing and deliberate misuse of power in relationships through repeated verbal, physical and/or social behaviour that intends to cause physical, social and/or psychological harm. It can involve an individual or a group misusing their power, or perceived power, over one or more persons who feel unable to stop it from happening (Australian Government Department of Education and Training, 2016).

This is not that different from definitions of bullying in schools in other countries. It bears many of the marks of the seminal contribution of Olweus's (1993) formulation, which has guided most researchers and educators in their work in many countries. From it we may infer that:

1. It involves an intention to do harm
2. It can include various means – verbal, physical and/or social

3. It involves a sense of powerlessness on the part of the target
4. It involves repetition of the behaviour
5. It can be perpetrated by individuals or by groups
6. Individuals and groups may be deliberately targeted
7. It is wrongful behaviour

But do teachers actually perceive bullying in this way?

Studies have been undertaken to discover how teachers do define bullying. One study conducted in England by Naylor et al. (2006) reported on teachers (N = 225) in schools catering for secondary school students who answered a questionnaire which included this open-ended item: 'Please say what you think bullying is.' The responses were categorized according to what features relating to bullying could be inferred. Mention was made by teachers of a wide range of behaviours, both direct and indirect. A minority (10%) of respondents limited themselves to mentioning direct forms of bullying, such as direct verbal or physical abuse. Approximately 70% of the teachers mentioned the existence of a power imbalance favouring the 'bully.' A similar proportion mentioned the harm that was suffered by the victim. Surprisingly, in view of the definition commonly employed by researchers, only 18% of teachers included the criterion of 'intention' or the criterion of 'repetition' in defining bullying. Only 13% mentioned social exclusion as a mode of bullying someone. From this study, it can be suggested that some of the criteria considered by most researchers as crucial to a definition of bullying in schools were not accepted by most teachers.

Arguably, this method of assessing how teachers view bullying depends on the readiness or ability to call to mind a variety of criteria that are essential in defining bullying. Defining something as complicated as bullying can be a demanding task. Easier to jot down whatever comes to mind when you think of somebody bullying someone. Hence, elements that might be included – with some prompting and more reflection – could have been omitted.

A recent study undertaken in Australia by Campbell, Wheirford and Hooijer (2019) engaged teachers in a less theoretical and more practical exercise. This small-scale study involved 52 teachers who were presented with 20 written scenarios, half involving cyber communications and half non-cyber bullying. A large majority of the teachers (90%) correctly identified cases that in the judgement of most researchers did constitute bullying. This piece of research suggests that whatever can be inferred from teacher answers to 'open ended' questions, there is considerable agreement between teachers and researchers when they make judgements about the same hypothetical situations.

A team of researchers from the United States (Maunder, Harrop & Tattersall, 2010) have suggested that there is much more to explaining the understanding that teachers have of bullying than making inferences from the definitions of bullying they adopt or are expected to adopt. They point out that the social, cultural and historical context may play a major role. In making a judgement of what constitutes a case of bullying, there are numerous factors that may influence teachers. Some of these relate to features of the social environment, both external and internal to the school. These may include pressures from parents who want to see the school act in certain ways in preventing and dealing with cases of bullying, and also views prevalent in the local community or expressed through the media. Within the school, teachers are influenced by the views of their colleagues and by what has come to be accepted as the appropriate attitude and response to bullying behaviour. Accepted professional practice within a school may be at least as influential in determining a teacher's perspective on bullying as directions provided by Departments of Education or implied in official definitions of bullying.

The 'historical context' can be taken in different ways. It can refer to the prevailing attitudes towards bullying at one point in time and place. As we have seen, teacher and community attitudes have changed over time, generally in the direction of recognizing bullying as a serious problem. But not all teachers appear to have gone along with the changes. Some remain sceptical. 'History' may also refer to what teachers have actually experienced in their observations of student behaviour and their personal interactions with individual students. Experience may have led some teachers to be highly critical of bullying behaviour and how it has – or has not – been handled. They may be aware of some cases of bullying that have had very serious consequences such as psychological trauma or suicide. Hence some teachers can become particularly sensitive to the harm bullying can do – and see bullying occurring when others do not.

The history, real or mistaken, of a child's involvement in bullying, may play a part in how teachers respond to a case of bullying. Over time some students gain a reputation for bullying; it is widely believed that someone has certain qualities that justify him or her being called a bully. In this way who is a 'bully' may be said to be socially constructed. This reputation may or not be a true reflection of how the student currently behaves. It nevertheless can play a big part in how a student's behaviour may be interpreted and labelled.

The perceived severity of actions taken to hurt another person may also be taken into account by a teacher in identifying a student as a bully: the more severe, the more likely it is to be seen as bullying. In general, teachers judge physical bullying as more severe and its consequences as more serious (Maunder, Harrop & Tattersall, 2010). One would expect such a judgement to be based in part on what others think, that is the prevailing view in the school, especially among staff members and educational leaders. This may sometimes result in non-physical and indirect forms of aggressive or negative behaviour being dismissed – or not regarded as bullying at all. Further, the 'fault' may actually be located in the person who is being targeted. This latter view has been reported as one held by a prominent Australian writer and sometime school principal, John Marsden. He concedes that 'real' bullying does occur, that is the extreme and egregious abuse of power, but most of it, he observes, can be described as the 'giving of feedback for unlikeable behaviour' (Ocelli, 2019). He opines that it is up to the 'victim' to recognize and acknowledge their 'unlikeable' behaviour and take steps to reduce it. As many of his Australian critics have pointed out, this is blaming the victim – and not surprisingly deeply resented by parents. It is unlikely, however, that Marsden is alone in attributing some responsibility to the victim for getting bullied at school. Few teachers would have the temerity to admit it.

Teachers are human and their likes and dislikes extend to their students. Hence within the body of teachers, personal or idiosyncratic judgements inevitably play a part in how they view cases of bullying. When a teacher becomes fond of a student and admires that student, he or she may be seen as doing no wrong. I recall an interview I had with a teacher who spoke of a boy who bullied others 'He is a real boy' she said.

Perhaps the most difficult area in which judgements are made is in cases of bully-victims; that is students who bully and are themselves bullied. It is hard for many teachers to be empathically disposed to a student who is being bullied, even seriously bullied, when he or she is repeatedly bullying or provoking others. A case in my own experience concerned a student who had been constantly speaking ill of a minority ethnic group and eventually became a target for them – and was himself collectively bullied. Action by the school was considerably hindered by the parents of the offended students who were aware of the provocative racial abuse. In fact, relations between the school and the parents deteriorated and the problem could not be satisfactorily resolved.

Teachers' views on bullying can be affected by their relations with the parents of their students and their attitudes towards parents. For some teachers, relations with parents over matters relating to bullying are tense and their attitudes to parents may be negative. This is a curiously neglected area of research. But it is, in my experience, an area in which a good deal of conflict can and does occur, especially when parents feel strongly that the school is not taking adequate action in dealing with the problem (see Chapter 8). This is not to say that many teachers are generally unresponsive to concerned parents and, of course, many teachers have children themselves, some of whom have experienced bullying. But what teachers may see as a case of bullying may be affected by interactions with parents, for better or worse.

An important contributory factor to the way teachers think about bullying is the social philosophy or ideology they adopt. At the current time, two contrasting ideologies that are clearly relevant to bullying include those who hold a strong belief in social inequality and those who do not. A belief in social equality can take various forms including opposition to any discrimination against ethnic minorities, racial groups, people of non-mainstream sexual orientation, disabled people or religious minorities. Recognizing the disadvantages that these and other groups experience can lead to a recognition of the harm that they experience and the need to give support and prevent discrimination against them. This may result in greater sensitivity to how they may be treated by other students. A contrasting view is that some humans are innately superior to others and believe that inferior types are less deserving. These superior types may include in some countries those who are white, especially if they are male, of high social status, heterosexual, able-bodied and orthodox in religious belief or unbelief. Unfair treatment of students who do not fit such categories may go unrecognized.

Undeniably in many societies, there are people who hold beliefs that are deeply prejudiced. For example, results provided by the Pew Research Center indicated that 83% of Blacks in the USA claimed to have been treated unfairly because of their race or ethnicity, more than twice that of other groups (Newport, 2020). One would like to think that school educators never contributed to racial prejudice. However, a recent study concluded on the basis of comparisons of results from large scale surveys that differences in racial attitudes between teachers and non-teachers were negligible and not significant (Starck, Riddle & Stacey, 2020).

The effects of negative evaluations of students by teachers can have important consequences. Early research by Rosenthal (1985) in the United States demonstrated that students about whom teachers had low or negative expectations were less likely to do well at school. A recent report provides evidence that black children are two or three times more likely to be punished for offences than other students in US schools (Losen & Martinez, 2020). Granted that there may be reasons other than bias for differential treatment, these findings suggest that, in some cultures at least, the attitudes of a minority of teachers do not promote inclusiveness in schools. Whether teacher attitudes to gay children and children from poor families are related to how some teachers view bullying behaviour is currently unclear.

Bullying between teachers and students

Relations between teachers and students can have important implications for relations between students and the capacity of the school to address the problem. A growing number of studies have reported that, at times, relations between teachers and individual or groups of students can be negative and can give rise to reciprocal bullying (Burns, Fogelgarn & Billet, 2020; Datta, Cornell & Huang, 2017; Twemlow et al., 2006).

What constitutes bullying of students by teachers is not easy to define. Teachers and other adults in schools have legitimate power over students and may appropriately criticize and discipline them in certain situations. How teachers treat students can be interpreted mistakenly by some observers as bullying. According to Twemlow et al. (2006), teacher bullying involves taking action that is meant 'to punish, manipulate or disparage a student *beyond what would be a reasonable disciplinary procedure*' (p. 191). What precisely constitutes bullying by teachers has changed over time, especially in the area of administering physical punishment, which is no longer permitted in many countries, including Australia. However, both anecdotal and systematic research suggests that teachers bullying students still constitutes a problem in some schools, judging from both reports by students who claim to have been bullied by a teacher and by teachers who admit to having sometimes overstepped the mark.

Explanations for teacher bullying may include (i) being overzealous in 'correcting' a child's behaviour (ii) seeking to establish control over an unruly class or unruly individual (iii) prejudice against a category of student, eg., due to his/her ethnicity or race (iv) failure to appreciate the harm that may ensue from bullying a child and (v) most rarely, an expression of a sadistic personality. Being traumatized by being bullied by a teacher or by observing a teacher bullying someone is possible, but a more likely consequence is that such behaviour stirs up resentment and damages student-teacher relationships with unfortunate consequences for a child's ability to make progress in his or her studies. In some cases observing the effectiveness of bullying by a teacher can elicit admiration and can lead to the teacher's bullying behaviour being emulated.

Sometimes negative attitudes of teachers towards students appears to be shared by the school staff. At the Grammar school that I attended as a schoolboy in England, the staff appeared to be united in disparaging and indeed sneering at children who had a working class accent or spoke in a [deplorable] Lancashire dialect. In Australia, I witnessed a fellow teacher ridiculing immigrant children from England who played football with a ball that was round, not the right spheroid shape that dinkum Aussies kick around. Trivial perhaps, but it did nothing to improve staff-student relationships.

Given the uncertainty of what constitutes 'reasonableness' in teacher behaviour by teachers, estimates of bullying prevalence by teachers are hard to evaluate. As expected, students tend to make exaggerated claims that teachers have bullied them. However, as many as 40% of teachers in the Twemlow et al study in the USA acknowledged that they had bullied their students on some occasions, and in the study by Burns et al. (2020) approximately 70% of Australian teachers reported that they had been bullied by students over the last 12 months.

The bullying of teachers by students is by all accounts not uncommon. It tends to be more prevalent in secondary schools, with some teachers (mostly female) far more likely to be bullied than others. When a class of students collectively bully a teacher the consequences can be serious and result in teachers leaving the profession. Some teachers are clearly more at risk than others, having characteristics that make them vulnerable, such as an inability to manage classroom behaviour; 'weird' personal idiosyncrasies, inexperience as classroom teachers; and lack of support from school authorities and other staff members. Such bullying, if not addressed, can have serious negative effects on the capacity of schools to address intra-student bullying and guarantee the safety of children.

As well as bullying between teachers and students, we must recognize bullying in relationships between teachers and parents and also among teachers. To the extent that such bullying occurs, it may detract from the task of addressing intra-student bullying, lower staff morale and increase the difficulty of promoting a peaceful school.

Cultural factors affecting teacher perceptions of bullying

What is judged to constitute bullying is to some extent culturally determined, as becomes clear when we examine how it is viewed in different countries. Most evident is the treatment of homosexuals. According to Wikipedia, the following countries may apply the death penalty for homosexual behaviour: Afghanistan, Brunei, Iran, Mauritania, Nigeria, Saudi Arabia, Somalia and the United Arab Emirates. Reports of cases of actual executions have become increasingly uncommon. Nevertheless, the existence of a statute in these countries legitimizing such a penalty sends a signal to schools that those who are homosexual – or appear to be – can be treated with contempt – without anyone being accused of bullying.

A degree of ethnic prejudice appears to exist in practically all countries, as revealed by experimental studies that assess the extent to which people of different ethnicity applying for jobs are successful in gaining employment, and in questionnaire studies in which respondents are asked about their preferences for people of different ethnicity to be their neighbours (Booth, Leigh & Varganova, 2012). As noted earlier, teachers may be as prone as others to discriminate in their treatment of people of different ethnic groups. Hence the need to promote inclusiveness in school policies and practice. This initiative appears to be effective in the light of findings in the Australian survey by Rigby and Johnson (2016) in which it was reported that children of minority ethnic groups (identified as indicating that they used a non-English language in communicating in their families at home) were not treated in discriminatory ways nor bullied at school more often than other students. Indigenous students, who make up approximately 6% of the Australian school population, did not report being bullied more often than other students. However, they did report being racially harassed at school significantly more often than other students.

Less obviously, views of what constitutes bullying may differ between countries with an individualistic culture and countries that have collectivist mentality. In South Korea, bullying is officially defined as 'any form of constant or repeated actions whereby *at least two students* inflict physical or emotional harm on a specific student or a specific group of students inside or outside of school premises, and then inflict pain thereon' (Statutes of the Republic of Korea, 2014). One-on-one bullying, according to students in an individualistic culture, is perceived to occur much more often than group-based bullying (Rigby, 2020). Thus, teachers in a collectivistic culture are less likely to identify bullying involving one-on-one incidents; in fact, they may conclude that it does not exist – by definition!

The teacher-researcher gap

Many researchers have commented upon what has been called the gap between the understanding or knowledge of educational matters of researchers and those of education practitioners (see Hirshkorn & Geelan, 2008; Procter, 2015). It is generally agreed that the gap is considerably wider than that between researchers in medicine and medical practitioners. Some educational researchers have expressed amazement at the very substantial gap as it exists. According to Cooper, Levin and Campbell (2009), 'It is virtually impossible for a reasonable person to disagree with the view that policy and practice [in education] should be based on the available evidence' (p. 161). Yet many teachers apparently do. How this gap appears as far as bullying is concerned was examined among Australian teachers in a recent government supported survey (Rigby 2018). This survey was conducted in Australia to ascertain similarities and differences in beliefs about bullying by teachers and researchers. A questionnaire was devised and answered online by 451 teachers. It contained 40 items about which researchers were thought to have a generally agreed position. The teachers were asked to indicate anonymously whether they thought each statement was true or false. On some items there was considerable agreement, for example, over 95% of teachers endorsed the view, supported by researchers, that 'bullying occurs when a person or group repeatedly abuse their power over someone,' and that, 'It is widely agreed that schools should adopt a whole-school approach.' However, there were many matters on which teachers were divided and disagreed with a position taken by researchers. Table 6.1 gives the percentages of teachers who agree with the research position on 11 selected items.

Do these disagreements matter? The answer in part depends on the validity attaching to the researcher's judgements and whether the teachers are really mistaken. Arguably on some matters, the professional experience of teachers may count, and further research may question what researchers have concluded. However, the results do illustrate the existence of notable gaps between the understanding (rightly or wrongly) of teachers and researchers.

At least equally important, is the fact that teachers did disagree greatly with each other on some issues. The differences suggest that there can be difficulties for schools in taking a whole-school approach on some issues. For instance, believing that bullies tend to lack adequate self-esteem may lead some teachers to believe that perpetrators can be reformed if they are indiscriminately praised. Further, denying the existence of genetic influence on bullying behaviour may result in a teacher failing to recognize that some students who bully (or are bullied) may require more than average attention and possibly a different approach in interventions.

Table 6.1 Percentages of teachers agreeing with judgements of researchers

1. Children are more likely to tell their teachers than their parents if they are being bullied at school. (F)	64.1
2. Bullying in schools is becoming more and more prevalent throughout the world. (F)	60.3
3. Most bullying nowadays is through cyber technology. (F)	57.9
4. The prevalence of bullying in school is much the same in all countries. (F)	54.3
5. Typically bullying occurs when no one is watching. (F)	53.4
6. Bullying at school is predictive of a greater likelihood of children engaging in crime as adults. (T)	49.2
7. School children tend to bully more as they get older. (F)	48.3
8. Victimisation (being bullied) at school tends to increase with age. (F)	40.4
9. Boys tend to bully more than girls, especially physically. (T)	39.0
10. Children with high self-esteem are less likely to bully others. (F)	33.5
11. Genetic factors can influence whether a child will bully at school. **(T)**	32.2

Note: The letters given in parentheses (T) for 'true' or (F) indicates whether it was assumed that researchers, in general, believed the item was true or false. The percentage in the Table indicates what percentage of teachers agreed with the researchers.

Further analyses of these data showed that male and female teachers did not differ in their responses overall. But two findings were of particular interest

1. The teachers who reported that they obtained information about bullying from reading professional journals rather than the internet made judgements significantly closer the those of researchers.
2. Given the opportunity to download the answers (for which a link was provided) and the sources related to the research judgments, only 44% did so. Those who did were in fact in closer agreement with the researchers. This suggests that some teachers are likely to be more open to research evidence than others.

This research suggests that in many cases perspectives on bullying are influenced only a little or not at all by what researchers have to say. As not infrequently observed, most schools do not have a research-interested culture. They prioritize professional experience. At the same time, there is increasing pressure on schools to adopt evidence-based strategies, the discovery and employment of which can arguably increase the effectiveness of both learning and anti-bullying initiatives (Godfrey, 2014).

Teacher perceptions of the magnitude of the problem of bullying in schools

How seriously are teachers taking the problem of bullying? There is little doubt that over time – at least since the 1980s – bullying in schools has been regarded in an increasing number of countries as a major issue. There have been numerous reports in quite recent times that teachers are seriously underestimating the prevalence of bullying in their school and have little knowledge of who is being bullied and by how much. There have been at least 15 relevant surveys of bullying in schools since 1998 in a range of countries including Australia, England, Finland, Kenya, Norway and the USA. In each of these teacher estimates of bullying prevalence have been compared with estimates derived from student reports (see Rigby, 2020). Reports from students on bullying prevalence have been regarded as the 'gold standard.' Lower estimates derived from teacher judgements have been used to support the view that teachers underestimate bullying prevalence.

However, when estimates, made by teachers and students of the overall level of bullying in a school using the same questions, findings suggesting that teachers underestimate bullying prevalence have not been supported. In the most recent study, conducted in Australia, the findings strongly support the conclusion that teachers actually believe *more bullying* is going on at their schools than students do (Rigby, 2020).

The Australian study differed from earlier studies in two ways. First, it made use of a multi-item scale of demonstrated reliability; secondly, it examined possible differences between teacher and student estimates of bullying prevalence for each of nine types or modes of bullying. These comprised the following: being made fun of; kicked or hit; having rumours spread about one; being ignored or excluded; being made afraid; receiving harassing text messages; experiencing cruel communications online; racial harassment; and sexual harassment. Respondents were asked to say how often they thought students at their school were being bullied in each of these ways: never, sometimes, often and very often. Scale scores were computed and averaged for teachers and for students. In addition, the mean percentages were calculated for judgements of more than 'sometimes' – that is 'often' or 'very often.'

The results suggested that, in general, teachers (N = 1606) produced much higher estimates of bullying prevalence than did students (N = 57). On the multi-item scale measure, the mean score for teachers was 18.84.; for the students, it was 15.87: a significant difference at the 0.001 level. Comparisons for each of the items are given in Figure 6.1. The differences between teacher and student estimates were statistically significant for the more common forms or modes of bullying (being made fun of; kicked/hit; rumour spreading; ignored/excluded' and made afraid) in each case with teachers giving a higher estimate. An important feature of these results is that students and teachers rated the items in practically the same order of magnitude, which suggests that the bases for their judgements were similar.

Percentage estimates of teachers and students of the prevalence of bullying at their school. Lines give the percentages of teachers and students indicating that the behaviour happened 'often.'

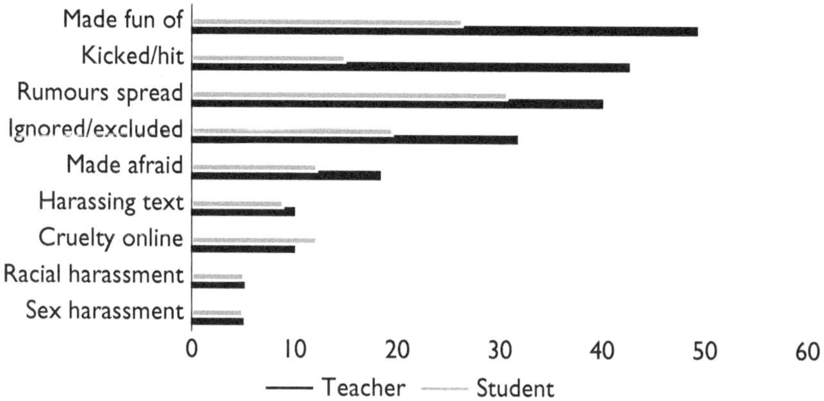

Figure 6.1 Percentage estimates of teachers and students of the prevalence of bullying at their school.

Does this mean that teachers are particularly observant as to which student is being bullied and if so how and by how often? Not really. Research has repeatedly shown that teachers' judgements of whether individual students are being bullied (as revealed by student self-reports) is no better than chance (Demaray et al., 2013). Given that most bullying is indirect and often covert this is hardly surprising. So why do teachers estimate more bullying than students? It seems likely that their judgements are influenced by what they hear or see in the media: more so, it seems, than by direct observations of what goes on in their schools. But whatever the explanation these findings in relation to Australian schools suggest that teachers are not underestimating the problem relative to judgements of prevalence provided by students.

Teacher views on addressing bullying

Currently, the overwhelming view is that action should be taken to develop pro-social attitudes and social and emotional competences among students to prevent bullying from taking place. To some extent, this view may be seen as a reaction against what was once the general view on what schools should do about bullying: schools: disregard it, or (if necessary) administer an effective sanction or punishment. As noted earlier, in many countries the proposed answer to bullying is to help students to develop high levels of personal wellbeing and appropriate skills through the use of instructional programs intended to develop social and emotional learning (SEL).

Discovering what individual teachers think of SEL using the usual questionnaire approach is greatly complicated – some would say made impossible – by the perceived need of teachers to acquiesce to Departmental directives, proposals or suggestions provided in many states and countries. In my experience, the desirability of SEL is not often discussed among teachers, despite its controversial nature, as it is for example examined by Ecclestone and Hayes (2019) in their book 'The Dangerous Rise of Therapeutic Education.' Their thesis in that book is that schools are not the appropriate places for psychotherapeutic techniques to be employed; such techniques (if required) should be left to trained professionals. They include in their anathema objection to the use of such techniques as Circle Time and Mindfulness. These and other 'therapeutic' methods are seen as encouraging introspection, which the authors see as often leading to a pervasive sense of vulnerability, associated anxiety, depression and a loss of resilience. The emphasis in schools should, in their opinion, be on discovering facts about the outside world – as is delivered through the traditional curriculum. How far individual teachers agree with this perspective is unclear. Certainly, many educational authorities disagree with Ecclestone and Hayes and believe that teachers have an important role to play in developing their students' SEL through using supportive counselling approaches, such as active listening and Circle Time (Hornby, Hall & Hall, 2003), as well as mindfulness meditation (Singh & Singh Joy, 2021).

Some research has reported on teacher attitudes towards SEL and its implementation in schools. Collie et al. (2015) reported that three factors could be identified (1) **Comfort,** as indicated by agreement with the item: 'I feel confident in my ability to provide instruction on social and emotional learning' (ii) **Commitment,** as in agreeing that 'I want to improve my ability to teach social and emotional learning,' and (iii) **Cultural support,** as in agreeing that 'the attitude of the school supports the development of children's social and emotional skills.' Each of these factors, they argue, needs to be present to optimize the chances of success of SEL and similar programs. The extent to which these conditions are present can vary from school to school. Some teachers do not feel comfortable in engaging in such programs and may lack the necessary skills. Recognizing this difficulty, it has been suggested that teachers delivering SEL programs should first be screened for social competence. Involvement or commitment of teachers to the program may depend upon their perceived competence to do so, their belief in the appropriateness of such programs; whether they think it would be possible to accommodate existing school curricula; and the support they could expect for the implementation of such programs (see Gorsek & Cunningham, 2014). In Australia, the infusion of SEL content into individual subjects rather than providing a series of sessions on SEL has been generally favoured. This seems more practicable in subjects like English and Health; less so for subjects like Mathematics and Chemistry. Despite the considerable hype associated with the promotion of SEL, there is no single school perspective on whether it should be applied and if so in what way.

Apart from the question of whether a comprehensive SEL type program should or should not be adopted and implemented by a school, there are various actions that teachers think would be effective in countering bullying. On some, there is little or no division. There is, in my experience, no significant disputes over whether a school should have an agreed anti-bullying policy, though disputes may arise as to its specific content. Differences may emerge over the relative effectiveness of pro-active actions teachers may take. This was evident in an Australian study (Rigby & Johnson, 2016) in which teachers from 25 schools were asked to rate the effectiveness of a number of actions that might take to reduce bullying. In providing answers to this and related questions, the principals of the schools were asked to nominate teachers who discussed together in a group what was generally the case of their school. Thus, although the sample of schools was relatively small the number of teachers pooling their answers was over 100. Whilst there were notable differences between schools, for example over whether peer mediation was helpful in reducing bullying, there was strong agreement that good classroom management could contribute to reducing bullying. This view is consistent with earlier research by Roland and Galloway (2002) that good classroom management with an emphasis on promoting student engagement in their studies and constructive ways of dealing with any classroom behaviour problem was conducive to low levels of bullying *outside* the classroom. The promotion of positive bystander behaviour was seen as important by most of the schools in the survey. It was believed that students should seek help from teachers when they were bullied, even if it involved cyberbullying outside the school. Teachers in Australian schools generally recognize that their responsibilities extend beyond the school gates.

There was agreement across the schools that some school initiatives were of little value in reducing bullying. These included peer mediation (it was generally thought that bullying was a matter that should involve staff only) and the use of school assemblies to address the problem (discussion with small groups of students was seen as preferable). In fact, some schools it was thought that giving formal one-way communication at school assemblies about bullying could be counterproductive.

As part of the survey conducted in Australia, students were presented with a list of possible actions that might be carried out by teachers in classrooms to counter bullying. (Advice in the selection of the items on the list was provided by Tracy Zilm, Curriculum Specialist, Health and Physical Education, at the Australian, Curriculum, Assessment and Reporting Authority). These items, as are presented in Table 6.2, together with estimates provided by students of the extent to which teachers in their experience actually carry out each action, along with their assessment of how useful each action was as a means of stopping bullying from happening.

Presented in Table 6.2 are the percentages of students who report that teachers do certain things, for example. 82.8% of the students reported that their teachers, 'encourage us to respect one another.' From its ranked position (1) it may be inferred that this is the most common student perception of what teachers do in helping to stop bullying. In the next column, we find what percentage of students find this 'encouraging respect' helpful, which is 42.6%, which is the activity endorsed by them as least 'helpful.'

Table 6.2 Student estimates of how often teachers carried out specified actions in class and how helpful they were in reducing bullying

School action	*% perceived as 'used often'*	*% perceived as 'helpful'*
1. Teachers encourage us to respect one another	82.8 (1)	42.6 (11)
2. Teachers expect us to include kids who are different	70.7 (2)	46.3 (10)
3. Teachers talk to us about what we can do if we see someone being bullied	48.5 (3)	54.2 (50)
4. Teachers advise us on what to if we are bullied	47.8 (4)	59.3 (1)
5. Teachers teach us how to keep safe online	47.3 (5)	53.5 (6)
6. Teachers discuss with us how to help students who are having a hard time	46.1 (6)	54.2 (4)
7. Teachers ask us to work with other students to solve problems	45.6 (7)	49.2 (8)
8. Teachers help us to understand how people might feel when bad things happen to them.	44.6 (8)	53.9 (3)
9. Teachers explain how to behave towards other when Using cyber technology	40.0 (9)	47.4 (9)
10. Teachers suggest ways in which arguments can be settled peacefully	36.3 (10)	52.6 (7)
11. Teachers make time for us to talk together in group	22.8 (11)	57.7 (2)

Note: Percentages perceived as 'helpful' include categories of 'helpful' and 'very helpful.' Figures in brackets give rank order of perceive 'often' and perceived order of being helpful *as a means of stopping bullying.*

For most students, the actions taken by teachers in classrooms were considered helpful in stopping bullying. Most helpful, according to students, was giving advice on what to do if one was bullied. Enabling students to discuss bullying issues, as in Circle Time was seen as helpful by more than half the students, but was also seen as happening relatively rarely. By and large, according to students many good things were being done by teachers in the classroom to counter bullying. However, there was no significant overall relationship between the perceived prevalence of particular kinds of teacher-directed classroom work and the percentages of students who found them helpful. Especially one may note that relatively few teachers (according to students) made time for students to talk together about matters, an activity that a relatively high proportion of students thought was particularly helpful. According to students, a good deal of time was devoted to encouraging students to respect one another and act inclusively and this was not considered by students to be all that helpful in stopping bullying. The perspectives of teachers appear to be general, whilst those of students more specific and practical. A further feature of the proactive actions described in Table 6.2 is that they were far more likely to be undertaken in primary schools than in secondary schools.

Teachers reacting to cases of bullying

In seeking to identify teacher perceptions related to cases of bullying, we may consider four questions

A. What do teachers think should be done, if anything, about cases of bullying when they arise?
B. What specific intervention methods do teachers choose to apply in cases of bullying and how effective do they think they are?
C. How effective is the action undertaken by teachers in addressing cases of bullying according to non-teachers?
D. How can one account for differences between teachers in their views on treating cases of bullying?

Teacher perceptions of what to do with cases

Relatively few studies have addressed the question of how teachers react to cases of bullying. An exception is a number of studies conducted cross-nationally using the Handling Bullying Questionnaire (HBQ) devised by Bauman, Rigby and Hoppa (2008). In this test educators are presented with scenarios describing a case of moderately severe bullying. For example,

> A 12-year-old student is being repeatedly teased and called unpleasant names by another, more powerful, student who has successfully persuaded other students to avoid the targeted person as much as possible. As a result, the victim of this behavior is feeling angry, miserable, and often isolated.

For this test, a list of 21 actions is provided and respondents are asked how they would respond using a 5-point scale from (1) 'I would definitely not' to (5) 'I definitely would.' Responses were subsequently scored according to degree of approval on each of five dimensions. These were:

1. **Discipline the bully,** e.g., 'I would make sure the bully was severely punished.'
2. **Enlisting other adults,** e.g., 'I would discuss the matter with my colleagues at school.'
3. **Working with the bully, e.g.,** 'I would discuss with the bully options

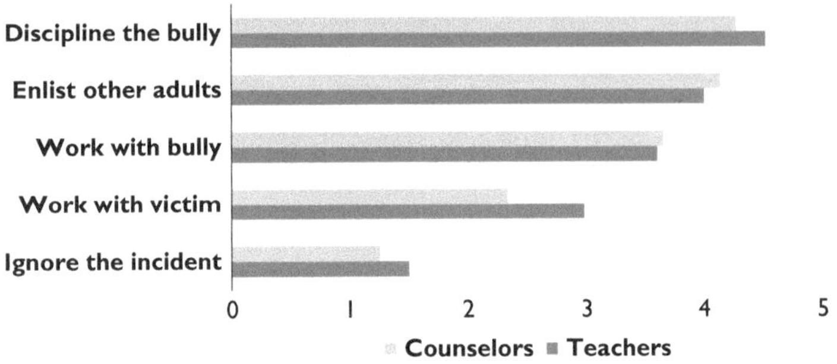

Figure 6.2 Mean endorsement of anti-bullying actions by counsellors and teachers in the USA.

from which he or she could make a choice in order to improve the situation.'

4. **Working with the victim, e.g.,** 'I would suggest that the victim act more assertively.'
5. **Ignoring the incident, eg.,** 'I would let the students sort it out themselves.'

In its application in the USA. the questionnaire was answered online by 254 teachers and (for comparison) 414 school counsellors. See Figure 6.2.

These results suggest that US teachers are generally very unlikely to ignore bullying incidents – or at least to say they would ignore any case of bullying! The use of a disciplinary approach is clearly the most popular (well above the midpoint of 3 on the scale). Differences between counsellors and teacher are small, with counsellors somewhat less inclined to endorse punishment and more inclined to work with victims of bullying

It should be understood that not all of the possible actions are mutually exclusive, apart from 'ignoring the incident.' A teacher may for instance, work with both the bully and the victim. These results tell us that the predominant perspective among teachers is that action of some kind should be taken in cases of bullying, with disciplining the bully the most preferred course, even in cases of relatively mild cases of bullying involving teasing and name-calling.

What specific intervention methods do teachers choose to apply in cases of bullying and how effective do they think they are?

Two similar studies have been conducted, one in England and one in Australia to discover what intervention methods teachers use and how effective they think they are. The earlier one was undertaken in England by Thompson and

Smith (2011) and the Australian one by Rigby and Johnson (2016). The studies entailed presenting teachers with possible intervention strategies in cases of bullying and asking them to indicate (i) which (if any) were employed at their school and (ii) how effective they think they were.

Clearly, this research strategy makes sense only if teachers are familiar with alternative or supplementary methods of intervention. This is especially important where some methods are not well understood or understood differently by different teachers or at different schools. Teachers in both countries were provided with descriptions of these four methods.

A. **The traditional disciplinary approach involving direct sanction.** Responsibility for the bullying is attributed to identified perpetrators of the bullying and sanctions or punishments are imposed. How the 'bully' is treated depends on the severity of the offence and may include reprimands, detentions, temporary loss of privileges, community service, meetings with parents, suspensions or exclusion.
B. **Restorative Practice.** Again responsibility for the bullying is attributed to the bully **and sanctions** may be imposed. Beyond this, the 'offenders' are required to attend a meeting with the practitioner and 'offended' to express remorse and undertake constructive action to restore the damaged relationship (See Thorsborne & Vinegrad, 2006).
C. The **Support Group Method** devised by Robinson and Maines (2008) is a non-punitive method which involves a meeting first with the victim, then with those identified by the victim as students who are doing the bullying. This meeting includes other students who are expected to be supportive of the victim. The victim is not present. The practitioner graphically shares knowledge of the victim's distress and encourages each person present to state how they will help the person who has been bullied. The situation is then carefully monitored.
D. The **Method of Shared Concern** devised by Pikas (2002), sometimes called the Pikas Method, is a non-punitive approach that begins with one-to-one interviews with students who are suspected of bullying someone (see Rigby, 2011). After the practitioner has shared a concern for the victim, each interviewee is asked to indicate how he or she will act to improve the situation. Outcomes are then monitored. The victim is then informed of the progress that is being made and offered support. Subsequently, the suspected bullies are required to meet as a group with the practitioner to discuss and determine how the problem is to be resolved. A final meeting is held, this time including the victim, to reach an agreed and sustainable resolution.

The Australian study included two additional methods not included in the English study.

A. **Mediation** involves inviting two persons in conflict to meet with a mediator to resolve any dispute or difference that may underlie or fuel any bullying behaviour. The mediator – a staff member or trained peer mediator – remains neutral and refrains from imposing a solution. In fact, the term 'mediation' as a method is sometimes understood differently by teachers, with some teachers including as mediation what amounts to 'forced arbitration' (Cremin, Sellma & McGluskey, 2012).

B. **Strengthening the Victim** This intervention consists of helping the victim to acquire appropriate skills, generally social skills that will render the victim less vulnerable to attack (Fox & Boulton, 2005). An element of confrontation may lie in ascribing some responsibility to the victim for permitting the bullying to continue or getting it to stop. In this procedure, the practitioner may explore with the victim possible ways in which he or she can respond to the bullying more effectively and provide advice and relevant training

One strategy was included in the English study only. This was the use of **School Tribunals**. A selected group of students in a school are appointed to 'try' students accused of bullying, according to agreed procedures. They determine the culpability of suspected bullies and recommend appropriate sanctions (Mahdavi & Smith, 2002).

For the study in England, it was possible to include ratings of the methods by Local Education Authorities, who as administrators rather than practicing teachers were able to provide a different perspective. The results are given in Table 6.3.

Table 6.3 Reported use of different forms of intervention and ratings for effectiveness, according to teachers and educational administrators in England and teachers in Australia

	Survey in England			*Survey in Australia*	
METHOD			*Mean ratings*		*Mean ratings*
	Use (%)	Teachers	*LEAs*	*Use (%)*	Teachers
Direct sanctions/ traditional approach	94	4.14	4	92	3.77
Strengthening the victim				100	4.04
Mediation				100	4.04
Restorative Approaches	73	4.18	4.4	92	4.14
Support Group Method	12	4.20	4.75	40	3.92
Method of Shared Concern	6	4.14	5	40	3.83
School Tribunals	2	4.26			

Note: Ratings of the effectiveness of the intervention were on a 5-point scale with 1 = very negative effect (increased bullying); 2 = negative effect; 3 = no effect; 4 = positive effect; 5 = very positive effect (decreased bullying).

As far estimations of how often the different intervention methods were used, there was general agreement between the results for England and Australia. The results for the English study and that in Australia both indicating that direct sanctions are used in a high proportion (over 90%) of cases, closely followed (or equalled) by Restorative Practices. The English and Australian findings also agree in reporting that the non-confronting approaches, the Support Group Method and the Method of Shared Concern are comparatively rarely employed, despite the evidence that they are at least as effective (or more so) than the much used traditional direct sanctions (see Garandeau, Poskiparta & Salmivalli, 2014; Rigby & Griffiths, 2011).

The mean ratings for each one of the methods of intervention are positive, as indicated by being above 3 – the midpoint of the five-point scale. Some differences are suggested between the two countries. Direct sanctions were rated slightly less positively by the Australian teachers; the non-confronting methods were rated higher in England. In general, one may conclude that the perspective of teachers in the two countries implies a belief that the reactive interventions are all positive and are expected to work.

The reported high use of direct sanctions corresponds to the high use of disciplinary measures used in the USA, as described earlier. Restorative Practices were used in some schools in the USA in cases of bullying (see Fronius et al., 2016) but their employment was much contested and teacher-based evaluations are unavailable. In Australia, its use is far less controversial.

Although these studies are suggestive of what reactive approaches are being used in schools in dealing with bullying cases, the evidence is limited, being derived from only a few countries. It is still not clear how some reactive methods can best be conceptualized and described to elicit the best account of what teachers do when they address a problem. For example, 'mediation' as an intervention method is variously understood and may include (1) entirely voluntary counselling from which students may withdraw or (2) part of what may be done in conducting sessions of restorative practice, from which the bullies (termed 'offenders') cannot withdraw.

The approach omitted from the survey conducted in England but used in the Australian study was 'strengthening the victim.' According to Australian teachers, this method is widely practiced. This is consistent with what Australian students who have gone for help from teachers have reported (Rigby, 2020). One may note that interventions may make use of one method or a combination of methods.

The effectiveness of actions undertaken by teachers in addressing cases of bullying according to non-teachers

Thus far the reporting on the effectiveness of teacher intervention in cases of bullying has been based on teacher judgements. There are in addition other sources of information that may be drawn upon, in particular, students who have sought help from teachers, parents of those students and educational administrators who are conversant with the work of schools.

Relevant data is available from a number of surveys conducted in England by Smith and Shu (2000); Thompson and Smith (2011); the USA by Davis and Nixon, 2011; the Netherlands by Fekkes et al. (2005); Germany by Wachs et al. (2019) and Australia or Rigby (1998); Rigby and Barnes (2002) and Rigby and Johnson (2016). The available results are presented in Table 6.4.

Examination of available findings from student surveys suggest that teachers overestimate the effectiveness of interventions in general. The results suggest that according to students 'no change' or 'got worse' was not an uncommon outcome and stopping the bullying from continuing has occurred in less than one in three studies. Similar results were obtained from the parent survey in Australia, described in Chapter 8. Very strikingly, results obtained from schools based on teacher judgements are far more positive than the figures derived from student surveys. Arguably, the bullied students were more likely

Table 6.4 Reported outcomes from interventions in cases of bullying in selected countries

	Bullying stopped	*Bullying reduced*	*No change*	*Bullying got worse*
Student Reports				
Smith & Shu,2000	26	29	28	16
Rigby, 1998		49	43	8
Rigby & Barnes, 2002		42	39	18
Fekkes, Pijpers, & Verloove-Vanhorick, 2005		49	34	17
Davis & Nixon, 2011		34	37	29
Rigby and Johnson 2016	29	40	23	8
Wachs et al. (2019)*	22	44	30	4
School Reports				
Thompson & Smith, 2011	67	20		13
Garandeau, Little, Kärnä, Poskiparta, & Salmivalli, 2011	78	20	2.	0
Rigby & Johnson 2016		78	19	4
Parent reports				
Rigby & Johnson 2016	27	33	30	10

Note: Figures in the boxes are combined categories only, as in 'bullying stopped' and 'bullying reduced' and for 'bullying reduced' and 'bullying worsened.' The findings reported by Wachs et al. (2019) are based on reports provided by a sample of students that included some who were not victims of bullying, for example, bystanders of the bullying incidents. Other student reports were from self-reports of victims.

to be able to report whether the bullying had stopped and that the perspective of teachers was more consistent with what they understandably wanted to think.

Given the major discrepancies between estimates of effectiveness by teachers and others, perceptual bias appears to be most apparent.

Differences among teachers in their views on addressing bullying

So far it has been suggested that teachers on the whole do not underrate the prevalence of bullying and are agreed on the need to address the problem in a concerted, 'whole school' way. They do, however, tend to exaggerate the success they have in dealing with cases of bullying. This is understandable: It is natural to believe that one's effort are to some avail – certainly not ever to make matters worse.

However, important differences between individual staff members emerge what there is discussion about the best form of intervention. Anyone who has been able to engage teachers in questions about what to do in cases of bullying will know that at times there are diametrically opposed views among them. Some will favour a strong disciplinary approach – a zero tolerance policy; others support an approach that is more educational and non-confronting. Explanations for these individual differences may be found in personality factors and/or in personal experiences that have shaped their outlook. These could include having been bullied at school and/or having a child who was bullied severely, such experiences possibly tending to influence one to adopt a punitive approach in all or most cases.

But not all teacher perspectives can be attributed to such personal factors. Most teachers were not severely bullied when they were children and most parents do not have children who have been bullied. One must also look for explanations that relate to the ideological or philosophical or religious positions that have been adopted. The most persuasive explanation for teacher differences in choice of intervention approach is that proposed by Australian researchers, Ellis and Shute (2007). They suggested that teachers tended to be divided between those who had a Justice Orientation and those with a Care Orientation The former emphasize the use of rules and sanctions in dealing with cases of bullying, whereas the latter adopting a problem-solving approach that avoids the possible use of harsh disciplinary action. Hence one would expect the former orientation to be favoured by supporters of the more traditional direct sanctions approach and the latter to support the use of Mediation, the Support Group Approach and the Method of Shared Concern. A teacher's perspective on what to do about cases of bullying would therefore be related to such orientations. In defence of the Justice Orientation, it could be argued that all children who bully should be treated in the same way – no favouritism! The Care Orientation may lead a teacher to be more concerned about the wellbeing of the child who bullies, as well as the victim, and measure success not by how fairly the rules have been followed, but by positive changes in the relationship between the students.

A further belief may also motivate teachers to act in one way or another. Belief (or disbelief) in a Just World, as defined by Lerner and Miller (1978) may also enter into judgements a teacher may make. Believing that the world by and large is 'just' would seem to imply that students who are victimized get what they deserve and are therefore likely to be ignored by teachers with such a belief. This may account for the minority of teachers who think no action is needed (see Bauman et al., 2008). On the other hand, a belief that the world is not 'just' may lead a teacher to express more sympathy for victims and seek to help them. Religious beliefs may also help to determine how a teacher acts in cases of bullying. A belief that suffering in this world is compensated for in the next world, in heaven or through reincarnation, might result in a teacher taking little or no action; whereas, a religion that encourages social action on the side of the oppressed may result in an opposite response.

Some conclusions

1. Teachers play a key role in addressing bullying, through the development of anti-bullying policies and their implementation.
2. There have been highly significant changes over the last thirty or so years among teachers in many countries in the recognition of the existence of the problem and its serious implications for student wellbeing.
3. Although teachers generally may not be able to define bullying as succinctly as researchers, they are similarly able to recognize actual cases of bullying.
4. Research findings about bullying are often not well known by teachers. Moreover, on some issues teachers disagree radically with each other. This can jeopardize the development and implementation of a whole-school approach. There is a need, recognized by many teachers, for better, more informed, research-based instruction in pre-service and in-service training.
5. Teachers do not underestimate the prevalence of bullying (at least in Australian schools) compared with estimations made by students. They are nevertheless often unaware of precisely who is being bullied in their school, as revealed by student self-reports.
6. Pro-active ways of addressing bullying have in recent years are being used increasingly by teachers, as in providing students with classroom lessons and activities that can help to develop greater understanding and competences to prevent bullying from occurring or continuing. This is well appreciated by students, especially in Primary Schools. Controversy nevertheless exists about the value and effectiveness of particular programs such as SEL and how they can best be applied.

7. Teachers generally recognize the importance of good classroom management as one means of countering bullying, including preventing bullying in the playground. They see that speeches about bullying at school assemblies have little or no positive impact and that the use of peer mediation by schools is of limited value.
8. Only a small minority of teachers believe that cases of bullying should be ignored. Generally, teachers favour the use of disciplinary means in addressing incidents of bullying although the use of non-confronting approaches is sometimes seen by a minority of teachers as more appropriate and effective in some cases.
9. International research suggests that, according to students, interventions by teachers in cases of bullying are effective in stopping the bullying from continuing in only a minority of cases. Teachers appear to overestimate the success of such interventions.
10. Substantial variations exist among the perspectives on bullying of teachers, as they do among non-teachers. This may be due to socially biased beliefs, personal experiences, inadequate knowledge of the subject, inadequate training and ideological and philosophical differences.

Chapter 7

Perspectives of students

We need to prioritize the perspectives of students. After all, it is shifts in attitudes and related behaviour among students that can ultimately determine whether bullying in schools will continue, increase or get worse. Knowing how students perceive bullying is therefore fundamental.

It has been reported that students tend to define bullying somewhat differently than do teachers being less comprehensive than teachers in what is included, for instance in not including non-physical forms of bullying such as social exclusion (Naylor et al., 2006). However, in the Australian study described in the last chapter, it was evident that students put the prevalence of different forms of bullying at their schools in practically the same order of magnitude Both students and teachers saw verbal and relational forms of bullying as occurring much more often than physical bullying. There was little evidence here that in general students and teachers saw things differently, although it is possible that some students may have included interactions between students of similar power, as in fighting or quarreling. In general, this suggests that students and teachers may share a common perspective on bullying, at least as far as identifying the relative frequency of different forms of bullying. This would be consistent with the fact that they share practically the same physical environment. They spend much of their time in classrooms together, they interact from time to time in the playground and other school contexts

However, there are two important differences between students and teachers. The first is that the perspectives students may have on school bullying are likely to based on actual interactions with their peers and the consequences of such interactions. They are likely to be based on direct experience, coloured by the emotions that were generated. Teachers are likely to take a more dispassionate view of what they see happening – and also to see less of what is actually going on between students than is reported by students. A second important difference derives from the greater variability in the characteristics of students compared with teachers. We have noted earlier that teachers do differ in the judgements they make about bullying, but the differences or variability among students are much greater.

DOI: 10.4324/9781315454450-7

The perspectives of teachers are more alike because teachers are more alike. They tend to have similar social backgrounds; they have opted for a particular vocation; they have received a similar education and training; they are to some degree directed or constrained by professional expectations and obligations. By contrast, students are as close to a random or representative sample of humanity as one can get. Practically everybody goes to school. There are large variations in personality types, and in government schools in Australia at least, large differences in social and ethnic background. Among school children, there are vast inequalities, both physical and mental, in part due to crucial age differences. There are then reasons for expecting that among students there would be substantial differences in what they see going on at school and how they appraise what they see. If we are to understand the variations in student perceptions of matters relating to bullying, we have to differentiate between the views of subgroups or categories of students. For instance, students who are repeatedly bullied are likely to have a different perspective on things than those who are rarely or never bullied. This latter category may include the large proportion of students who are not bullied at all at school, a small minority who are frequently bullied and some who are bullied rather more often. A distribution of reported bullying frequency is given in Figure 7.1 based upon a survey of 682 boys and 828 girls in Australia in 2015 (Rigby & Johnson, 2016).

In Australia, as elsewhere, the percentage of students who report that they have bullied others at school appears to be lower. Differences in categorizing prevalence make precise comparisons impossible. However, the estimate of 14% provided by the Australian Institute of Health and Welfare (2020) for

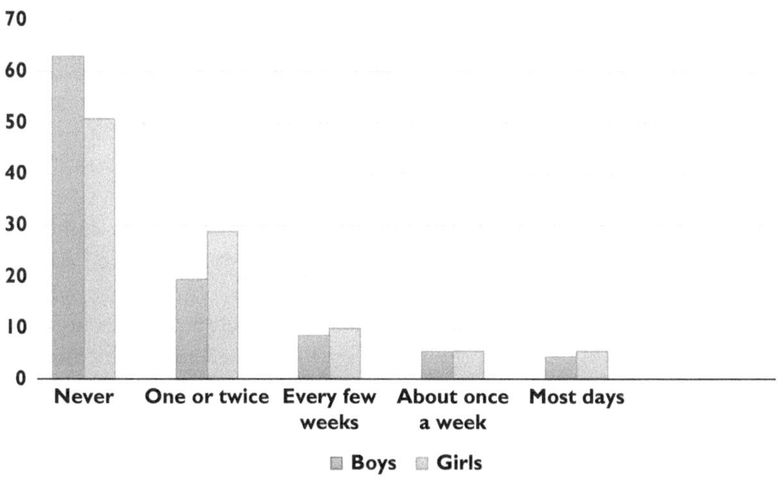

Figure 7.1 Percentages of boys and girls reporting on how often they had been bullied over the last 12 months.

students aged 12–13 years who bully suggests they are far fewer than those who are reportedly victimized. In the Netherlands, it was reported that 5.5% of students were reportedly engaged in 'regular active bullying' (Fekkes et al., 2005). Still, these figures must be treated with caution. Even in an anonymous questionnaire students may wish to conceal the fact that they had bullied someone. Some students who report that they have not bullied anyone may regard their bullying as harmless teasing or understandably avoiding someone they don't like – and not bullying at all.

There is nevertheless a reasonably high level of agreement among students as to what may be considered as bullying. This is apparent when we examine the correlations between the frequency one form of bullying and another as reported by students. Students who say that they have been bullied in one way are very likely to say that they have been bullied in another way. For instance, if they have been repeatedly physically or verbally abused they are more likely to say that they have been deliberately excluded or have been cyberbullied. Multi-item self-report scales assessing frequency of being bullied show a high degree of internal consistency. There can, however, be variation in the hurtfulness of bullying actions.

Perceived hurtfulness of bullying behaviours

Some forms of bullying are viewed by students as more hurtful than others. One Australian study by Rigby and Bagshaw (2001) drew upon student ratings of the hurtfulness of a range of different treatments that students reported they had observed at their school. In that study, 289 boys and 353 girls, who were Year Nine students (aged approximately 14 years) attending eight schools in South Australia, rated the hurtfulness of 30 negative treatments as experienced by students. These included ten treatments that involved relational aggression, eg. being deliberately excluded and having rumours spread about them; ten described verbal aggression, eg., being called names and remarks made about one's personal appearance; and ten described physical aggression, e.g., being hit or having one's face slapped. Relational aggression was reported as by far the most hurtful, followed by being physically attacked, with verbal aggression being least hurtful. Some gender differences were found: being physically and relationally targeted was seen as more hurtful by girls. Not included in this study were forms of cyberbullying.

How hurt students are by being cyberbullied is a disputed area. A common perception is that cyberbullying is the more hurtful and serious. The difficulty confirming this judgement is that students who are cyberbullied are generally bullied in traditional ways as well (Waasdorp & Bradshaw, 2014). Rather than assess the degree of harm experienced by those who were cyberbullied (and who may have suffered even more by being bullied in other ways), the more valid method of making a judgement on this matter may be to ask students which forms of bullying are more hurtful. Research suggests that for most students traditional or face-to-face bullying is more hurtful than cyberbullying (Ortega et al., 2012; Smith et al., 2006). There are clearly exceptions, as cases of suicide subsequent to cyberbullying are sometimes reported (Hiduja & Patchin, 2010). Being cyberbullied may increase the hurt experienced from other forms of bullying.

Who are (or seen to be) the bullies?

As noted earlier, bullying is sometimes conceived mainly as an outcome of activities located in networks. The notion that bullying may be the outcomes of volitions and associated actions undertaken by a single individual is seen to be usually, if not always, mistaken. Consistent with this view, Monks et al. (2009) opine, 'bullying rarely takes place between two individuals in isolation' (p. 154). Social groups are commonly thought to be directly or indirectly responsible for episodes of bullying. Individual targets may be unaware of who exactly the 'bullies' are. This may explain the helplessness of some victims when they are asked to identify the perpetrators. Female politicians in Australia in recent times have been ridiculed for the vagueness of their accusations in describing the bullies as 'male politicians.' School children may be similarly at sea in identifying the source of their troubles.

The judgements or attributions that victims of bullying make of those who are bullying them were examined in an Australian study reported by Rigby (2020) in which students (N = 1688) from 36 state schools were asked how often this year they had been bullied by (i) one person and (ii) by a group of persons. The results are presented in Figure 7.2.

The most common category was 'never bullied' followed by being bullied by individuals and groups. Only slightly less common were students bullied by individuals. Being bullied by groups only was relatively rare. We should bear in mind that the results describe 'perceptions,' and in some cases students may be unaware of the support being provided by groups of students. It may be unclear to some students that a so-called 'henchman' is acting under the influence of a group. It may be hard for them to recognize that the actions of individuals, for instance in excluding someone repeatedly, may be traced to normative pressures from groups of students or from one person, a group leader, who is orchestrating the bullying.

On the face of it, however, attributing bullying behaviour quite often to one person may not be delusionary. Such a conclusion is consistent with a study involving students (N = 918) attending school in the Netherlands (Veenstra et al., 2007). Data were gathered from children relating to 13,606 dyadic relations. Student reports from both dyad members indicated that the perpetrators tended to be relatively aggressive and domineering and the victim unassertive and personally vulnerable. This suggests that interactions between children with contrasting personalities, with one more powerful than the other, may account for more bullying than is sometimes acknowledged. At the

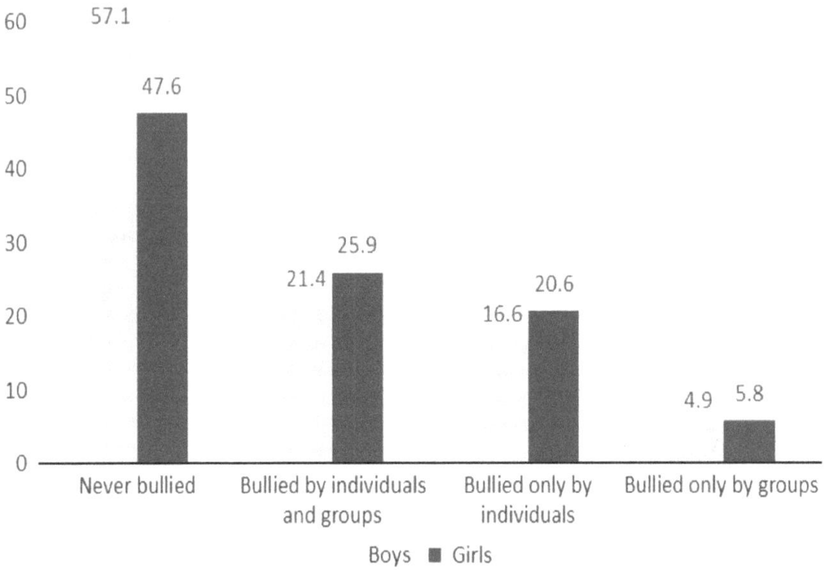

Figure 7.2 Percentages of boys and girls reporting being bullied (or not bullied) in different ways.

same time. it seems likely that the ambient culture may account for differences in who are identified as responsible for bullying. In collectivist cultures such as South Korea and Japan group bullying is reported to be much more common.

One important result from the Australian study found that students who attributed bullying more often to groups reported more serious emotional distress, indicated by measures of being upset, angry, frightened and depressed (Rigby, 2020). It appears that the perception or actuality that a group of students are seeking to bully a targeted child may have greater significance in producing negative consequences than the form of the bullying or its reported frequency.

Student roles in bullying

Differentiating between categories of students regarding bullying, for research purposes, is a necessary albeit controversial area. Unfortunately, once a speaker utters or writes the words 'bully' or 'victim' sensitive people sometimes shriek with horror. Both terms suggest a person who is that and nothing else but that. Commonsense and common observation tells us that people are rarely, if ever, one of these all of the time. Hitler, they say, had his kinder moments. Abductees may exhibit a Stockholm syndrome and become fond of their abductors. Having been labelled a bully or a victim, the label can stick, whatever changes may occur, however, they behave, and however, they are treated. But if we are to understand the perceptions and perspectives of students one must use these dangerous or unpopular terms, or some circumlocution thereof. In examining the involvement of students in bullying, we are concerned with the roles different students may play, as in bullying someone, being victimized or being a bystander. On different occasions, a student may play a different role. However, it is clear that some students are far more prone to act as a bully, or be a victim or be a bystander or remain uninvolved. Hence the terms bully and victim (offensive to some ears) will be employed, bearing in mind that we are concerned primarily with the roles they play.

The victim

We may define a 'victim' as one who is repeatedly targeted and treated in a negative way by another individual or group. This would include victims of non-malign bullying where the perpetrator's intention may not be to hurt someone but rather to improve one's own status in a group. Needless to say, the targeted person may feel under increasing pressure as the perceived bullying continues, just as person who is the butt of repeated jokes, intended to amuse everyone, may be feel bullied. How do the perceptions of victims of what is going on differ from the perceptions of others? In the Australian survey, the responses of students who had identified themselves as victims of bullying over the last 12 months were compared with responses to other students who answered the same questions.

As indicated in Figure 7.3, bullied children were less positive than others about the bullying situation at their school and what was being done about it at their school They perceived far more bullying, both by individuals and by groups. They were more likely to see students at risk of being bullied if they couldn't defend themselves. They were more likely to see bystanders as

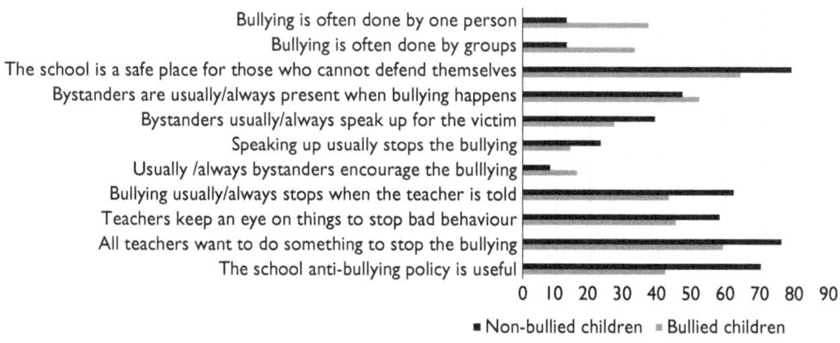

Figure 7.3 Views expressed by bullied and non-bullied students about bullying and response to bullying at their school.

unhelpful or likely to encourage the bullying. They were less likely to see teachers as helpful and the anti-bullying policy as less useful. On only one of the issues was there little difference. Both sets of students were similarly aware that bystanders tended to be present when bullying occurred.

Social perceptions and emotional arousal

It was suggested that the differences between the perspectives of bullied and non-bullied students could have been due to the heightened sensitivity of bullied students to what was actually going on around them. However, a further explanation is plausible. It could be that the bullying had affected them emotionally so that their perceptions were affected. That being bullied does affect students emotionally, sometimes very seriously has been widely reported (see Ortega et al., 2012; Rigby, 2020). In these studies being bullied by others was seen as contributing to relatively high levels of depression or sadness, feeling angry, being upset and afraid. Such emotions can affect how individuals perceive on-going events and subsequently report on what happened around them (Keltner, Ellsworth & Edwards, 1993). It is therefore possible that the estimates of bullying provided by bullied students could, to some extent, be coloured by their personal experience and as a consequence become somewhat distorted.

Here, however, we may remind ourselves that this book is primarily about how bullying is perceived rather than its objective nature. The evidence thus far presented is that the world of the victim of school bullying is often one of recurring fear and disappointment.

Student perceptions of the classroom climate

How students who are involved in bullying, either as bullies, victims or bully-victims evaluate their classroom environment was examined in a study by Yoneyama & Rigby, 2006). It was conducted in Australia with Year 8 and 9 students (N = 531) in five secondary schools. Measures were obtained of (i) the perceived quality of their classroom environment (ii) the frequency with which they experienced bullying at school and (iii) how often they bullied other students. As expected, victimized students and also bullies tended to be less positive about the classroom climate than other students. This was especially true of those boys who were bullied and were themselves bullied, that is, the bully-victims. Comparisons on the scale assessing perceived quality of the classroom environment are given in Figure 7.4, with standardized scores above the mean of zero indicating positive evaluations. The findings of this study suggest that the perception of the classroom climate depends to a significant degree on whether the perceiver has been or is being bullied at school. But it is not quite as simple as that. It is evident that bullies too are somewhat less positive about the classroom environment, especially students who both bully and are bullied at school.

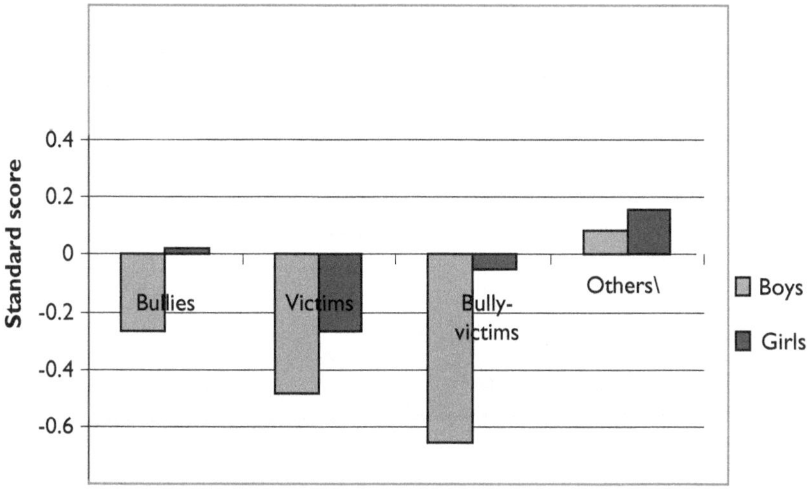

Figure 7.4 Perceptions of classroom climate according to self-reported status of the student, as bully, victim, bully-victim or other.

One may surmise that children who are bullied are inclined to feel negatively about being in class and threatened by the presence of some other students in the classroom whom they fear may bully them in the playground when the lesson is over. Students who bully may have their perceptions of the classroom climate affected by antagonism that could exist between themselves and their teachers, especially if they are seen as acting aggressively. One implication of such findings is that signs of negativity in the classroom on the part of some students may signal to the teacher that involvement in bullying could be a cause of such behaviour.

Self-perceptions of victims

it is hardly surprising that many victims think badly of themselves. They are treated badly and are apt to feel at times that they deserve the negative treatment they receive. They may feel that there is little or nothing they can do about it. Various studies of the self-esteem of victims, as noted earlier, support this contention. However, this can be an overgeneralization. Attributions as to why one is repeatedly bullied by different students may sometimes result in a victim refusing to accept that the fault lies within. This is more likely to occur if the bullying is directed towards a group of which one is a member, as for instance when bullying is directed at members of a racial or ethnic group. It is true that a victim might bemoan the fate of being part of an unpopular racial minority, but more often the reaction towards such bullying is unlikely to seriously affect one's self-esteem, especially if one is part of a support group that is being treated in the same way. This does not lessen the culpability of the bullying, but it may make it easier to withstand. It may not injure your self-acceptance as much. It is when the reason for being bullied appears to be due to personal flaws that the effect appears greatest.

A study conducted in Australia has examined how students see themselves. Rather than focus on self-esteem, the research made use of a measure of self-acceptance. This concept developed by Berger (1952) sought to provide a more comprehensive measure of how students feel about themselves, one that was related to the notion of resilience. Berger defined self-acceptance as maintaining a positive attitude towards oneself regardless of acknowledged defects, successes or failures, or negative judgements made about one by others. It suggests a deep sense of who one is. As Popeye put it 'I yam what I yam.'

The Australian study was undertaken as part of a mixed-methods study of student attitudes relating to bullying in Australia (Rigby & Bortolozzo, 2013). Students (N = 116) from primary schools and students (N = 96) from secondary schools in South Australia completed a questionnaire. This included a reliable multi-item scale developed for use with schoolchildren by Rigby and Bortolozzi, based on a measure that was developed for adults by Berger. The new measure contained 20 items assessing acceptance of self. In addition, students completed a sentence completion test designed to elicit qualitative data on how students at the school thought about themselves and others. The incomplete sentence was: 'My honest opinion about myself….' Another question asked them to provide an estimate on how often they had been bullied at school over the last 12 months. Three categories were provided: (1) never bullied; (2) bullied sometimes; and (3) bullied often.

Acceptance of self on the Scale was significantly lower for those who had reported being bullied. Sentence completions by victims of bullying provided strong supporting evidence of how victims saw themselves. For example, 'I am a nobody'; 'I am stuperd (sic)'; 'I don't like my life'; 'I don't fit in,' 'I'm always the odd one out'; 'I am not happy the way I am'; 'Maybe the world would be better if I wasn't there'; 'I am fat and ugly'; 'Sometimes when people talk about me my gut cries out.'

This study and others raise the question of whether children can learn to accept themselves despite the negative things that are happening to them as individuals. Bortolozzo, my co-researcher and educational practitioner in schools in Australia believes that quite young children can learn to think positively about themselves as a consequence of instruction provided through rational-emotive behaviour therapy (REBT), as described by Albert Ellis (2004). See REBTOZ: Bully for You! – An REBT Approach to Bullying

Help-seeking behaviours and attitudes of victims of bullying

Clearly many, if not all, children who are bullied need help of some kind. The advice given by schools is almost always 'TELL.' They advise students to seek help from a teacher or counsellor. Research shows that some do, but many do not, sometimes preferring to put up with it or to ask a non-teacher or school counsellor. In a study reported by Rigby and Johnson (2016) students who had been bullied at school over the last 12 months were asked to say from whom they had sought help. Figure 7.5 shows that the main source for help consisted of another student or students and parents or caregivers. Girls were slightly more inclined to ask for help from other students. Teachers and counsellors were the next most likely to be approached for help. A small minority of students sought help from counsellors or counselling services outside the school, such as the Kid's Help Line. A smaller minority indicated that they had sought help from the Police. These students tended to be boys exposed to serious assaults at school.

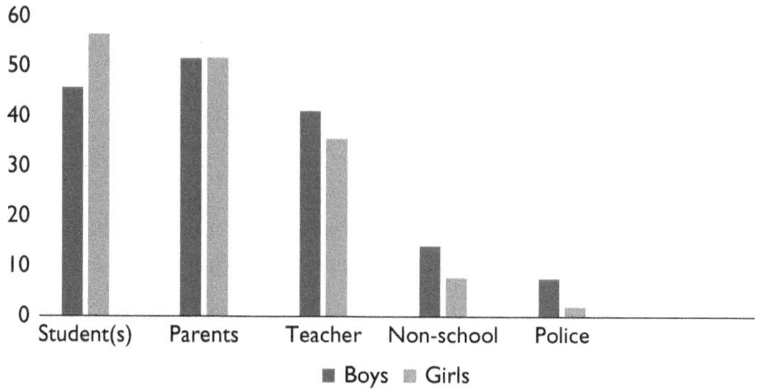

Figure 7.5 Who bullied children go to for help.

Note that the category of 'teachers' included counsellors on staff; 'parents' included 'caregivers'; and, 'non-school' refers to counselling services outside the school. In some cases, students sought help from more than one source.

Given that teachers urge students to tell them if they are being bullied and need help – and that teachers are commonly in the best position to provide such help, it may come as a surprise that teachers are not the most favoured source of help. Most teachers indicated in answers to the knowledge quiz, previously discussed, that they believed they were the ones the bullied students were most likely to seek help from. Why then are not teachers the first port of call?

Students who had been bullied and did not seek help from a teacher or counsellor were asked in an anonymous questionnaire why they hadn't done so. A variety of answers were given, as summarized below:

1. **Uncertainty about the role of teachers in addressing cases of bullying.**

   'It is none of their business.'

   'They are here to teach us.'

2. **Bullying is a personal matter.**
   'I don't feel comfortable telling someone I don't really know.'
   'There is no-one in the school I can trust.'
3. **Lack of belief that they would take the bullying seriously.**
   'They might laugh. I have seen them brush off students' problems.'
4. **Fear of repercussions**.
   'I don't want to be teased because I told a teacher.'
5. **Not wishing to get others into trouble.**
   'The people [the bullies] were my friends and I don't want to lose them.'
6. **A sense of personal inadequacy**.
   'I would feel weak and embarrassed.'
7. **Having a preferred option.**
   'I can get help from friends and parents.'

A wide range of reasons may influence whether a teacher is informed, including the severity of the bullying and the age of the student. Some of the reasons given point to a capacity to get help from other sources, such as friends and parents. However, some convey negative perceptions of what teachers might do, as in being unable to improve matters; indeed, some fear they may make matters worse. There is also a suggestion that it is not the role of teachers to help solve student difficulties associated with bullying. The relationships they have with teachers is for some too impersonal to permit discussion about intimate matters of interpersonal relations. Getting advice from a friend or a parent was seen by many as a better course of action.

The perceptions of bullies

How those children identified as bullies see their peers and teachers does not permit a single, simple answer. In the first place, those we label as bullies are not bullies all the time (nor are 'victims' victims all the time). Yet, for some, there is a largely consistent attitude that appears to be at the root of much of what children who bully do and think.

A model outlined earlier suggested that bullying commonly involves a negative attitude to others and is related to a desire to hurt or dominate others. If this is so, one would expect children identified as bullies to be generally hostile and non-accepting of others. The Australian study by Rigby and Bortolozzo, discussed earlier in relation to the acceptance of self, included a reliable measure of Acceptance of Others based upon the Berger formulation of that concept. As expected, the bullies, as identified by self-reports, score significantly lower than others on this measure. This finding was consistent with results from a sentence completion test in which students were asked to provide a completion to one beginning 'Children at this school'... Bullies were more likely to produce completions like these: 'are stupid, mean, bitchy, stuck-up and unkool (sic)'; 'are idiots and don't know a thing.' By contrast, most other children produced positive responses such as, 'are kind, helpful and trustworthy'; 'are great people to be with and trustworthy'; 'are respectful and nice.' It should be added that it does not follow that children with negative attitudes towards others will have a desire to hurt or dominate them and will invariably express it, if they can, by bullying them. But it does suggest that a basic attitude of hostility to others is more likely to be present among those who bully. Where the hostility is particularly pronounced, acts of violence such as the Columbine massacre in the United States in 1999 may well follow (Brown & Merritt, 2002).

Although some children may engage in bullying virtually anybody they can bully and become serial bullies, it is often the case that the targets of the bullying are largely determined by their possession of characteristics against which there is good deal of bias or prejudice. As noted earlier the selected targets may vary cross-culturally and possibly from school to school. A large-scale study of students (N = 162,034) attending schools in the United States has provided data on the frequency with which some categories of students are bullied (see Figure 7.6)

The origins of bias against particular social categories can sometimes be traced to the home backgrounds of students and the transmitted prejudices of parents and family members. More generally, prejudiced beliefs may derive from the community and may be reinforced by legal or quasi-legal injunctions, as may be the case when bullying is directed against people of non-orthodox sexual orientation or religion. From the point of view of the perpetrator, the actions are justified on the grounds that the targets are exhibiting unacceptable behaviour or holding an unacceptable belief. The grounds may be related to

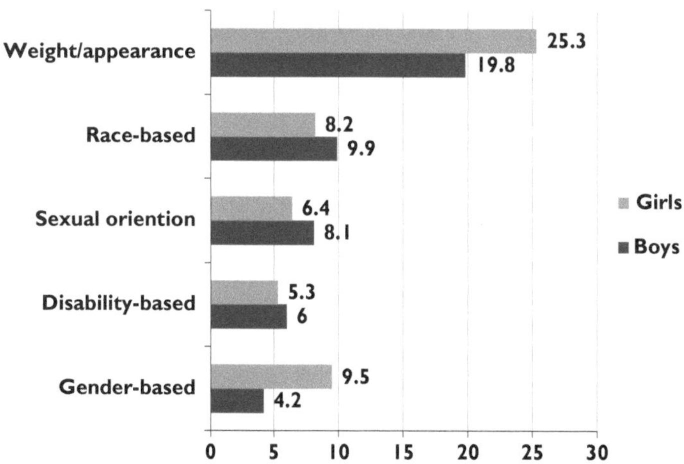

Figure 7.6 Percentages of students in the sample of US students reporting being bullied for different reasons.

firmly held, internalized values, which may be, for instance, racist or homophobic. Alternatively, they may derive from identification with a leader or group holding a seemingly attractive and empowering view, or be simply a superficial conforming response which it pays to adopt.

Conforming to what others would like a person to do may result in bullying without prejudice being involved. It is enough that one's status, acceptability to the group or even personal safety may be at stake. My own realization of the force of this motive for bullying came when an old friend and I were reminiscing one night about our schooldays – and bullying. He told me that he never had any desire to hurt anyone – which knowing him I could well believe. Yet, he confided, he had relentless engaged in minor acts of bullying as a schoolboy because he knew that if he didn't his friendship group would doubt his loyalty – and quite possibly turn against him. Does this confession explain why so many good Germans went along with Hitler's anti-Jewish pogroms?

We naturally distinguish between the culpability of acts of bullying by placing them on a continuum of minor acts of avoidance and mild teasing at one extreme and horrendous acts of ostracism and physical violence at the other. Given that is hard to be sure of how damaging any act of bullying may be to a target, such differentiations can be difficult to sustain. The perpetrator may, in all conscience, not intend the harm that is experienced by his 'innocent' joking. When is a tease more than a tease is a conundrum, to which the only the answer is when it is seen as hurtful and the teasing persists. There is however a sort of bully who continues to hold that the target ought not to take offence and should be further humiliated for being so vulnerable.

At the other end of the continuum is the sadist – or so it is claimed. The sadistic personality has been defined as 'a person who humiliates others, shows a longstanding pattern of cruel or demeaning behavior to others, or intentionally inflicts physical, sexual, or psychological pain or suffering on others in order to assert power and dominance or for pleasure and enjoyment' (O'Meara, Davies & Hammond, 2011, p. 523). The term however, thus defined, is controversial and disputed as a descriptive category among clinical psychologists. Certainly, some people are regarded as having sadistic impulses that give rise to bullying behaviour of an extreme kind.

Sexual harassment

Sexual harassment is commonly considered to be one aspect of bullying, involving unwelcome behaviour of a sexual nature, which can include both verbal and physical actions, as in making comments, gestures or suggestions and/or physical advances as in touching or grabbing a person in a sexual manner. Like other forms of bullying, it involves an imbalance of power, usually (but not always) that of a male person relative to a female. Contrary to some definitions of bullying, the behaviour may occur on just one occasion.

Conceived in this way, there is considerable evidence that sexual harassment not infrequently occurs in schools, more commonly in secondary schools, but not confined to such schools.

Student perspectives on sexual harassment may be inferred from how students respond or think they would respond in cases of sexual harassment that they observe. In a study conducted in South Australia by Rigby and Johnson (2004) 100 boys and 100 girls, in years 8 and 9 attending co-educational secondary schools, were shown cartoon pictures of a boy sexually coercing a girl by grabbing her breasts from behind, despite her vigorous objections. Some 19% of respondents reported seeing this kind of thing happening every day or most days at school; 25% less often; and 65% hardly ever. There were no significant gender differences. From these results, one might conclude that some students were particularly observant and some others were not, or possibly some preferred not to report what was happening. At any rate, around 50% of students were aware of sexual harassment taking place at school. How objectionable or otherwise was this behaviour? Not surprisingly, there was a marked gender difference with 62% of girls indicating that they would certainly object when they saw it happening compared with 45% of boys who indicated they would object. Significantly more girls indicated that they would tell a teacher. Among boys 13% thought they would probably or certainly support the boy in coercing the girl, and 2% of girls thought the same! From this study it is apparent that the perspectives in general of boys and girls on sexual harassment differed widely; but within the gender groups, there was much variation. In this study attitude to victims was a significant predictor of whether the girl victim would be supported, after controlling for the gender of the respondent.

It is often assumed that sexual harassment is limited to interactions between males and females. An Australian study reported by Rigby and Bagshaw (2001) suggests that 'being touched in a sexual way against my will' was experienced equally often by boys (N = 386) and girls (N = 340) at secondary school in Year 8, with 15% of both boys and girls reporting that this had happened to them. Approximately one-third of both boys and girls reported that they were hurt 'a lot' by the experience. This issue, often involving intra-gender sexual harassment, is rarely addressed and must affect a substantial proportion of both boys and girls in schools.

A more recent study has examined the prevalence of sexual harassment among adolescents (N = 4,098) attending Australian secondary schools (Xiaojing et al., 2020). They estimate that approximately 40% of students have experienced one form or other of sexual harassment – a similar percentage for boys and girls. They conclude that 'sexual harassment is a pervasive problem in Australian high schools and needs to be acknowledged and dealt with specifically' (p. 349).

There are great difficulties in addressing this sensitive issue. This is in part because of the shame and embarrassment experienced by the victim. I became aware of this problem several years ago when I learned of a teenage girl who was being harassed by two boys who were sitting behind her in class. When they got her attention they accused her of staring at a supposed bulge in one of the boy's trousers, admonished her for 'keeping looking at John's penis' – and asked her to stop. This was repeated on other occasions. She was greatly upset and didn't know what to do. However, it did come to the attention of the school counsellor who arranged for a meeting of the three of them. Nor surprisingly she refused to come.

Is the motive for sexual harassment sexual? It may seem so, but not necessarily. Sexual interest and sexual gratification are likely to be involved but also demonstrating dominance over another person and even an element of sadism may play a part.

Bullying as a means of advancement

Here I have in mind a perspective that focuses on the practical gains that can be achieved through effective bullying, as distinct from an action that is more of an emotional response based on biological impulses, psychiatric abnormality or social conditioning.

Into this category are cases of extortion, whereby a target is continually forced to give the bully what he or she wants. It may be money or items of value, or a service of some kind. In extreme cases, it may involve a kind of slavery. In the old English school system the process was institutionalized and called 'fagging.' From the perspective of the school, one might say that it wasn't bullying at all; indeed some schoolteachers at an Australian private boarding school I visited several years ago argued that affording privileges to senior students and the right to punish juniors for misdemeanours or slackness was a good way of maintaining social order. It is sometimes justified in advice given to the young students: Don't worry: your turn will come. And it does. Old perspectives have the habit of persisting long after you think they have gone away.

More commonly, instrumental bullying is directed towards acquiring less tangible items or services. It may, for instance, be seen as a means of achieving or maintaining social status. Reducing the status of another may increase the relative status of one's self – and serve as a stepping-stone to higher things. What matters with bullying of this kind is its effect on the pecking order. This perspective of bullying, driven by social competitiveness, is encouraged more in some schools and some societies than others.

The school ethos and attitudes to victims

We have seen how social contexts have a highly significant effect on the prevalence of bullying in schools. For instance, countries vary very widely in the tables of statistics describing the prevalence of bullying. At a more local level, the school ethos can exert a powerful influence. The school ethos may influence and be influenced by the classroom ethos which may, to some extent, be determined by the class management and teaching skills of the teacher or teachers. But beyond this, a school ethos is also a product of the attitudes of students, how they regard others, especially (in the case of bullying) those students who are bullied.

In one Australian study (Rigby & Slee, 1993) 82 boys and 82 girls aged 12–15 years were asked to complete a sentence beginning, 'Children who complain about being bullied…' Analysis of the completions indicated that just over half (51%) of them were supportive of the victim, some 21% were neutral and 28% were negative. Those who were supportive of the victims made such comments as, 'Is fair enough because you would if you were being bullied'; 'are usually telling the truth'; 'I feel sorry for them'; 'should be listened to and believed by people who will do something about it.' On the other hand, there were those who viewed the complainers negatively, describing them for instance, as 'wimps who are trying to get people into trouble'; 'normally asking for it'; 'losers,' 'poo dicks,' 'pussies' and a 'pain.' Boys tended to be more critical of the 'complainers,' especially older boys.

Some students had mixed feelings, sometimes inclining them to be sympathetic in their attitudes, sometimes indifferent, sometimes conflicted. For example, 'I feel sorry for them, but sometimes they deserve it'; 'sometimes they're over-reacting and want attention and maybe sometimes some kids need help with this.' 'I pity them but laugh with everyone else.' 'They are people I feel sorry for, although I hate to admit that sometimes I just don't care and I'm glad it's not me.'

A later Australian study of students (N = 213) adopted a quantitative approach in which students completed a reliable 10-item Attitude to Victims Scale in which 5 items were coded positive such that agreement indicated positive views of victims and five items were coded such that disagreement indicated a supportive attitude. In this study reported by Rigby and Bortolozzo (2013) more than half of the students indicated that they agreed with each of the items supporting victims, with some being unsure, and around 10 % of students disagreeing (see Figure 7.7).

Responses to the remaining five items (negatively worded) provided consistent results. Here students mainly disagreed with items that were critical of victims, as indicated in Figure 7.8.

From the results presented in Figures 7.7 and 7.8, it is evident that students in general are supportive of children who are bullied, that is they agree with statements that are made in support of them and disagree with statements that are critical of them. At the same time, they reveal that a minority of students have little or no sympathy for children who get bullied and may in fact despise and ridicule them. A somewhat larger group of students are, 'on the fence' and seemingly unable to make up their minds.

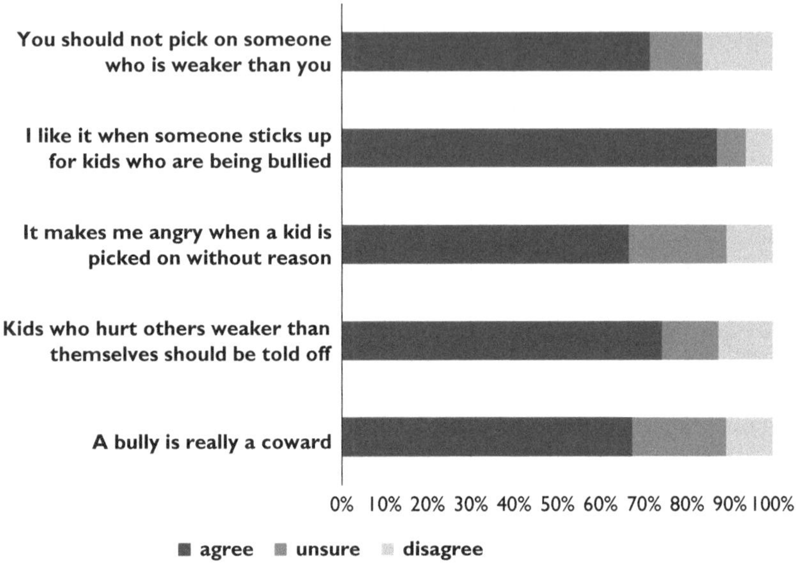

Figure 7.7 Students agreeing with supportive statements about victims.

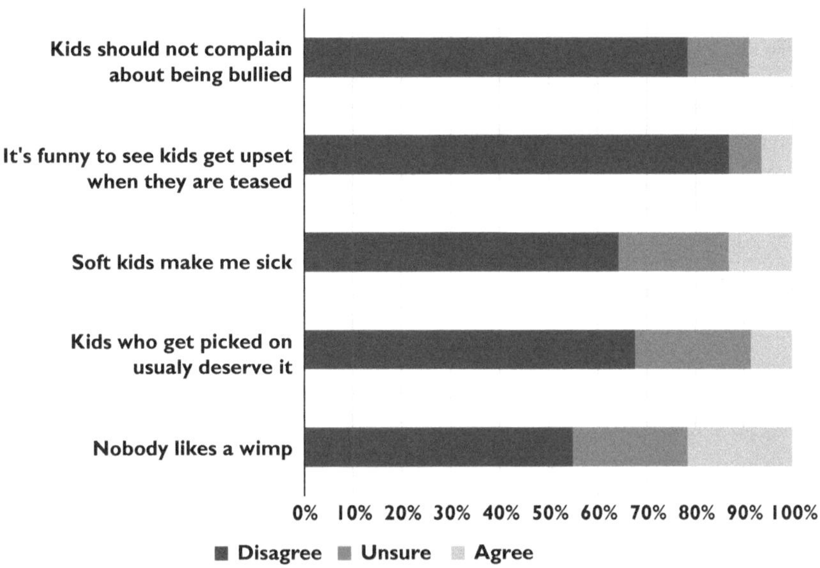

Figure 7.8 Students disagreeing with negative views about victims.

Views of bystanders

In a survey of 400 Australian students, half of whom were in Years 6 and 7 in Primary Schools and half in years 7 and 8 in Secondary schools, approximately 40% indicated that they would intervene if they witnessed bullying as depicted in illustrations that they were shown (Rigby & Johnson, 2006). These illustrations provide examples of physical and verbal bullying with bystanders watching. Approximately 15% thought they would not or probably would not intervene. A substantial difference appeared between the intentions of primary and secondary students with the latter, especially boys, saying they would not intervene.

A number of factors were identified in this study as making it more like that students would say that they would intervene. The most powerful factor was simply attitude towards victims, as assessed by the Victims of bullying Scale, followed by having intervened in the past. A further significant factor was what they thought friends would expect of them, followed by what they thought their parents expected of them, especially their fathers. Gender played a role only in primary schools, with girls more ready to intervene. What they thought teachers expected of them was not related to whether they would intervene.

The respondents were also asked to give their reasons for intervening or not intervening A wide variety of reasons were given. Many explained that their decision was based on a belief that bullying was simply wrong, as in these examples:

> 'It feels like the right thing to do';
> 'It is wrong to harass someone like that';
> 'It is not right to bully.'
> 'I am not a mean person'

One added: 'I don't know why, I just would.'

Some students 'related their actions to an empathic concern for the victims.

> 'I feel sorry for them and do not want them to get hurt;'
> 'I don't like seeing people's feelings being hurt';
> 'They [victims] are usually the ones who can't stand up for themselves;'
> 'They need support—they may be scared';
> 'I can imagine how the person [the victim] would feel'
> 'I have been in similar situations and I know what it feels like to be bullied.'
> 'It has happened to me before and no one stuck up for me and that made me feel angry.' 'I don't want other people to go through what I went through in Year 3.'

A few noted the possible rewards for helping

> 'If I helped someone they might help me,'
> 'It is nice to help and I would probably make a new friend if I did.'
> 'I could become a hero!'

Not all answers were positive. For some students it was none of their concern:

> 'It is not my problem if someone I don't know is getting picked on';
> 'It isn't nice to intrude on someone's business';
> 'They can solve it all by themselves';
> 'None of my business.'
> 'It's the responsibility of the person being bullied'
> 'He [the victim] should stick up for himself.'

Some were reluctant to act because of the fear of negative consequences

> 'I would be scared it would happen to me';
> 'The people may turn on ME!';
> 'Everyone would be on the insulter's side so I'm not going on the insulted side because I would get drilled.'
> 'If I got involved I would probably get bashed';
> 'I don't want to be a "sissy" by telling a teacher.'

There were students who thought any action would be futile:

> 'They would not take any notice of me'
> 'It might make matters worse'
> 'If I ignored it, it might stop, because they are not getting any attention.'

Sadly, there were some students who supported and admired the bully:

> 'The person insulting the other person is cool and ROCKS.'
> 'The person pushing [the victim] is me or my friend and you gotta be cruel.'
> 'Some people deserve to get their heads kicked in because they are dickheads.'
> 'Every kid likes to have fun and I am part of it.'

These comments and others expressing similar viewpoints illustrate the wide spectrum of attitudes and beliefs that underlies the behavioural intentions of students on this important matter. Most responses suggested positive attitudes or values, especially among younger students and female students, who generally exhibit a higher degree of empathy. At the same time, it should be noted that good intentions are not easy to carry out in some complex bystander situations.

A major implication from this study is that the direct influence of teachers in affecting what students intend to do as bystanders is often ineffective or quite limited. Facilitating student discussion of the pros and cons of intervening can be a better way of proceeding. As the research shows students are much more likely to be influenced by what fellow students think. Given that a large majority of students are in fact sympathetic to victims and supportive of them, teachers can help individual students to be aware of this. Many do not realize this. They typically experience what has been termed pluralistic ignorance, a cognitive bias that leads individuals to believe mistakenly that others do not share their personal opinion (see Shamir & Shamir, 1997). The revelation that many students hold the same positive beliefs as themselves can be an important motivating factor – and change their negative or neutral perspective about bystanding.

Prospects of student-cooperation in addressing bullying.

From the research described in this chapter, it is evident that although, on the whole, students deplore bullying, are broadly supportive of victims, and would like to see it stopped, there are substantial numbers of students who are sceptical or critical of what is being done to counter bullying. Evidence is scant regarding whether student perceptions of whether they should or can co-operate with staff to address bullying have been changing in recent times. Some Australian studies may throw some light on this important matter.

It should first be acknowledged that the prospects of students and teachers working together depend not only on the views of students but also on the views of teachers or school authorities. About twenty years ago I received an email from a 16-year-old male student who informed me that he had a strong interest in helping to reduce bullying in his school. As a start, he had constructed a questionnaire to identify the scope of the problem and how students were being affected. He had sought help from the Deputy Principal who, to his surprise had told him to 'back off' as it was the business of the school to address any such problem. He was somewhat shaken and disillusioned. It is fair to say that I received another email from a female student at another school who said how pleased she was that her teachers had welcomed her initiative and were very supportive. How receptive in general schools were (and are) to student-teacher collaboration in addressing bullying has been the subject of a few surveys involving students.

In the mid-1990s I conducted a survey of students (127 boys and 155 girls) in one co-education secondary school in Tasmania, Australia to find out whether the students were interested in working with staff to address the problem of bullying at their school. Student self-reports indicated that around 35% of them had been bullied more than once over the last 12 months (see Rigby, 1995). Being bullied at this school was found to be associated with feeling unsafe at school and with absenteeism. Students were also asked through anonymous questionnaires whether they would be interested in talking about the problem of bullying at school with other students to see what could be done to stop it. Among boys 11% said 'yes,' 40% were 'unsure' and 49% said 'No.' Among girls the response was somewhat more positive: 22% said 'yes'; 54% were 'unsure' and 25% said 'No.' Thus only a quite small minority (around 16%) were interested in being part of a discussion on what could be done to stop the bullying. Among girls (but not boys) who wanted to take part, there was a higher proportion of students who had evidently been victimized. From this study conducted over 25 years ago, it appeared that in general students in secondary schools students were not interested in working together with teachers to counter bullying – at least not at a meeting organized by their teachers. There were several shortcomings to this study. It drew on data from one school only and the school could obviously be non-representative. Secondly, the question was posed as if it was the teachers who were requesting the students to collaborate – and the students were young teenagers for whom school authorities were perhaps not their favourite people (see Rigby, Schofield & Slee, 1987). A more age-representative sample could have perhaps produced different results.

Around this time a much larger, more representative Australian survey was conducted drawing on questionnaire responses from over 38,000 students between the ages of 8 and 18 years (see Rigby, 1998). In it students were asked in a questionnaire whether they thought teachers *were interested in stopping the bullying* at their school. The belief that teachers were usually or always interested in stopping the bullying was held by approximately 75% of younger students (under 13 years) and 61% of older children. These results suggested that for the most part students appreciated that teachers were trying to stop the bullying, though as the students got older more of them were sceptical.

Several years later Rigby and Bagshaw (2003) addressed the question of whether students thought that students and teachers should work together in dealing with bullying. The students were in the first year of secondary schools, aged approximately 14 years. The results are summarized in Table 7.1.

Table 7.1 Student views on whether students and staff should work together to stop bullying

Student responses			
	Yes	*Unsure*	*No*
Boys (N = 4017)	49.6	36.0	14.3
Girls (N = 2977)	57.3	33.8	8.9

In contrast to the results reported 10 years earlier a majority of students thought that they should work together with staff. Earlier the recorded percentage was more than 4 times less for boys and around 3 times less for girls. Although the former study was based on student responses from one school only and probably seen as a request by the school to cooperate – the scale of the differences suggest that there had been an increase in the readiness of students to work with staff on the problem. But there was still a long way to go with almost half the students believing that they should not work with teachers on the problem or were unsure whether they should do so.

Why were so many students not ready to commit themselves to working with teachers. A series of questions sought to find out. Some reflected on the belief that teachers did not know how to work on the problem. Some indicated that they thought that teachers would handle cases of bullying unfairly – this was especially evident among students reporting that they had in fact engaged in bullying. In short, there appeared to be a lack of trust evident earlier in the reasons given as to why many students prefer to go for help from others rather than from teachers.

A study conducted more recently pooling data from 36 Australian schools (Rigby & Johnson, 2016) provided a much more positive picture of teacher motivation to counter bullying. In this later study, approximately two-thirds of students opined that 'all' of their teachers always wanted the bullying to stop (see Table 7.2).

Thus in the latest Australian survey conducted in 2015 only a relatively small percentage of students (around 10%) across a wide age span saw teachers as usually not interested in trying to stop bullying. A large majority of students express support for victims and abhorrence of bullying, and recognize that teachers are sincerely committed to the task of stopping bullying. To this should be added the finding reported earlier that at least half the students believe that the efforts of teachers through classroom instruction and related activities are 'helpful' or 'very helpful' in stopping bullying behaviour. Only around 10% reported that they were not helpful. Such beliefs held by students augers well for student-teacher collaboration, at least in the Australian context.

An evaluation of a proactive intervention to reduce bullying in the UAE has also provided largely positive feedback from students who had received a

Table 7.2 Student estimations of how many of their teachers want to stop bullying

Student responses					
	None	*Most don't*	*About half*	*Usually*	*All do*
Boys(N = 706)	1.4	2.5	8.6	20.4	67.0
Girls (N = 847)	0.8	1.9	5.9	22.6	68.8

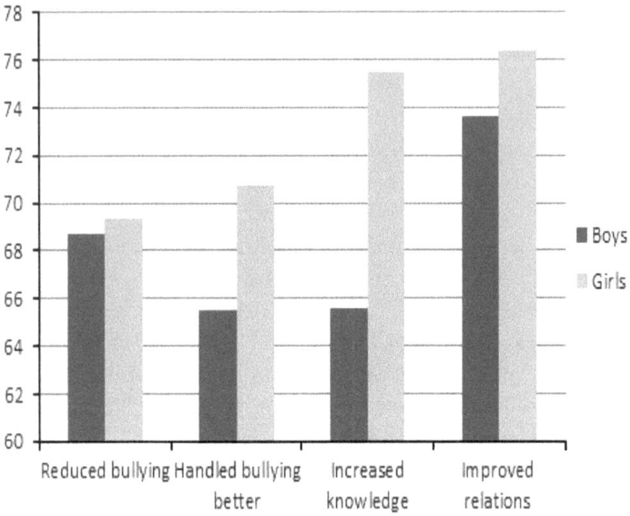

Figure 7.9 Percentages of boys and girls in schools in the UAE evaluating a classroom intervention as positive in different ways.

series of six lessons directed at promoting social skills and social competence and on responding effectively to bullying (Rigby, Haroun & Ali, 2019b). An evaluation based on measures of prevalence of bullying before and after the intervention indicated that bullying had been significantly reduced among girls but not among boys. However, positive effects were reported by students, especially by girls, in a number of areas, as indicated in Figure 7.9.

Of particular importance, students reported that the sessions had improved their relations with other students. How the students thought about the sessions was conveyed by comments from most of the students', examples of which are provided below (Note 'b' or 'g' indicates gender next to which is the year of the student).

- All activities are beneficial (g, 9)
- I enjoyed my time (b, 7)
- is very good and very beautiful (b, 9)
- It is beneficial because it has taught me to build friendships. (b, 9)
- The skill-based activities reinforced the knowledge of students (g, 9)
- Student collaboration and support for teachers (b, 6)
- Thank God, I am happy with everything. My school is beautiful and great (g, 9)
- I liked the activities that were implemented (b, 7)

  Numerous recommendations were made by the students
- Apply to all schools (g, 8)
- Do these activities once a week (g, 9)

- Increasing the activities because there are students who do not respect each other, so suggestions should be put to improve this thing (g, 9)
- Provide beneficial activities to improve morals (g, 9)
- Add an awareness session per week (g, 8)
- Have every day a session for development or activities (g, 7)
- Increase the number [of activities] and make them for all categories and levels of students (g, 9).

These results suggest that the work of teachers in seeking to prevent bullying through social educational sessions was greatly appreciated by students in contrasting cultures.

Further prospects of student-teacher collaboration

An essential element in future collaboration to address bullying involves a recognition on each side of the good will of the other. But beyond that, devising the means by which effective collaborative action can be taken is by no means an easy task. Some years ago when I was visiting schools in Australia I got into conversation with a teacher in a primary school who had engaged her students to act as peer helpers to sort out problems involving conflict or potential conflict between their peers. The selected helpers had received special arm bands to show who they were. The teacher explained what subsequently happened: 'They behaved like a lot of little Hitlers,' she said, with an air of gentle derision: 'You do this because I say so.'

The idea of engaging students as peer helpers or peer mediators is not new. As long ago as 1994, the New South Wales Department of Education trialled peer mediation in schools and mandated two weeks of training for teachers to act as trainers. The scheme continues to be controversial. In the 2016 report on bullying in Australia by Rigby and Johnson, nine of the 25 schools rated peer mediation as negative as a means of addressing bullying. Only one school strongly approved of its use. Certainly, there are students who want to fulfil the role of peer helper or peer mediator. There appears to be a gap between the perceptions of many teachers and probably between many students over what is do-able in this area.

Greater agreement is evident over what teachers and students can do in class to promote more effective responses to bullying. As noted earlier most students appreciate much that is being done proactively in classrooms in Australia to help them cope with bullying and how they might help others. Yet, in one area, again a gap occurred. The use of student-centred discussion groups, as in Circle Time, was given a much higher priority by students.

An old idea promoted by the grandfather of research into school bullying, Dan Olweus (1993) continues to have much appeal to schools wishing to engage students proactively in anti-bullying work. His suggestion was that students should discuss in class what rules they should follow and display what they agree to prominently for all to follow – or be reminded. The examples he gives are:

- We will not bully others.
- We will try to help students who are being bullied.
- We will try to include students who are being left out.
- If we know of somebody who is being bullied we will tell a teacher who can help.

Statements like these, derived from students working together were to be displayed prominently in classrooms and around the school as testimony to what students think how students should behave towards one another. Its value and impact comes from showing how students themselves see things – or would like things to be. Many students have been happy to assist in designing and displaying posters to promote anti-bullying campaigns at their school.

The suggestion is sometimes made that students themselves can deal with cases of bullying according to some agreed procedure as in the use of Bully Tribunals, discussed earlier. Although the research suggests that students can put on trial peers accused of bullying and make recommendations acceptable to the schools, this approach has not been seen by teachers generally as justified. With a growing acceptance that students may act responsibly using procedures based on the practices of law courts, the time may come when this approach, or something like it, can be welcomed and incorporated into school policy

Somewhat less controversial, but not widely practiced, are methods that engage students, not as virtually independent persons but as collaborators through group discussions about how situations involving bullying, or suspected bullying can be handled. As discussed earlier, these include the Support Group Method and the Method of Shared Concern. Both require a shift in the traditional way of viewing bullying incidents and how those involved as perpetrators of the bullying can be brought to see things differently, without blame and coercion.

How perceptions of others may be changed successfully through engagement in the Method of Shared Concern may be illustrated in an evaluation of this mode of intervention in Australia by Rigby and Griffiths (2011). Central to this form of intervention is the requirement that the practitioner listens non-judgementally to each of the students involved in the bullying – both suspected bullies and the victim, to enable the perspectives on the incident or incidents to emerge and to provide a realistic basis for a negotiated solution. The findings from the application of this method confirm the readiness of many students who have participated in bullying to work together to resolve a problem, commonly of their own making. An evaluation of 17 cases in which the Method was employed in schools in Australia – in South Australia, Tasmania, Victoria and Western Australia – reported a 90% success rate in stopping the bullying.

How individual students described their experiences of taking part in the series of meetings in which the method was employed may be illustrated from student comments in post intervention interviews that were conducted, importantly by someone other than the practitioner of the Method. In each of the following quotations 'T' is in place of the name of the person who was targeted by the group of bullies.

1. Good, me realizing how much I was doing it; T feels better, so do I'
2. We stopped giving him a hard time and apologized for our behavior'
3. 'We are going to be finishing Year 7 soon and when we look back on primary school, we want to have happy memories and for T to feel OK and us to feel good about ourselves'
4. I'm happy for myself because I've been helping people and helping him to feel better about himself'
5. 'It was good, because we are kinder to T and not teasing her any more'

The process itself was seen as positive

1. Both sides of the story were heard and it was possible to speak freely'
2. 'I enjoyed the process, as I didn't feel as though I was going to be punished for my actions'

Participation appears to have resulted in a positive sense of achievement in improving the happiness and wellbeing of others.

1. 'I think because of these meetings it has improved the friendships T has made'
2. 'T looked happier because we all said nice stuff'

What is most striking about these observations is that they were made in response to a process of guided interaction in which multiple perceptions of events occurred, resulting not only in greater awareness of how others saw things, but also of how one could act responsibly to improve a dire situation.

In this chapter, practically all the evidence relating to the various student perspectives on bullying has been taken from studies conducted in Australian schools. Although there has been a notable increase in studies of bullying in different societies and cultures in recent years, there has not been as yet any close examination of how the perspectives of bullying by students and others is different in different cultures. The general impression is that in collectivist cultures like South Korea and Japan, bullying is perpetrated by groups and often reinforced by social norms that are difficult to change. Student perspectives on bullying may therefore differ in different cultures. At the same time, the evidence is accumulating across some cultures that teacher initiatives, both proactive and reactive, are well appreciated by students. With increased understanding of how students and teachers perceive bullying and make efforts to combat it, one may look forward to greater and more productive collaboration.

Concluding points

1. Students estimate the frequency with which different forms of bullying occur at their school in much the same way as teachers do and rate indirect forms of bullying as the most hurtful.
2. Perspectives of students on bullying are closely related to whether they have experienced being bullied at school. These consist of approximately 50% of all students.
3. Victims of bullying tend to identify the perpetrators more commonly as individuals rather than as groups.
4. Students who report having been bullied consistently regard the consequences of bullying as more serious. They also think badly of themselves, especially if the bullying is done by groups, and are more critical of how their school seeks to handle cases.
5. The classroom climate is viewed more negatively by students who are bullied and/or bully others.
6. Students who bully tend to be unaccepting of others and be morally disengaged. In some cases, they are under pressure from their friendship group to act anti-socially or engage in bullying out of a misguided sense of fun.
7. Much bullying is directed towards unpopular social groups against which there is a significant prejudice, such as minority ethnic groups and children who are gay or thought to be gay.
8. In general, students are sympathetic towards those who are bullied. However, a minority despise victims and believe that they have only themselves to blame.
9. Only a minority of students who witness bullying act to support the victims. They are influenced in their bystander behaviour partly by the values they hold and also by what they believe other students think they should do, rather than by what teachers or parents tell them.
10. In Australian schools, there has been a trend over time towards more students seeking to collaborate with teachers in addressing the problem of bullying.
11. Courses delivered by teachers in classrooms to improve interpersonal relations and social competence have been much appreciated by students, for example in the United Arab Emirates. In Australia non-confronting interventions in cases of group bullying have been successful in resolving conflict by engaging students in constructive discussion.

Chapter 8

Perspectives of parents

What parents think about school bullying is important for a variety of reasons. The first is that actions taken by the school, both proactively and reactively, are likely to be more acceptable if they are in agreement with the perspectives on bullying taken by parents. Schools can act with greater confidence in what they do if they believe that their actions accord with the perceptions and judgements of parents. This applies most obviously to schools that are private and fee-paying, but can apply also to a large extent to state-run schools that are less dependent on parent support. Secondly, there are times when close teacher-parent collaboration is needed on what is to be done in particular cases, that is, when it is claimed that a child is being bullied and action, by both teachers and parents of the victim and parents of the suspected bully, needs to be taken. The third reason for understanding parent perceptions on bullying relates to the judgements parents make in the course of rearing a child who will enjoy positive interpersonal relations with peers, being neither a bully nor a victim.

My own understanding of parent perspectives on bullying was much affected by a series of emails I received from parents of children who had been bullied, mainly from the United States, seeking my help. Until that time, my understanding of how parents reacted to bullying had been largely theoretical. Of course, I knew that parents were troubled when they discovered that their child or children were being bullied at school, but I had little conception of the profound emotional effects of such discovery, especially when effective steps were not taken to stop the bullying or help the child to cope. I did my best to provide advice and support, but felt almost wholly inadequate. I was never able to meet any of them. I did, however, write a book that was intended to help parents of bullied children and their teachers to work together better (Rigby, 2008). One email cited in the book, in particular, conveyed to me the profound sense of horror that parents can feel at the discovery that their child is being bullied and is in deepest despair.

> My 10-year old daughter went through hell due to being bullied, and as for people to say it does children no harm is absolutely pathetic. I am totally disgusted in them for even thinking that.

DOI: 10.4324/9781315454450-8

> She did not tell me she was being bullied but asked me a question which will haunt me for the rest of my life. The question was: mummy how do parents know that when children kill themselves that they did it because of bullying? I just said they leave a letter, not thinking that she was talking about herself. Two days later I got a phone call from my friend whilst I was at work to tell me my daughter had just been battered and had her head rammed in a wall by 6 girls; then it dawned on me my daughter wanted to kill herself. … I went home and checked her room where I found the letters to say she was sorry and that she loved us. Luckily I found out in time. I had to hide all tablets and medicines, can you imagine how that feels? And then as we were taking her and another girl for a trip to a holiday resort, she asked me to put a song in for her, one I had not heard before, called 'The happiest day of my life is the day that I die.' I talked to the school who did nothing. So I changed schools for her and I have since found out that the [previous] school has been under investigation for bullying. Thank God I found out in time. … I always advise parents to waste no time and get the bullying sorted out asap – because you never know what a child is thinking.

Not all cases of bullying are so traumatizing to a parent but in different degrees they can be very disturbing, especially when they see how their child is constantly upset and unhappy, not only at school but also everywhere else.

A few years ago, I conducted an Australian Government survey, previously described (Rigby & Johnson, 2016), in part designed to obtain more objective data on parent views of bullying involving their children. Schools agreeing to take part in the survey contacted parents through their students with a note asking them, if they wished, to complete an anonymous online survey. As it turned out, approximately half of the 160 parents who took part had a child who was being bullied or had been bullied at school. One question asked them to say how they believed their child had been bullied. The most common form of bullying reported was 'cruel teasing' with 38% of parents saying that this happened 'quite or very often' to their child at school. This was followed by 'being left out on purpose' (33%); then 'lies being told about him/her' (31%); being the target of online bullying was experienced by 12%; being afraid of being hit 10%. Often the bullying was carried out by one individual, but sometimes by a group, sometimes by both individuals and groups. In many cases, students were reported as being bullied in a combination of ways. According to the parents, 96% of the students were to some degree upset, with 80% of parents saying they were 'quite' or 'very often' upset. Staying home from school because of bullying was reported as occurring in 64% of cases, with a further 5% of parents saying they were 'unsure.' Such results are in agreement with student reports on the relative frequency with which different kinds of bullying occur in Australian schools and also with the student-reported emotional consequences.

Can one trust the data provided by parents? Some have thrown doubt on the validity of the information provided by teachers regarding their perception of the prevalence and hurtfulness of school bullying. It is sometimes suggested that parent reports are not reliable and their perspectives should be challenged. It is said that parents become emotional when they believe their children are bullied and this clouds their judgement, just as it clouds the judgement of students who claim to be bullied.

Sometimes I have heard this point being made in a more judgmental manner. At a national conference, recently I heard the head of a State Teachers' Union berate and ridicule parents for reacting in such an absurdly oversensitive way to the minor difficulties their children experienced at school with other children. They needed to toughen up. To get real. This perspective is perhaps understandable from one whose role may be seen as giving support to teachers being harassed by worried parents. It nevertheless flies in face of what is known about the disturbing social and mental consequences of bullying on children as reported in mountains of published research. Many parents often have much to be concerned about.

A related view is that parents define bullying differently from how it ought to be defined. How it ought to be defined, so it is said, is the way researchers, or most researchers, say it must be defined. It is clearly in the interest of researchers to have a precise operational definition of the object of their investigation. Replication of findings cannot be made unless the same or equivalent measures are employed; otherwise researchers cannot build upon the findings of their predecessors. Agreed definitions serve a useful purpose. Whether they should be used to invalidate the perceptions and judgements of those who think otherwise is nevertheless questionable. At any rate, some researchers have chosen to use what they claim are the widely agreed criteria (among researchers) as comprising the gold standard according to which the perceptions of parents are to be judged: the 'correct criteria' being: intention to harm; imbalance of power; and repetition over time.

Two research strategies have been employed in a survey reported by Ey and Campbell (2020) examining the way Australian parents (N = 201) of children aged 5–10 years define 'bullying.' One strategy required parents to provide a definition of bullying, 'in their own words.' Responses were subsequently analysed and criteria inferred as to what parents saw as constituting bullying. The most commonly employed criterion was 'intention to harm' followed by 'repetition.' Much less commonly noted were references to a 'power differential.' Some referred to 'aggression' generally and some 'the harm caused.' Comparisons were made with the 'true' definition of bullying, which was seen as including all three criteria – intention to harm, imbalance of power and repetition. By this standard, only 8% of parents were seen as getting it right.

The second strategy made use of a test containing 20 scenarios, each describing an incident that involved interactions between students that might (or might not) be seen as bullying; half of them using traditional means and half cyber technology. Parents were asked to tick TRUE if they thought it was an example of bullying and FALSE if they thought it was not. For each scenario, a majority of the parents gave the approved answer. The median percentage of parents giving the correct answer was 96.5. Clearly, this strategy provided a much more positive endorsement of the capacity of parents to make accurate judgements of what constituted bullying.

Where parents gave what the researchers saw as 'inaccurate' responses to the test are of particular interest. Consider this scenario which received the least accurate judgments from parents.

> Once after class Max grabbed Peter's schoolbag and emptied the contents onto the floor in the classroom. Peter got Max's bag and emptied its contents. They both started to punch each other.

Some 57.7% of the parents indicated that this constituted bullying. The assumed 'correct' answer is that it doesn't. Arguably, they were fighting, it wasn't that one was bullying the other. Anyway, it was a one-off incident, not repeated.

Consider now how a parent might have visualized the incident. The teacher wasn't there when it started – it probably wouldn't have happened if she were. The teacher hears the scuffling and shouting and dashes back into the room. Pandemonium. The two boys are still embroiled; everybody is shouting. Not everybody, a few are hiding behind the furniture. Then a stillness. The teacher strikes a pose of authority. Seeing the mess on the floor: 'Max, Peter! What are you doing?' Not waiting for an answer. 'Off to the Principal's Office, the two of you!' Then the questioning, the cross-questioning, maybe phone calls to the mums. Perhaps the truth will emerge. Was it bullying? Did Max intentionally seek to hurt Peter? Looks like it. Doesn't look like a joke. Has Max behaved like this before – with Peter, with others? Did Peter actually provoke it? Was there an imbalance of power? Probably Max thought so. But who knows – we will have to wait and see. Still (it will be said) Peter is fighting back, so it is a fight. But isn't that what victims so often do or try to do anyway?

One can imagine the bemused parent, pen hovering over the questionnaire item, building a picture of what might have happened. No category of 'unsure' or 'don't know,' just a binary. The researcher decrees: it can't be both bullying and fighting? But why not?

In my own survey of parent perspectives (Rigby, 2019), my first research question was whether the 80 parents of bullied children had the same or different perspectives to those parents whose children were not being bullied. In some ways, they were not different. Parents of both bullied and non-bullied children were alike in believing that most teachers talked to students in class about bullying, were encouraging students to help bullied peers and to seek help from teachers if they were bullied. The two sets of parents did not differ in their evaluation of their school's anti-bullying policy (66% of all parents thought it was 'good'). In one area, there was a difference. Parents of bullied children were more likely to think that teacher supervision of student behaviour was less good. These findings do not on the whole suggest that parents with concerns about bullying are emotionally fired up so as to condemn the school.

Perceived actions of the school to cases of bullying

When the parents of bullied children were asked about how the school dealt with their child being bullied the results were disappointing. Of the 80 parents who reported that their child had been bullied at school, 52% reported that the school did something about it; 36% reported that nothing was done; and 12.5% reported that they did not know what, if anything, was done. These figures indicate that these parents saw the school taking action in about half the cases. This does not mean that the school took no action in these cases. But it does suggest that either no action was taken or the school did not communicate what it had done to the parents.

For comparison parents of non-bullied children were asked what they thought the school would do if their child was bullied. Possible actions were suggested. As indicated in Figure 8.1, there were consistently higher percentages of parents of non-bullied children who thought the school would carry out the suggested action than the parents of bullied children believed had actually happened.

A further question was asked to parents of bullied children to indicate the outcome following help being sought from a teacher or counsellor. Other parents were asked to say what they thought the outcome would have been if their child had been bullied (Figure 8.2).

If we compare the reports provided by the parents of bullied children with the *expectations* of the other parents in the study *if their children* had been bullied and teachers informed, we find a striking contrast. Every one of the parents of non-bullied children reported that they expected that the bullying would stop or be reduced. Approximately 40% of the parents of bullied children reported that there was no change, or things actually got worse for their child.

Parents of bullied children for the most part thought the case could have been handled better. Some 58% indicated that it could have been handled better, 30.7% were unsure. A small minority of parents (10.5%) reported that it could not have been handled better. From this, one might infer that among parents of bullied children there must be a good deal of disappointment.

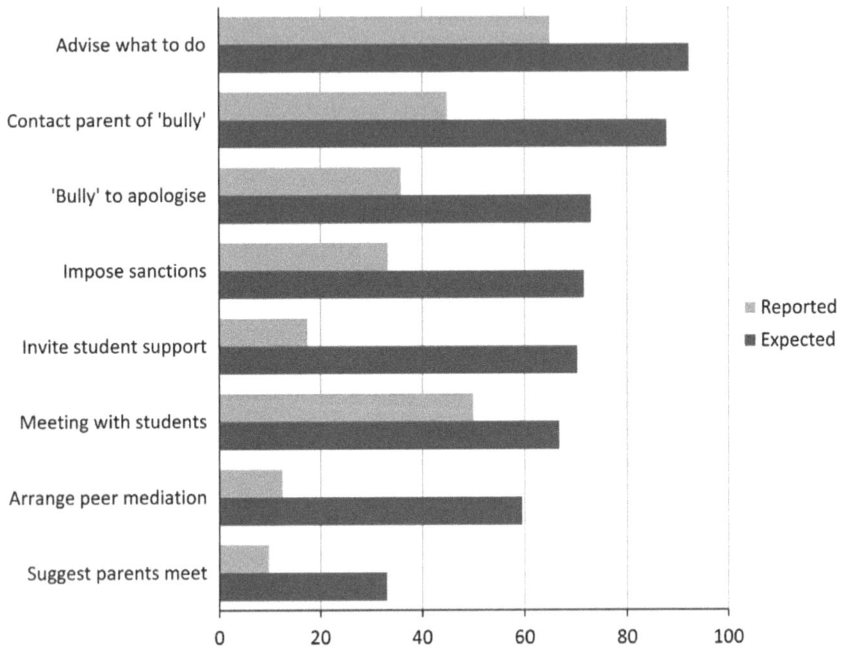

Figure 8.1 The reported outcomes of what the school did (or did not do) in response to the cases of bullying in comparison with what other parents expected if their own child had been bullied.

In a qualitative study of parent perspectives on bullying in North West England, Hale, Fox and Murray (2017) provided an in-depth account of how parents of bullied children viewed their role as parents with respect to bullying. Twenty-one parents took part in semi-structured focus groups and interviews to share their experiences. The researchers go on to discuss how parents see their role as being a 'good parent.' Fundamentally, it entailed protecting their child – a basic instinct, one shared with all creatures, at times with the utmost ferocity. As one parent expressed it, 'as a parent you become a tiger.' Compare this with the role of the teacher who understandably has a less emotional response when one of her many charges has problems with peers. From the parent's perspective, the teacher is in loco parentis. In practice, this is a kind of legal fiction. The teacher has obligations by virtue of her position; the parent normally has a passion when it comes to her child being bullied by virtue of her relationship as a mother or father.

Unsurprisingly, these different perspectives may lead to frustrations and dismay on both sides. Hale et al. report numerous complaints on the part of parents in the course of interactions with focus group members and parents who were interviewed. These included:

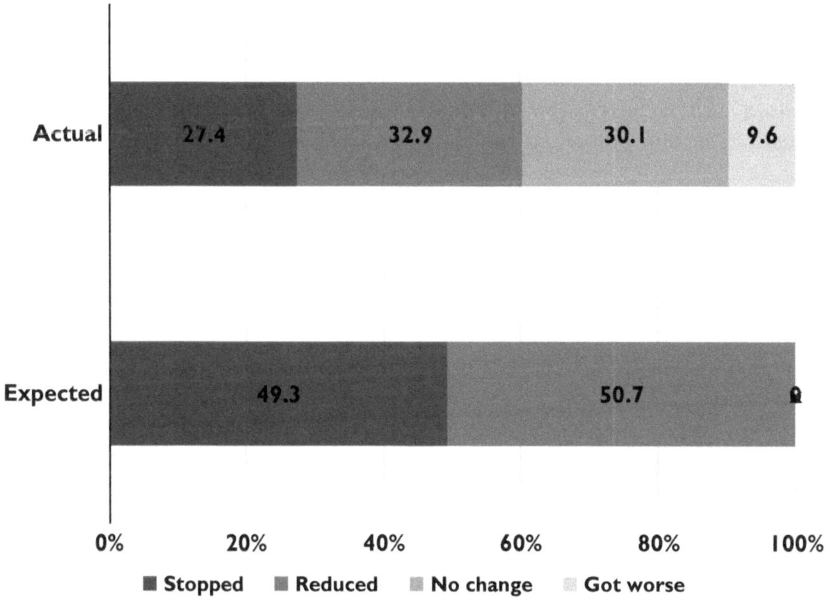

Figure 8.2 Actual reported outcomes of what Australian schools did according to parents of bullied children and what was reported as expected outcomes from other parents if their child had been bullied.

- Astonishment that the school was unaware that her child was being bullied – or actually in denial about what they must have known.
- Not being approached by the school to report bullying incidents that are of concern to parents. Usually, it is the parent who contacts the school.
- Not applying the school anti-bullying policy; in particular by not disciplining the bully, as required.
- Being unable to contact the school to make complaints about what was happening to one's child. Contact person not available. An appointment to be made several weeks ahead.
- Not being informed regarding what action was taken by the school in response to complaints.
- Non-physical bullying such as verbal abuse and social exclusion not being taken as seriously as it should.
- Being unreasonably expected to collect 'evidence' of one's child being bullied, such as photographs of injuries and copies of abusive emails, in order to convince the school of the need to respond.
- Defensiveness of teachers when concerns expressed that seemed to threaten their authority.
- 'Everything has got to be on [the teachers'] terms, and I mean I don't know about you, but you feel inadequate enough already.'

Feelings of parental inadequacy were frequently mentioned. The question of whether they had unwittingly contributed or even caused the problem weighed heavily on some. Had they contributed to the bullying by how they had behaved as parents, as for example, telling their child not to respond forcefully when he or she is being bullied? Or, perhaps through over-protection, having prevented the child from acquiring the interpersonal skills needed to thrive in a rough school environment?

Not all parents were negative about teachers.

> I dropped my son off the next morning and the learning support teacher came running across the car park and said: 'I sorted it for you; the boy has admitted it and he will be punished for his actions.' I was happy with that, my son was happy with that, so I was extremely happy.

Hale et al. note that parents in their study typically wanted the bully to be punished. As noted earlier, a substantial proportion of teachers agree that this is the best way of dealing with cases is through the use of direct sanctions. But some do not, and increasingly schools have come to see that non-confronting methods, such as the Support Group Method and the Method of Shared Concern, may be a better option for some selected cases. This can be a source of conflict between parents and teachers.

Parent perspectives on what teachers should do about bullying

Parents were also asked to say what advice they would give to teachers at the school in addressing bullying. Their comments could be summarized under seven headings, as presented in Table 8.1, with examples.

The comments reflect a critical perspective on how their school is responding to bullying and to the concerns of parents. At the same time, here and there, are attempts to 'educate' the teachers, for example, in stressing the need to address non-physical bullying more adequately, the use of mediation and the application of anger management. Such advice, however well intended, is likely to threaten the professional standing of teachers and result in hostility towards some parents. Add to this, accusations that teachers may be abusing their power by treating some students unfairly.

Perspectives of parents of children who bully

The perspectives of parents of children who bully have received comparatively little attention; certainly little sympathetic attention. It is often assumed that they are the ones to blame for the inadequate parenting which has led to their child bullying. There appears to be some justification for this attitude. Research into the parenting styles of parents of bullies indicates that they are

Table 8.1 Advice to school by parents of bullied children

1. *Recognize bullying (including non-physical bullying) and be sensitive to the hurt that may result* 'Exclusion can be just as detrimental to a child's self-esteem as physical bullying and should be treated seriously.' 'There is a more subtle form of bullying where one of the cool kids ostracizes another child and the others bow to peer pressure.' 'Identify the bullying as covert bullying'
2. *Confront the bully and apply appropriate sanctions* 'There are not enough consequences for the children doing the wrong thing' 'Remove the child from the playground each time an incident occurs' 'They could be given a stern warning – don't be gentle to the bully!'
3. *Supervise student behaviour closely* 'Keep an active watch on the child to ensure he keeps his hands to himself' 'As the bullying was done in school playtime better supervision would have prevented the bullying' 'He [the bully] should have been monitored more'
4. *Communicate with parents more adequately* 'As a parent I could have been informed earlier in regard to the actions taken.' 'I would have liked a phone call explaining the situation to me.' 'The school did not inform me about it. Not until I rang up was any of it discussed with me'
5. *Act promptly* 'My child was quite upset and completely sick of it. It should have been stopped earlier.' 'The school should have acted on it ASAP. The delay was unacceptable.' 'We wanted a mediation between the bully and our daughter but this never happened. The bullying got bigger over time. It was left too long in our view.'
6. *Act fairly* 'As the bully's parents had made a stance previously, the teacher couldn't be seen to reprimand the bully.' 'The school chose to ignore the situation and turn a blind eye as the bully was a very intelligent student and the school didn't want to disadvantage her in any way.' 'My son was moved into a new class halfway through term, whilst the group of boys involved in the bullying all remained together.'
7. *Promote the acquisition of appropriate social skills* 'Give the kids a chance to express themselves in a non-confronting way that might expose bullying earlier.' 'Practical options to the child being bullied. One-on-one role plays with the child being bullied.' 'The child's [i.e. the bully's] anger management should have been addressed and my child given the right tools to cope with this child.'

more likely than other parents to relate to their children in a cold, authoritarian way, enforcing obedience through punishment or the threat of punishment, and also, in some cases through a failure to monitor and set limits, if needed, to possible anti-social behaviour (Rigby, 1993; 2013). How the parents themselves behave in their relations with others may provide a model, sometimes a negative one, for their children. Teachers often remark that when they meet such parents their child's bullying at school is understandable. Yet as a total explanation for bullying behaviour, this is far from adequate. Genetics can play a part. 'Like father like son' can however be misleading. Some children react against parental control and decide, 'I'm not going to be like the old man.' Yet something may 'rub off,' for example, ethnic prejudice and the prevailing community attitudes mirrored by some parents. These may foster bullying of targeted individuals whose social identity is disrespected.

A distinction should be made between the kind of bullying that is generally thought to be criminal, as in repeated physical assaults, and bullying which employs non-criminal though often equally deplorable and hurtful means of bullying. Relatively few parents encourage or justify bullying of the first kind. Yet some are not displeased to hear that their son or daughter dominates and bullies at school. Quite the contrary. This is well illustrated in cartoon by Michael Heath in 1988 which depicted a group of middle-aged men celebrating over drinks … One of them informs the others:

> I just got the most wonderful news from school – my son's a bully
>
> (see Search Results for 'I just heard' | PUNCH Magazine Cartoon Archive)

Whilst some fathers may really want their children to physically bully and dominate others at school, they tend to be quite few. More often parents want their children achieve dominance and status by what they say. A cartoon in the New Yorker by Emily Flake (2013) in the New Yorker captures one mode of parental influence, as a father instructs his boy: 'Son, if you can't say anything nice, say something clever but devastating.' The verbal put-down can be a form of bullying that accounts for much more bullying than the inflicting of a physical blow and can be at least equally hurtful.

In conceptualizing the bully, it is common to have in mind the entirely proactive perpetrator of abusive behaviour; the target is absolved from all blame. In fact, as studies have shown a substantial number of students who bully are also victimized, and are known as bully-victims. Being bullied themselves, they are inclined to 'take it out' on others whom they may be able to bully. The parent of such a student may be very much like the parents discussed earlier, that is parents of bullied children – and share some of the perspectives of those parents. Their child is being bullied and the school is not stopping it! To the extent which they identify with their child they may feel that there is some sort of justification for being aggressive, even though the child expressing the aggression may lead to a worsening of the situation. He or she has provoked the bullying and must suffer the consequences – that is justified bullying. Here is an example of a case I became familiar with.

> An Australian adolescent student of mainstream ethnicity thought that some other students somehow deserved to be ridiculed because they were

from Italian families, hung out together, had distinctive ways of talking, ate unusual food and kicked around a round football – the 'correct' shape being oval – as in Australian Football League. So he took opportunities, when it seemed safe, to make fun of them, call them names and spread rumors about them. Unfortunately for him, they were not amused and got together and did whatever they could to make his life a misery. In desperation he sought help from a student counsellor who decided she would call the Italian 'bullies' together and 'counsel them.' But first she was obliged to notify the parents of Italian boys, whereupon all hell broke loose. Their boys were the victims! How dare the school .... So much for this abortive intervention.

Adult involvement

Although bullying among schoolchildren is typically seen as arising out of interactions within a school, feuds involving parents and their families and – sometimes their extended families may play an important role in determining the perspectives of parents of school-age students. Such feuds may go back many years and generations. The disputes and perceived wrongs may be lost in time, but the animosity persists and may affect relations between children at school and rekindle mutual hostilities among adults, which in turn may make resolution of cases of school bullying difficult or impossible. With the virtual demise of the extended family and the influence of the clan, the perspective derived from feuding has become more and more rare. Nevertheless, it continues to be alive and strong, especially in some rural areas, where bullying may be seen as war and, as such, without civilized rules.

Can parents of the 'bully' and the 'victim' meet and resolve the conflict? I have from time to time been told of cases where parents of each 'side' have met and things have got much worse. One case involved two doctors who shared a country practice. The son of one of them began to bully the son of the other at school. The doctors met to talk it over, the problem escalated, and one of the doctors felt constrained to leave his surgery and move to the city. The black comedy directed by Polansky (2011) 'Carnage,' based on the French play, 'Le Dieu du carnage' by Yasmina Reza, examines the futility of the parents of bullies and victims seeking to resolve their children's fraught situation – and how disastrous it can be, with relations between the two families in tatters and relations with each of the families seemingly beyond repair. Nevertheless, despite the seemingly primitive perspectives of parents involved in defending and justifying the behaviour of their children there are cases revealed in the Australian survey of parents meeting and actually resolving the problem. Much depends on the prior relationships of the two sets of parents and/or the services of an expert mediator.

Concluding points

1. Parents are commonly deeply affected emotionally when they learn that their child is being bullied at school.
2. To add insult to injury, they are apt to be accused of being over-sensitive and over-reacting to the normal rough-and-tumble of school.
3. Parents of bullied children not uncommonly blame themselves for the bullying that has occurred.
4. Parents are sometimes thought to be deficient in failing to distinguish between bullying and fighting, two phenomena that often overlap and cannot be readily differentiated.
5. Parents of bullied children tend to report far less action being taken by teachers to help their children than is expected by other parents if *their* child was bullied.
6. The reported outcomes of teacher interventions are much less successful in stopping the bullying than is expected by parents of non-bullied children.
7. The parents of bullied children generally acknowledge that their school is taking appropriate educational initiatives in addressing bullying, but tend to be highly critical of the way cases are handled by the school.
8. Parents of bullied children are generally eager to advise schools on how they should identify and respond to cases of bullying, especially in keeping them informed of the actions they take and involving them in what can be done.
9. Whilst few (if any) parents actually encourage their child to bully, they are generally not strongly motivated to restrain or counsel their children, especially if they are involved in non-violent bullying.
10. Meetings between the parents of a victim and parents of a bully to resolve the issue have been reported as resulting in a worsening of the case, as each set of parents tend to see responsibility for the bullying differently.

Chapter 9

Perspectives of bullying of institutional and other authorities

If you would know who controls you, see who you may not criticize.
Tacitus

As in many of our judgements, we are influenced by a wide range of authorities. Each may have a distinctive perspective on matters relating to bullying. In some cases, that authority has the power to require obedience in some areas of conduct, for example, a Department of Education may require that every school has an anti-bullying plan consistent with a prescribed anti-bullying policy. In addition, a Department of Education may provide advice to schools on how bullying may be addressed. Where a body is seen as having legitimacy in requiring people to do certain things and to deliver negative consequences if they do not and rewards if they do, it can be referred to an 'institutional authority.'

According to Collier (1992), institutional authority may be distinguished from other kinds by its reliance on the force of persuasion unaided and unhindered by institutional context. Collier calls this 'intellectual authority,' which he defines as 'the authority exerted by arguments that make their way by virtue of superior rationality and do not depend for their impact on the lines of power and influence operating in an institution.' In this chapter, we will examine the perspectives of institutional authorities as far as school bullying in concerned, in particular Departments of Education and the Law. In addition, we will examine the perspectives of bodies that do not have the distinctive quality of being able to insist on obedience but rather derive what power they have from a recognition that what they say is authoritative and not compelled.

Whether authorities *can* impose their perspectives on particular individuals depends in part on the extent to which they are compliant, that is their attitude to authority. That there is a generality to institutional authority such that people are predisposed to respond positively or negatively to authorities such as teachers, the police and the Law has been extensively demonstrated (Rigby & Rump, 1979). Furthermore, the roles that people adopt in their

DOI: 10.4324/9781315454450-9

work and social relations can largely determine how compliant they behave (Milgram, 1965; Zimbardo, 1969). Hence, the effectiveness of institutional authorities can vary depending upon the characteristics of people and the situations in which they find themselves.

Departments of Education

These are bodies whose responsibilities are defined and considered legitimate and authoritative with respect to schools. They may be run by national or state governments or by other agencies, such as by religious bodies, and have jurisdiction over areas and/or populations varying in size. Globally, there appears to have been no estimation of their number or any detailed examination of differences in the roles or tasks they perform. Broadly, however, there is agreement that one of their functions is to ensure as far as possible that children are not bullied at school. As summed up in a declaration made by one Australian Department of Education:

> Every school is expected to have a safe, supportive, respectful and positive learning environment free from bullying, harassment, discrimination and violence.

A distinction can be made between central or National Departments of Education and local or State Departments of Education. Their functions typically differ. The National Department has a broader and less 'hands-on' role and is concerned primarily with giving general advice, gathering and disseminating information and funding educational research. For example, the Australian Department of Education has provided a document known as the National Safe Schools Framework (2010) with subsequent revisions, and has funded research aimed at assessing the prevalence and effectiveness of anti-bullying strategies in Australian schools (Rigby & Johnson, 2016). One may conclude that the perspective of the national department is that bullying can be more effectively addressed in schools if the work in countering bullying in schools draws upon information that is evidence-based and related to a general framework of understanding.

This distinction between Departments of Education at a national level and Departments of Education at a localised or state level is to be found in many countries, as for example in the United States, Canada and Australia. There is some overlap in function, with States also providing schools and their communities with information about bullying and the need to address the problem. Because of my greater familiarity with the work of State Departments of Education in Australia, I have chosen to examine the perspectives taken by these Australian authorities.

Departments of Education at the local or state level in Australia pre-date the establishment of a central department. The origins of the State Departments of Education date back to the latter half of the 19th century. The South Australian

Department of Education, for instance, was formed in 1875. It was only in 1901 that the States and Territories of Australia were federated; the Federal Government in Canberra acquired 'residual powers'; the States retained much of what they had acquired as self-governing ex-colonies, including Education.

Over time, changes have taken place in how the Departments are structured and operate. At the national level between 1966 and 2020, the Education Department has been renamed and has been variously known as The Department of Education and Science; The Department of Education and Youth Affairs; The Department of Employment, Education and Training (DEET); The Department of Employment, Education, Training and Youth Affairs (DEETYA); The Department of Education Training and Youth Affairs (DETYA); The Department of Education, Science and Training (DEST); The Department of Education, Employment and Workplace Relations (DEEWR); The Department of Education; Department of Education and Training; and (currently) Department of Education, Skills and Employment. The rationale for such changes is often unclear. It does however suggest that there has been, and is, considerable uncertainty among politicians and among bureaucrats as to how the administration of Education at a national level should be structured, and where, for example, 'bullying' fits. At the State or local level, one may observe many similarities between government and non-government education authorities with some minor differences.

Concern over the safety of children

A common perspective related to bullying is the safety of children in schools. Especially, it is recognized that some children are at much greater risk of being harmed through bullying or harassment than others. I became aware of this perspective when 25 years or so I interviewed an Education Department Official in one of the smaller Australian State Departments. I gathered that the Department placed considerable emphasis upon the problem of bullying and was promoting appropriate policies in their schools. These policies were well documented. They related to gender, especially being female, race or ethnicity and disability. The perception was that if the safety of persons in these categories could be ensured there was nothing more to be done. Twenty years later, there was added in some quarters LBQT, that is Lesbian, Gay, Bisexual and Transgender, which resulted in much controversy in Australia and elsewhere, with some Departments of Education taking different stands. Gradually, the Departments' perspective of who is potentially at risk has enlarged and it is acknowledged that under some circumstances *any* child can be bullied.

Concern over the safety of the Education Department

Departments of Educations sometimes worry over whether an acknowledging that some children are unsafe at school will be seen as their fault.

I have found this reluctance to accept that maybe at times schools can be really unsafe for some children is evident among both principals of schools and staff in Departments of Education. This anxiety is evident in the National Safe Schools Framework, the first sentence of which reads:

> Schools are among the safest places in the community for children and young people.

In justification of such statements, it has been maintained that more children are murdered in their homes than at school. Being 'safe' is equated with not being murdered! What if parents became aware that some children on some occasions are not safe in some other ways, as in being bullied? Votes may be lost. Heads might roll.

A second argument is that calming statements must be made to avoid panic. Recently being invited to write a booklet on bullying for an Australian State Education Department, I was admonished for describing the problem of bullying as 'serious.' The use of that term in the context of bullying behaviour had evidently been cancelled. It would be unfair, however, to suggest that all the Departments are tarred with the same brush. Some have been open and frank about what almost everyone knows and have introduced ways in which the safety and security of young students new to a school can be promoted, for example, through the use of a buddy program in schools in Victoria in which younger students are paired with older helpers (see trkpp6.pdf (education.vic.gov.au)).

The provision of helpful resources

A perspective on bullying shared by Departments of Education in Australia has for some years been that resources that are helpful can be provided to schools to address bullying proactively and/or reactively. A leader in this field is the Education Department of Victoria through a series of resources made available via the Internet, known as Bullystoppers (https://www.education.vic.gov.au/about/programs/bullystoppers/Pages/default.aspxI).

In the introduction to this resource, this statement is made:

> Bullying can be a real and serious issue in our schools. It can happen to anyone, anywhere, anytime, and can have devastating consequences.

It asserts unequivocally that bullying is indeed a serious problem and that it involves more than identifying and helping children who can be neatly described as fitting particular social categories. It also recognizes that stopping bullying requires the cooperation of all the stakeholders, including teachers, principals, parents and students, and evidence-based resources are needed to help each of these in working together.

Rather than take a 'do-it yourself approach,' the Victorian Department of Education engaged experts in the area of bullying prevention and intervention and worked closely with them for some months in order to provide agreed evidence-based tools and advice that they were able to convey to schools. Unlike some other Departments of Education, detailed advice is provided on when and how different methods of intervention may be employed as appropriate, given different circumstances.

What should stakeholders be told?

Departments of Education are faced with choice of what is to be communicated to whom. One answer given by one department is that they are not to be 'told' anything; they are to be engaged with! Taken to its logical extreme, this perspective neutralizes any expert opinion or indeed the expression of any reasoned opinion. In practice, all departments seek to influence what is to be done to counter bullying or to handle cases of bullying. This includes having an anti-bullying plan based upon an acceptable policy, such as that set forth by the NSW Department of Education. In fact, not to have such a policy or plan and a failure to carry it out can, in extreme cases of bullying, result in legal action being taken against a school. However, the line between directing what a school should do and what it should be left to decide what to do can be a difficult one to draw and Departments may be seen as erring on one side or the other.

Who are the experts?

Given the conflicting views of researchers and educators in the field of bullying, Departments of Education can be forgiven for feeling uncertain as to who are the real experts. Some resolve the problem by drawing on the views of 'in house' experts, who unfortunately are commonly unaware of what actions are supported by credible evidence. This is not to blame anyone. Department staff rarely have the time or opportunity to master even a part of the ever-increasing research literature on bullying. In my interactions with Department staff, I have noted that many members do not sit in the same chairs for long and must be continually seeking to grasp what they need to know before they are moved on. Hence – and sometimes reluctantly – they have to call upon 'experts' from outside, often university researchers whose acquaintance with schools is from when they were schoolchildren themselves, although they might be well acquainted with theories of bullying and wonderfully adept in the use of multivariate statistics.

The perspectives that Department of Education staff choose tend to be either ones that strike them as commonsense as generally understood in the community and communicated by 'wise old heads' such as the eminent and respectable Australian ex-government minister, Graham Richardson, who writes in The Australian (August 21, 2020, p. 10).

> If bullying is to be stamped out in schools the perpetrators must be named and shamed. Imagine being shamed before the whole school. Bullies never prosper when light is shone on them. They work well only in dark spaces.

As we now know, bullying more commonly takes place in broad daylight with bystanders present, many just standing there, a few trying to discourage the bullying; a few actually egging the bullying on. As for shaming, it can have the unintended consequences of making the bully into a martyr whose friends and supporters will continue to bully in ways that are at least equally harmful and more difficult to identify. Generally, Departments have recognized the negative effects of shaming and have sought to promote Restorative Practices as a better approach (Ahmed, 2001).

Alternatively, someone in the Department may have been impressed by the view that bullying can, like any other behavior, be decreased through the use of negative reinforcement or 'consequences' (a buzz word from years ago) and, perhaps more acceptably by positively reinforcing desirable behavior along the lines proposed by proponents of Positive Behavior Support. Ten years ago, this was the orthodoxy for addressing bullying espoused by the Queensland Education Department and some others. As a resident consultant to that Department, I was much surprised that there was in fact no discussion of the pros and cons of this approach – and virtually no opportunity to do so. In fact, it was very difficult to engage with anyone on the matter of approaches to dealing with bullying, apart from one true believer in 'consequences' and with whom I had many interesting arguments. Other people were very busy.

More recently, the orthodox perspective on bullying is to be proactive and especially to conduct lessons on social and emotional learning (SEL). This approach is proving to be popular in most States in Australia in part because it fits well with the perspective that has been growing in popularity in most quarters, in a large part because it relates to the goal of enhancing the wellbeing of students and their capacity to succeed academically. The revision of the National Safe Schools Framework in 2013 included both an emphasis on safety, bracketed, as it were, with the promotion of wellbeing, as the following quotation illustrates:

> All (sic) Australian schools are safe, supportive and respectful teaching and learning communities that promote wellbeing.

The assumption is commonly made that SEL will increase the overall wellbeing of students exposed to related instruction and classroom discussions and exercises. The enhanced wellbeing will result in fewer students being bullied or bullied less severely and fewer students will engage in bullying others. As discussed earlier, research evidence is mixed, with some studies reporting positive changes and some not. However, the efficacy of SEL as an antidote to bullying constitutes a perspective that currently is being strongly promoted by some Australian Departments of Education. In part, it is attractive because it avoids entering into any difficult and dangerous controversy about what is to be done about actual cases of bullying. The assumption is that bullying will simply be prevented by students equipped with the cognitive and emotional skills to stop it happening. 'As if', as my children used to say.

Sexual orientation and bullying

In recent years, Departments of Education in some parts around the world have had to grapple with the question of what is to be done about the over-representation of bullied students among those who are not of mainstream sexual orientation, now commonly referred to as LGBT. Although figures differ – sometimes widely – about the proportion of students in this category and the proportion actually bullied, it cannot reasonably be disputed that they comprise a substantial and very vulnerable group and that the consequences for individuals in that group of being bullied can be devastating, with numerous reports of youth suicide following bouts of severe bullying.

In Australia, the initiative to provide greater support for LGBT students in schools came from a body known as the Safe Schools Coalition. Some Education Departments encouraged schools to consider accessing and utilizing available evidence-based and age-appropriate information, resources and professional learning to help them prevent and respond to bullying and discrimination based on sexual orientation, gender identity or intersex status. This was seen as potentially involving a review of school policies and practice, professional development for school staff, or establishing a student-led group to help create a more inclusive environment. Controversy arose and perspectives differed. Whilst the intention of this initiative to help a particular category of students to be safe from being bullied at school was generally supported, it was pointed out by some that the program was being presented as a general anti-bullying policy when it was in fact somewhat narrowly conceived and might more reasonably form part of a much broader-based policy. Also, there were aspects of the Safe Schools initiative that went beyond what was thought acceptable to the community, especially in getting young people to consider or reconsider their gender and sexuality and act accordingly. Finally, it disregarded the interests of parents who were the legitimate authorities in guiding their children in such matters. Here, we may see a clash of perspectives that are difficult to reconcile.

Community involvement

Recognizing that bullying in schools is not simply a consequence of individual students possessing characteristics that incline them to bully or be bullied, nor is limited to the effects on interpersonal relations of the school culture or milieu, Departments of Education may draw attention to sources of the problem that lie beyond the 'school gates' and emphasize the need to collaborate with external organizations that can help to promote positive and respectful behavior in the wider community and in so doing reduce bullying in schools.

The South Australian Department of Education has promoted this approach in a recent publication in 2020: 'A community approach to bullying prevention within the school gates and beyond' (S.A. Department of Education, 2020). This involves developing and/or strengthening relationships between the Department and a range of relevant community organizations and agencies with which it can work. These include, among others, organizations concerned with helping families in need; promoting health and wellbeing of young people; providing positive recreational activity; devising and applying appropriate laws relating to bullying; engaging with non-State educational bodies (Catholic and Independent); and, working with the Media. The rationale is that such organizations can act, individually or together, to improve the quality of interpersonal relationships and contribute to lowering rates of bullying in schools. The perspective of the Department is that bullying can be reduced through collaborative connections within the community at large and for which it can provide a catalyst.

This view is certainly consistent with what is known about community influence. As reported earlier, there are extreme differences between communities, as defined by national boundaries and by social and economic considerations, and these correlate with the prevalence of bullying in schools. Within countries, there are communities that are relatively peaceful and those in which civic conflict is rife. What happens in such communities affects what happens in schools. Addressing such conditions is one way of reducing bullying. But is it realistic to think that significant changes to counter such forces can be brought about by the actions of Departments of Education? True, some headway can be made by Departments in collaborating with some community organizations, especially ones that share a common concern about bullying and can help each other in practical ways. But as a central or major initiative, it might be said that addressing problems within the school community would pay a higher dividend in the drive to reduce bullying.

Media relations

Departments of Education are understandably concerned about public relations. Their authority and acceptability depends largely on how they address and deal with issues in schools. Teachers may be unhappy if they believe that they do not have the legitimate support of the Department. Equally, parents may be critical if a problem that concerns them personally is not handled to their satisfaction. The media plays an important role in reporting and commenting upon issues that may reflect well or badly on the work of the Department. This can result in a Department cultivating positive relations with media persons. The media for its part may refrain from negative comment if it is to receive newsworthy bulletins it can print and broadcast. At the same time, sensational disclosures sell news, therefore, a delicate relationship may exist between the Department and one or more media outlets.

My own realization of the Department's situation came as a shock. Working at one time within a Department of Education, I was asked to respond to a request from a media organization for an interview by phone on some aspect of bullying. To my surprise, I was accompanied to the phone by two ladies who sat on either side of me. The first question was why I thought that bullying in schools was increasing so much. Rather than tactfully obfuscating, I asked why my interviewer thought that was the case – as research showed that it was declining in prevalence. Big mistake. My lady minders on either side shook with annoyance. As an academic, I was used to saying what I thought; as a sort of Department representative, I had still to learn the rules. As I noted earlier, I was left alone for months to visit schools and write my report; rarely did anyone discuss what bullying was about. I was, however, in demand when the Department Head was under pressure from someone who was complaining about something that had gone wrong – and the media wanted an explanation. I began to understand the depth of the insecurity that was inseparable from her position in the Department.

The media as a public educator

Beyond its relations with Departments of Education, the media acts as a public educator or in some cases mis-educator. The accuracy, intentions and impact of the messages conveyed about bullying may vary between media sources. A recent study by Moreno et al. (2019) has provided a detailed assessment of newspaper articles covering bullying or cyberbullying across regional and national US newspapers over a six-year period. In interpreting the results, the study drew upon Framing Theory according to which communications tend to select certain aspects of reality and make them more salient, while leaving other aspects absent. The main conclusion from an examination of 463 articles was that the writers were concerned mainly with emotional aspects of bullying, and the fearfulness of situations faced by young people. The threat posed by cyberbullying was seen as especially alarming with repeated references to the prospects of induced suicide. The temptation to gain attention by sensationalizing events is ever-present. At the same time, in my experience, journalists are interested in what researchers have to say and seek to convey research findings in language that is readily understood. This can be difficult given that many research papers tend to be highly technical and easily misunderstood. One important aid in helping newspapers and other media is an intermediary with an understanding of relevant research language. In Australia, this is currently being provided by an organization known as the Media Centre for Educational Research (MCERA). But even with this useful service, misunderstandings still arise. For example, a published paper of mine was interpreted by the local journalist to imply that teachers were exaggerating the prevalence of bullying in schools, when in fact they were simply making an estimate that was greater than that made by their students. Who knows who was right? But listening to all sides or interpretations of the story would seem to be essential if the media is to do the best job it can.

The Law

The perspective of those who support the Law as a means of addressing bullying can be stated simply. Legalized sanctions need to be applied to perpetrators of some forms of bullying behavior. In addition, sanctions need to be applied to schools that neglect their duty of care in failing to take appropriate action to prevent or deal with cases of bullying. It should be added that in setting out what legal actions may be taken in relation to bullying, the Law may at times play a role in the formation of desirable community attitudes.

Bullying per se is not regarded as a punishable offence by law, but certain forms of bullying behaviour may be regarded as criminal and incur penalties. Such behaviours may differ according to their perceived severity and nature. For instance, persistent stalking, serious threats and physical assault are commonly regarded as justifying legal consequences. In some States in Australia and elsewhere cyberbullying may fit into this category.

The severity of the bullying is not easy to gauge. As noted earlier, there are differences of opinion regarding the hurtfulness of different forms of bullying. One framework for assessing the severity and seriousness of episodes of bullying based upon suggestion by Rigby (2002) was subsequently adopted by a leading Australian Professor of Law, Butler (2006) as follows:

Low severity – commonly involving thoughtless teasing, name-calling and occasional exclusion, and regarded as annoying and unpleasant.
Intermediate severity – victim is subjected for a time to forms of harassment that are both systematic and hurtful, including cruel teasing, continual exclusion and some threats or other relatively mild physical e.g., pushing or tripping.
High severity – where the harassment is particularly cruel and intense, especially if it occurs over an extended period and is very distressing to the victim, frequently involving serious physical assaults, but may still be severe when the bullying is non-physical as in total or almost total exclusion from groups.

Since 2006, cyberbullying has come to be regarded as a particularly serious form of bullying and in some States any suspected cases must be reported to the police. It should be observed that the harmfulness of such offence, as inferred from student reports, suggests that in general this form of bullying may be less severe or serious than bullying involving traditional forms. Given that most students who are bullied are bullied in a variety of ways, judgements made solely on the presence of one form is hard to defend. Differentiating between the culpability and therefore the treatment of offenders in this area – and avoiding a blanket and equal condemnation of all bullying, as is sometimes suggested by the term 'zero tolerance,' is a perspective sometimes taken by the Law. It is also generally recognized that most bullying is of a relatively low level of severity, as suggested by Figure 9.1 and is distributed along a continuum of severity.

It follows that a case can be made for less confronting or punitive methods of intervention being applied where the severity is seen as low. Judgements, however, differ according to where to draw the lines. Hence, there can be much tension between the advocates of legal penalties and advocates of counselling methods in dealing with cases. A further difficulty in applying sanctions in dealing with cases of bullying arises when a group is seen as the source of the bullying and apportioning the blame to individual group members is problematic. Here, intervention methods appropriate for working with groups of suspected perpetrators and supporters of victimized students may be the most appropriate way to intervene. Unfortunately, practitioners of the law (and some teachers) are often unaware of alternative approaches and see the use of sanctions as the only way of proceeding.

A second area in which the law may be called in to address school bullying appears when a school is charged (usually by a parent) with having

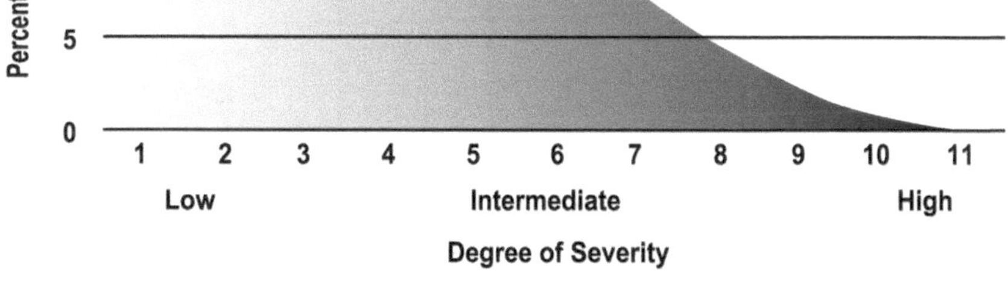

Figure 9.1 Continuum of bullying severity.

neglected its duty of care in failing to take reasonable action to prevent a case of bullying from occurring or continuing. In such cases, the focus is on the obligations that the school has, as indicated in its anti-bullying plan and policy, and whether it has acted accordingly. In deciding upon the culpability or otherwise of the school, it is common to take into account the consequences of the bullying as far as harm is concerned. Decisions can be made more readily regarding physical harm experienced by the victim; possible psychological injury, especially long-lasting harm, is often hard to establish.

Given that a connection between the bullying and serious negative outcomes can be established, one increasingly accepted way of proceeding is to examine whether the school could be held responsible for the harm because (i) the risk of the bullying of the targeted person was foreseeable; (ii) the risk was more than insignificant; and (iii) a reasonable teacher would have taken precautions (Figure 9.2).

Much emphasis is given to being 'reasonable' in defining bullying as it might occur in the workplace. It seems to suggest that bullying cannot be broken down into constituent elements. It comes down to exercising sound and sensible judgement – as the court decrees.

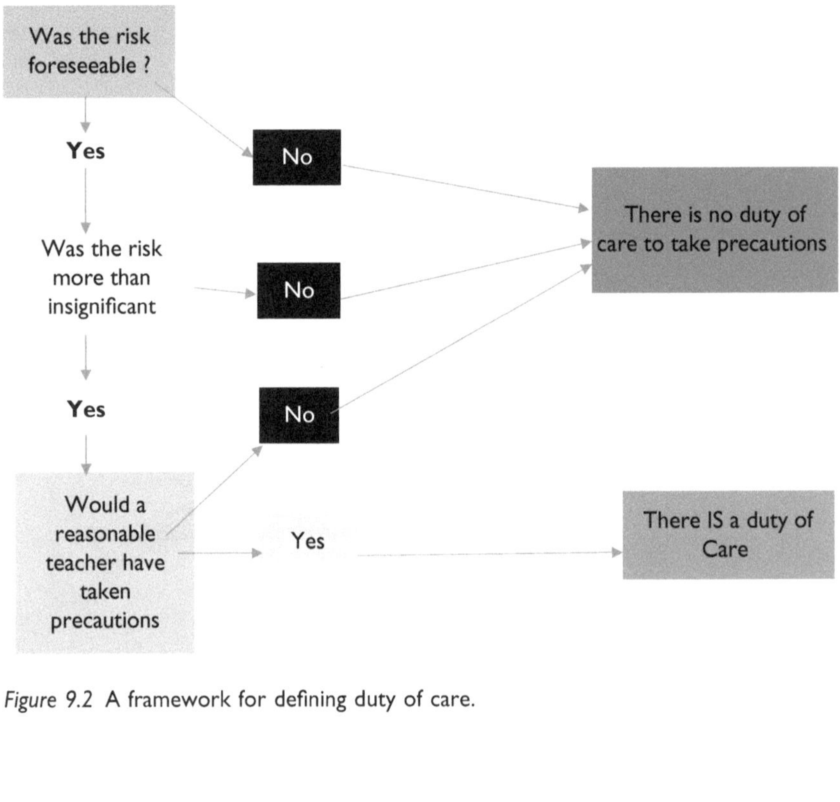

Figure 9.2 A framework for defining duty of care.

Intellectual authority

I have adopted the term 'intellectual authority' following the categorization coined by Collier. I hasten to add that I am not equating those who can be discussed under this heading with 'intellectuals.' Actually, the term seems to have gone rather out of use. As the popular historian, Andrew Marr has said: 'Once upon a time, there were intellectuals. They wore pebble glasses and stern expressions, sat around in cafes and acted as the collective conscience for politics: they provided a bridge between philosophy and power.' Here is meant something rather less pretentious, namely a source of possible knowledge based, it would seem, on facts and reason unaccompanied by any threat of harm if you don't actually believe it. Intellectual authority works, if it works at all, it works through persuasion. It should not be thought that Institutional Authority is bereft of intellectual authority and may not convey accurate information and reasoned judgements. The distinction I am making pertains to the legitimized power of institutional authority to command, at least in some areas of behavior.

It can be added that intellectual authority is sometimes accompanied by charismatic authority that works at an emotional level, as when one is awe-struck by the personality and conviction of a skilled orator, of which there are a few around giving masterful sermons on bullying and how to stop it dead. Or how to eliminate or absorb its toxicity in an atmosphere of euphoric wellbeing.

The perceived sources of intellectual authority are diverse. They have provided access to knowledge and understanding of bullying in schools in a variety of ways: in pre-service education and training for teachers; through in-service professional learning sessions held in schools; at conferences and workshops; through Internet sites; in printed material (books and articles); in videos; and through telephone contact with advisors or counsellors. Within communities, and sometimes internationally, persons identified as 'experts' commonly provide input at conferences, through the media and at workshops. In Australia, these have included Dr Martin Seligman from the United States, Professor Peter Smith from England, and Professor Donna Cross, a leading authority on school bullying in Australia.

Over time, a large number of organizations have been formed with the aim of addressing bullying in the community, more especially bullying in schools. They provide information and suggestions as to how bullying should be countered, in some cases drawing on research evidence, as in the Olweus Bullying Prevention Program (OBPP), prominent in the United States; the Anti-Bullying Alliance in England; and the National Centre against Bullying (NCAB), and Bullying No Way, in Australia. Many more organizations fulfil a similar function, based less upon research evidence and a strong conviction that bullying is a social evil that should be opposed. These include secular organizations in the United States, such as Stomp out

Bullying; Stopbullying; Speak; Up; and Stop Bullying.gov; as well as religiously motivated bodies such as Protectors, a Faith-Based Anti-bullying program. Increasingly organizations concerned with the health and well-being of young people have included the promotion of anti-bullying initiatives as part of their mission. Examples in Australia include Wellbeing in Schools Australia (WISA), and Resilient Youth Australia, both of which draw on research findings. A further important resource is provided in Australia (with counterparts overseas) to help children and parents concerned about bullying and needing help to talk by phone with qualified counsellors through the Children's Help Line.

Human rights

The authority of some influential bodies derives from their role in the promotion of human rights. These have asserted the importance of human rights as they apply to bullying. Governments worldwide periodically express their support for a range of human rights including a right not to be bullied or harassed. Specific bodies make it their business to promote tolerance and respect for others. In Australia, there is the Australian Human Rights Commission; in England, a similar function is performed by the National Human Rights Commission. They identify categories of people who need special protection, such as those in minority ethnic or religious groups, the disabled and those who are victims of sexual harassment.

The limitations of the work of such bodies is evident in the failure of some nations to agree as to what constitutes human rights or to apply the principles. Despite authoritative declarations widely endorsed by nations as members of the United Nations in 1945, in practice global agreements are sometimes difficult to sustain: witness the withdrawal of the United States from the United Nations Human Rights Council (UNHRC) in June 2018.

One of the consequences of identifying selected groups for special consideration consistent with human rights has been the de-legitimization of opinions expressed about outsiders. The proverb 'only the wearer knows where the shoe pinches' has in some circles been interpreted to mean that no one but the wearer (or who imagines being the wearer) can have a valid opinion on any related subject. Often now ridiculed as 'politically correct,' a perception has arisen in some quarters that expressions of opinion that are critical of the 'correct' perspectives ought to be cancelled. Such cancellations in practice amount to bullying – what we may call mono-perspectivity.

This perception is satirised in a cartoon by the Australian satirist, Leunig. He has produced a cartoon that is the obverse of the famous Voltaire exhortation for us to defend the right of people to say things with which we may strongly disagree. In it, he depicts an immensely large figure towering over a very small person and lecturing him as follows:

> I don't agree with what you say and I will defend to your death my right to stop you saying it. (See Cartoons – Leunig)

How does this relate to bullying in schools? First, it acts so as to prevent, as far as possible, the expression of any opinion by any student or teacher that does not accord with the approved right way of thinking, and to cancel out those that have the temerity to think otherwise. Second, it acts so as to gag would-be contributors to the debate on how bullying should be understood and responded to. It serves as a filter so that only those views that are acceptable are to be heard. Thirdly, it provides a bandwagon on which those who care more about getting on and gaining the support of the authorities, regardless of any commitment they, as individuals, may have to telling it as it is.

Universities and political correctness

Universities have traditionally been considered as the intellectual authority to which people should turn for the best evidence and the most rational interpretation. The media generally considers the opinions of academics and scholars as reliable and informs readers or viewers of what they have to say. But of late in some countries, for instance, Australia, there has been a change. The gap between what many people believe and what most people are expected to think has in many areas widened. The disallowing of the expression of views that are politically incorrect has been frequently noted. Thus, a prominent Australian researcher, Bettina Arendt, honoured as an exceptionally able social researcher has expressed the view that the prevalence of sexual molestation of women on university campuses has been much exaggerated. This has led to a chorus of demands that she should recant (shades of Galileo) – or at least be deprived of her prestigious Order of Australia medal. Following this, an Australian scientist, Peter Ridd, who questioned global warming and its alleged negative effects on the Barrier Reef on empirical grounds was summarily dismissed from his position at his university.

Australia is of course not unique in providing egregious examples of academic cancellation. In a recent case reported from Canada, we learn that an Associate Professor of Anthropology, Kathleen Lawry, has expressed the view that 'transgender identity' should not supersede biological sex in policy decisions, and has been summarily dismissed from the University of Alberta (David, 2020). To some extent, university authorities may act because of a concern that some people may feel uncomfortable on reading such an opinion expressed. One may legitimately question whether such feelings justify the severe penalty that has been imposed (Haidt & Lukianoff, 2018). They suggest that the movement towards cancelling in universities may be attributed to the growth of a bureaucracy of 'safetyism' driven by government mandates, risks of lawsuits, and a consumerist mentality on the part of students who want to be told what they need to believe to be 'with it.' This explanation may well apply to some other institutional authorities.

It would nevertheless be unfair to view the perspectives of universities, at least in Australia, as simply defenders of what is politically correct. There is still a diversity of views, for instance on school bullying, as my earlier review of research perspectives showed, ranging from the conservative advocacy of some leading researchers such as Olweus in Norway and Farrington in England, drawing largely upon quantitative data, to the more radical supporters of the use of qualitative data valued more highly by such researchers as Thornberg et al. in Sweden. In addition, whatever its limitations, researchers working mainly in universities are generally vetted to a degree through a peer review system, a valuable source that other 'authorities' do not draw upon.

Ethical bodies

The perspectives of bodies that decide what is ethical practice in the study of bullying can have far-reaching consequences for researchers and the findings that get published. These bodies function within universities and within Departments of Education. They exist in part to protect the sources of information, such as students and parents, from exploitation and harm, for example, by being asked questions that are too intrusive and/or disturbing. Often ethical decisions are a matter of opinion and empirical methods are rarely used to provide justifications. An exception relates to methods of obtaining samples of respondents, whereby potential respondents are asked to take part by opting into the study, an active approach, or opting out, a passive approach. The latter leads to obtaining larger, more representative samples and therefore more reliable results (Shaw et al., 2015). Hence, decisions may involve a trade-off between what is considered the right thing to do and the value or usefulness of the likely findings. Ethics committees typically act cautiously and seek to minimise risk. As a consequence, research is often delayed by long deliberations, and this may result in much frustration experienced by potential researchers. In recent years the authority of ethical bodies has tended to expand and it is a matter of opinion as to whether this has led to improvements in ethical standards in educational research.

Charismatic authority

One has only to go to conferences or workshops where school bullying is discussed to appreciate the diversity of types of presenters who seek to inform and influence their potential followers. There is the academic who impresses with a knowledge of research; the teacher who explains what her school is doing about bullying; the man or woman from the Department who assures us that everything is under control; and the wizard from nowhere who has the answer. We listen spellbound. Later we may think he or she was off the planet. But for the time being ... This is charismatic authority.

According to the authority on authority, the sociologist, Max Weber, periodically, people come along who have extraordinary personal qualities that resonate with those they seek to influence. Knowledge is superfluous. Their influence is personal, emotional – and generally short lived, except for a band of fervent disciples. Given the great uncertainty about what can be done about bullying, whether progress can be made, and the desperation people feel, the charismatic authority is apt to bind us with its spell.

Moral authority

Little has been said thus far about moral authority, yet many would say that bullying is at root a moral problem. It is implied in some things that are said, but seldom said out loud. For better or worse we live in postmodern times and have a profound distrust of absolutes. God is a con. A Catholic archbishop is widely declared guilty in Australia before he is tried. Unwelcome news is fake. Still, some cling to the belief that moral authority implies a respect for the facts and the role of reason. Does it extend to an acceptance that there is a repository of known knowledge about bullying which confers authority on those who possess it? Increasingly, the answer being given is no.

Several years ago, I was invited to a meeting of so-called experts on bullying, as were about 20 others. It was held in the seat of government in Canberra and presided over at times by the then Australian Federal Minister for Education, Peter Garrett. At one stage a member of this august group, the leading and most respected Australian authority on bullying in schools, made, a brave proposal. Could there not be formed, she asked, an accredited body of experts on bullying who would decide what had been truly established by research based on irrefutable evidence, and advise accordingly? The politician smiled indulgently – and passed on the next question.

Concluding points

1. Authorities play an important role in determining attitudes and perceptions relating to bullying, either through their legitimized status which enables them to require compliance in some areas and/or by their actions in promoting persuasive ideas and suggestions.
2. Departments of Education, Government and Non-Government exercise their authority with respect to bullying principally in determining what schools must or may or may not do in their dealings with teachers, students and parents. Variations exist between Departments in the policies and programs they devise, promote or insist upon.

3. Departments of Education tend to be risk-aversive and guard against taking or approving of actions that may conflict with political interests or reflect badly on the Department.
4. For advice on addressing bullying Departments commonly turn to recognized experts in the field, at the same time being careful not to support or endorse opinions that appear critical of the Department or its current philosophy.
5. Ethical bodies seek to discourage or disallow research and practices that are thought to be harmful to individuals who may be involved. As a consequence, controversy may arise regarding the wisdom of some ethical judgements.
6. The Law is primarily concerned with identifying cases of bullying to which schools have not responded appropriately and may be held culpable. As a conservative institution, the law tends to assume that some form of disciplinary action is needed in dealing with cases of bullying, a view that is sometimes challenged by educators who see that alternative non-confronting methods are sometimes justified and at least equally effective.
7. Reporting of bullying by the press is often regarded as contributing to misleading perceptions of the current situation, largely because of a tendency of some media outlets to sensationalize incidents and catastrophize events.
8. At the same time, responsible and accurate accounts of evidence-based reports can be helpful in informing the general public, including teachers. This can be achieved through closer collaboration between researchers and the media, if possible through an intermediary who can bridge the gap between specialized research terminology and everyday use of language.
9. Numerous organizations and presenters of information about bullying have made themselves available to help educate people, especially teachers and parents, about bullying in schools. At the same time, the appearance of self-styled gurus with little or no knowledge of the evidence relating to bullying has been an unfortunate feature of our time.
10. As in many areas of modern life, ideas and points of view considered to be 'incorrect' have been stifled, censured and cancelled, thereby preventing a free and open discussion of the subject of bullying.

Chapter 10

Reflections

> There is no reason at all for hating the bad. For just as weakness is a disease of the body, so wickedness is a disease of the mind.
>
> Boethuis: Consolations of Philosophy

This book has sought to examine the subject of bullying in schools through the lens of multiperspectivity or, if you like, through a multiplicity of lenses. In part, it may be seen as a reaction to a failure on the part of educators and researchers in this field to reach anything like a consensus on how bullying can best be understood and addressed in schools. Hence, it is natural to turn one's attention to how and why people view bullying as they do, in the belief that at least some of the mutual misunderstandings may be overcome and greater collaboration becomes possible.

First, however, consider a serious objection to the line of thinking that may seem to characterize multiperspectivity, namely that in seeking to attribute validity to every point of view one may lose all sense of objectivity and conclude that perceptions are all that there are. One person's perspective is no better than another's. All views are compatible.

A story told by Rokeach (1960) in his book on the 'Open and Closed Mind' illustrates the point.

> One day there came to visit the town Rabbi a man and wife who were in dispute over a marital problem. In accord with tradition, the Rabbi was to hear both sides of the argument and then decide who was right. He first heard the husband's side of the story and, when he was finished, the Rabbi said to him: "You are right." Then he heard the wife's side of the story. "You are right," the Rabbi said. When they both left, the Rabbi's wife stepped from her hiding place behind the draperies. She had overheard everything. "But how could they both be right?" she asked. The Rabbi answered: "You are right." (Rokeach, 1960, p. 3)

Here, Rokeach was concerned with the illogicality of the utterances, a characteristic of the dogmatic mind. The Rabbi's two pronouncements, if

DOI: 10.4324/9781315454450-10

sincerely meant, were clearly incompatible and were justified, if at all, as a means of relationship building. In any event, the Rabbi was not telling the truth. Multiperspectivity is not a philosophy that justifies illogical thinking. It is not akin to zen Buddhism.

Nor does it deny the claims of morality. An important distinction is made between the right to hold and express an opinion that is controversial and seen as objectionable to some people, and the expression of an opinion that can reasonably be expected to cause serious and unjustified harm. Determining what ought not to be said and whether and how it is best to discourage it, is clearly a matter – often a difficult matter – of judgement. Adopting a multi-perspective approach does not solve this problem.

Adopting a non-judgemental view may be seen as offensive. A personal anecdote may show what I mean. About 20 years ago, I was invited to attend a meeting in South Africa on bullying in schools that was attended by academics, school educators and parents. At one point I launched into an account of the Method of Shared Concern extolling its merits. I was suddenly interrupted by a scream from an angry parent who insisted on being heard. Her son was a paraplegic; he had for years been confined to a wheelchair. He had been continually bullied at school and was now attending university. Little had changed. A favourite game his fellow students played on him was to push his wheelchair into a place from which he was unable to move it – and must remain stranded for hours. Nothing that could be done to those idiots could be bad enough. Shared Concern indeed! Considerably chastened, I reflected on how I would have felt if he had been my son.

However understandable this is, it does not invalidate the principle that we must hear out what people have to say before we pass judgement. All too often we make assumptions about why a person has done certain things or intends to do certain things. Here is an example from an academic peer-reviewed article in the journal *Social Psychology of Education* by Shevlin and Gill (2020). Writing about the Australian anti-bullying safe schools program they describe the attitudes of parents as, 'their imagined (sic) concerns being central to the debate' (p. 891). Parental concerns are dismissed as imagined, that is not 'real.' What they mean apparently is that they don't agree with them, they shouldn't have them, so they aren't real.

This view may be contrasted with that expressed by Kierkegaard (1973) in his discourse on responding to views expressed by those with whom you do not necessarily agree. It could be applied to a student who you think might have been involved in bullying someone. It involves suspending judgement, at least for the time being and really listening. This is how he put it.

> Surely I must understand what *he understands. If I do not know that, my greater understanding will be of no help to him. If however, I am disposed to plume* myself on my greater understanding it is because I am vain or proud, so that at bottom, instead of benefitting him, I want to be admired. But all

> true effort to help begins with self-humiliation: the helper must first humble himself under him he would help, and therewith must understand that to help does not mean to be sovereign but to be a servant, that to help does not mean to be ambitious but to be patient; that to help means to endure for the time being the imputation that one is in the wrong and does not understand what the other understands. (pp. 333–334)

This is not to imply that in listening non-judgementally, one is agreeing with what is being said. But decidedly one is doing one's best to understand how the student actually sees a situation – his or her real perspective on the matter. This approach in interviewing children who are suspected of bullying someone is central to the first stage in the Method of Shared Concern as proposed by Anatol Pikas. Contrast this with a method of interrogation sometimes practised with suspected criminals whereby the accused are relentlessly pressured – and disbelieved – until they break.

One may distinguish between how you may seek to help students whom you suspect to have abused their power and caused distress in others, from reasoning with those who hold a different view from oneself in a situation in which a resolution is needed. Here, the emphasis is on what each thinks, although how they feel may be relevant. But the principle is the same, as expressed by the philosopher, John Stuart Mill (1860). He comments upon a situation in which a person really knows his own side of an argument.

> His reasons may be good, and no one may have been able to refute them. But if he is equally unable to refute the reasons on the opposite side, *if he does not so much as know what they are,* he has no ground for preferring either opinion. Nor is it enough that he should hear the opinions of adversaries from his own teachers, presented as they state them, and accompanied by what they offer as refutations. He must be able to hear them from persons who actually believe them. He must know them in their most plausible and persuasive form.

Therein lies a counsel of perfection to which we rarely attain, but to which the philosopher would have us strive.

Although the prime focus of this book has been on bullying in schools, the subject is so entwined with what is happening in the broader society and what needs to be understood from an historical perspective that any attempt to view bullying in any context, whether in the home, the workplace or wherever, needs to take into account as far as possible the much larger picture. An examination of the historical context shows that the fundamental and central characteristic of bullying, the systematic abuse of power, has been present among humans for as long as there has been historical evidence – and probably in prehistoric times. One need not espouse an evolutionary theory of bullying as a plausible explanation for the persistence of bullying through the ages to conclude that the behaviour we call bullying is extremely resistant to change.

Yet, as Pinker has meticulously documented, there has been since the Middle Ages in Europe a diminution in violent interpersonal behaviour – and we may surmise a reduction in other forms of negative interpersonal behaviour in the community, largely attributable to the increasing establishment of legal means of control, the capacity to identify criminal behaviour and the use publicly acceptable means of punishment. As far as bullying is concerned, States have stopped short of declaring bullying to be a crime, although some aspects of bullying such as physical assault and stalking and, in some places, cyberbullying, are listed as crimes.

As noted earlier, accompanying the ever-expanding application of the law to bring about a reduction in undesirable interpersonal behaviour has been the assertion of human rights. As Kolstrein and Jofre (2012, p. 2) declare,

> Bullying undermines the fundamental principles of the Universal Declaration of Human Rights (UDHR), which establishes the following in its First Article: "All human beings are born free and equal in dignity and rights. They are endowed with reason and conscience and should act towards one another in a spirit of brotherhood." Fine words. But as we have seen, countries continue to dispute whether the above sentiments are being applied, and there is continual debate as to what actions are needed to match the rhetoric. We agree in theory that much can be achieved through the inculcation in children of fundamental values. But what values?

The question of values goes to the heart of the fight against bullying. In Australia, a National Framework for Values Education has been provided for all Australian schools in the 21st century. It contains nine values for Australian schooling. Teachers, students and parents are urged to come together to implement them. They are as follows: (1) Care and Compassion, (2) Doing your best, (3) Fair go, (4) Freedom, (5) Honesty and Trustworthiness, (6) Integrity, (7) Respect, (8) Responsibility, and (9) Understanding Tolerance and Inclusion. Each is said to be grounded in the experience of being Australian – in the 21st Century!

Contrast this with what has traditionally been believed: that values do not belong to countries, nor to particular centuries; that they are not a modern invention applicable now but subject to change as people change; that they require no rationale beyond what it is thought people may think; and that they are limited in their application to particular localities. For thousands of years, people have believed, or have been expected to believe, that values had an eternal quality, apprehensible by humans and binding on how they should behave. The listing of values or virtues is in part a recognition of the need for moral guidance in a world that has increasingly dismissed the need for enduring, unquestioned standards.

Since it seems impossible at this point to avoid metaphysics, I think we should, in reflecting on the problem of bullying, consider belief in free will. The domination of Science with its amazing technological successes has led to the virtual abandonment of the belief among social scientists that the will is in some sense free. What we think and do is seen to be determined in much the same way as everything else in Nature. Eminent thinkers of the past puzzled by the notion of free-will sought, we might think naively, to locate its bodily source. Aristotle thought the decision-maker or 'Self' was in the heart; centuries later Descartes claimed to have located the Self in the pineal gland of the brain. More recent research whilst abandoning the quest for objective evidence for this entity has inquired as to where people think it is. Perhaps surprisingly, experimental subjects have been happy to point confidently either to their heads or to their chests; the latter has been reported being more prone to make decisions based on feelings (Fetterman & Robinson, 2013). That the heart is in some sense involved in decision making is an old idea made famous through the writings of Pascal in 1670 (Pascal & Trotter, 1931) and his famous dictum: 'Le cœur a ses raisons que la raison ne connaît point' (The heart has its reasons that reason does not know). The poet Wordsworth (1800) took the idea further and advised his readers to stop learning from books.

> Enough of Science and of Art;
>
> Close up those barren leaves;
>
> Come forth, and bring with you a heart
>
> That watches and receives

Regardless of whether the 'heart' as a metaphysical entity somehow exists and can inform our judgements, as a psychological concept, belief in free will has been shown to have predictive value. Beaumeister (2008) has reported research claiming that disbelief in free will is related to cheating, aggression and not helping others. He concludes that 'belief in free will is conducive to better, more harmonious social behavior' (p. 18); therefore, one may surmise, less bullying. A popular science writer, Appleyard (2011), has pointed to the limitations of current scientific thinking in explaining forms of behaviour, citing a famous poem by Emily Dickinson, 'The brain is wider than the sky,' and concluded that simple solutions or half solutions do not work in a complex world. Applied to bullying, it seems we may have more to learn.

We have reached a point at which explanations of bullying and the models constructed to describe how and why it occurs appear to assume at least partial freedom of the will, despite the current scientific zeitgeist. Thus, the model suggested by the Tattums (Figure 5.4) built around the view that bullying originates as a desire to hurt, assumes that an individual can within limits decide whether such a desire can be expressed or suppressed in one situation but not another. The now very popular ecological model of bullying posits the existence of two influences on behaviour, including bullying behaviour – what Lewin called P (the person) and E (the environment). P and E are distinct entities. They are said to interact to produce B (behaviour) that may or may not involve bullying. Presumably, P can, in some circumstances, play a decisive role. But *what is* the P that can act decisively? Curiously, this is a question that never seems to bother us. Traditionally, this has been answered by asserting the existence of the soul or spirit. We have, it seems, in practice a general acceptance of some such entity – that is, we act as if we believe we have the means to decide but theoretically reject the possibility.

Bullying as a moral issue

Here and there in this book, I have noted that some people take a distinctive moral perspective on bullying. Within the social sciences, this has been largely limited to explanations for bullying as due to 'moral disengagement.' Little has been said about its opposite: moral engagement. Discourses have tended to be confined within religious or theological contexts. Yet in the everyday world there has been and still is a great deal being said about the relevance of 'character' which may be roughly defined as 'personality' from a moral viewpoint. Within traditional philosophy and in some modern philosophizing the nature of moral thinking and acting has been of central concern.

Broadly, three strands of thinking about moral behaviour can be distinguished. These are (i) deontology – doing one's duty; (ii) consequentialism – doing what produces the desired outcome; and (iii) virtue ethics – being the sort of person one should be. The first, doing one's duty would seem to depend on a positive response to an authoritative directive, as in killing in the enemy in time of war, or a recognition of the validity of relevant rules. 'Consequentialism' may be seen as a utilitarian philosophy that sees moral behaviour in terms of achieving personal and community satisfaction, as in 'the greatest good of the greatest number.' For some, it is step forward (for others a step back) to promote the case for 'virtue ethics,' especially in circumstances in which the rules are unclear or conflicting and when it is difficult to see what the consequences might be. The question, however, is what virtues are relevant to bullying and how can they be inculcated.

Some philosophers have sought to establish a general principle. According to Kant, there is a principle that all rational beings must accept. This is, 'Act only according to the maxim whereby you can at the same time will that it should become a universal law.' More simply, 'Do as you would be done by.' How this might be done has been suggested by a modern philosopher Rawl (1999) who suggested a cognitive device known as 'the veil of ignorance' whereby one pretends to know nothing about oneself; for instance, not knowing whether one is a bully or a victim – and then, let us say, imagine you are a victim – and walk in that person's shoes for a while – and reflect.

In an innovative article, Webber (2017) describes how promoting discussion and reflection on alternative views held by philosophers on moral behaviour as part of a course on bullying at a Canadian University not only increased knowledge and awareness of moral viewpoints but also motivated students in a School of Education to develop video resources and work with schoolchildren to help them to appreciate and evaluate how they were interacting with peers at school. An important aspect of this procedure lay in the stimulating of thinking about moral behaviour being undertaken by trained students a little older than the schoolchildren, rather than by school authorities who might more directly tell them where their duty lay. The distinctive value of this non-directive approach is supported by Harrison (2015) who worked effectively with students in schools in England to promote moral thinking as an antidote to cyberbullying, a phenomenon in which the relevant rules to be followed are particularly obscure and the perceived consequences of actions of cyberbullying are often hard to imagine.

The attempt to produce an acceptable list of virtues (as distinct from values) has been, it seems, generally abandoned, except in more antiquarian religious circles, where 'faith, hope and charity' have been identified as theological virtues (as proposed by St Paul) with supplementary virtues: prudence, justice, fortitude, temperance (attributed to St Thomas Aquinas). More demanding are the pre-eminent virtues of humility and self-effacement favoured by Quietists, such as Francois Fénelon (1699/2007) and the polymath, Aldous Huxley (1946). In a world in which self-assertion and the virtue of self-esteem are so often praised, these sentiments are apt to fall on deaf ears.

In recent years, both community and academic interest have grown rapidly in the subject of 'wellbeing.' The Oxford Dictionary defines wellbeing as 'the state of being comfortable, healthy or happy.' According to a measure of the frequency of the use of the word in published literature (the ngram viewer accessible online; see Google Ngram Viewer), the period of its most rapid increase occurred after 2000. The increase over this period was approximately three and half times. A similar trend occurred over this period in relation the word 'bullying,' although there are signs now that it is levelling off. How are 'wellbeing' and 'bullying' related? First, I think it is now widely accepted that being bullied is liable to produce a serious decline in personal wellbeing. Much of the motivation to address bullying in fact derives from this belief. The possible effects of levels of wellbeing on bullying behaviour are less understood and this can have important implications for actions that at school may take.

As discussed earlier, there is a persistent (unsupported) belief, held by some researchers and most teachers that at least one element of wellbeing, positive self- esteem, tends to be lacking in bullies. This belief underpins much of what is proposed as a means of reducing bullying behaviour in schools. Proactive intervention programs have been seen as justified because they may help to develop positive qualities, such as empathy, self-control, assertiveness and mindfulness that will eliminate or at least reduce bullying behaviour.

An alternative view is that such programs can have limited effectiveness. Comfortable, healthy and happy children (to take a common definition of wellbeing) may bully others and cause enduring misery. Hence, programs that are directed towards promoting the qualities that are conducive to wellbeing, as it is commonly understood, need to be supplemented by programs that can help children to develop and sustain a moral outlook. Traditionally, this view has been associated with preaching and pious platitudes and now is apt to be laughed out of court. Yet there is still a recognition that the desire to hurt others is a recurring feature in everyday life and underpins a good deal of bullying from an early age. We recognize that moral disengagement is a root cause of bullying, but fail to agree on how moral engagement can be brought about. How to incorporate this insight into anti-bullying initiatives in schools remains a basic problem of our time.

I have argued in this final chapter that it is not enough to adopt a simple relativistic perspective in seeking to understand and address school bullying. We must also be prepared to make personal judgements and say why we are making them. Some such judgements may be logically based, as in the non-acceptance of mutually contradictory propositions. Some may be evidence based including what has been found to work. Some may be morally based – and lead to a search for and adherence to firmly held and justified values. But, if I am right, one element is often missing in our search for what to believe and what to do, and this is the capacity to hear what people say, regardless of its current level of acceptability. The latest and loudest is not always the best.

The urge to blame is particularly strong when we think about bullying; I have it myself. Who is to blame then? There are two slogans that come to mind that seem to encapsulate two extreme perspectives. Both are by humourists, one, Australian; the other American. The Australian is well-known in Australia as a television producer, interviewer and comedian: Andrew Denton. He has ended his TV performances straight-faced, with the faintest touch of mischief: 'Remember folks, Society's to blame!' The American is the late master-cartoonist, William Steig, creator of Shrek. Again, tongue in cheek, hardly detectable, he tells us 'People are no damn good!' I suspect we all concur from time to time with these extreme, though opposite, judgements. Trouble is that in some people they become more or less permanent features of how they continue to think, thereby rendering the problem of relating to others practically insoluble. It is the thesis of this book that we must nevertheless listen to what is being said, especially, I think, to what Andrew Denton and William Steig are parodying.

A way of responding to those with whom we may agree or disagree has been attributed to C.S Lewis. He suggested three ways of responding:

> There is much in what you say (General acclamation).
> There is something in what you say (Balanced agreement).
> There may be something in what you say (Respectful agnosticism).

Sadly, one's instinctive response is all too often Denunciation: there is nothing in what you say. Go away! Hence our need to listen.

Listen to what? I have in this book made suggestions that can be briefly recapitulated.

Summary and conclusions

1. Read History. Bullying conceived as an abuse of power is not new, even if its justifications and modes of operation may be new and generally less cruel. It should not surprise us that bullying in all its forms is so difficult to reduce, let alone eradicate.
2. Note however that positive changes have occurred over time in how extreme forms of interpersonal abuse have been addressed, principally through the application of the Law and in the recent past the assertion of fundamental human rights.
3. Get to know what the researchers and educators are claiming and what evidence they see as supporting their assertions about bullying.
4. Do not accept non-critically the definitions of bullying that are dogmatically insisted upon. They may serve some purposes, but they can get in the way of being open to what people are saying.
5. Distinguish between the perspectives of the primary stakeholders: students, teachers, parents and Departments of Education and ask why there should be such differences.
6. Compare the views of those who have been negatively affected by bullying at school, with those who have never experienced being bullied. You will get different pictures.
7. Find out, if you can, why people feel and think as they do before you enter, if you must, into any arguments.
8. In cases of bullying, always listen non-judgmentally to what you are being told by the participants; failing which you are likely to misperceive, alienate your informant(s) and act unwisely.
9. Be as clear as you can about the values and virtues that are guiding your actions and those of others.
10. Learn from (but question) authorities. Often enough, they too have their agenda.
11. Consider your own perspectives on bullying as you would the perspectives of others. A difficult task in part because we like to think well of ourselves and are prone to deny having prejudices and also because our perspectives commonly change with the situation or mood we happen to be in.
12. Reflect on the words of the uncouth Scottish poet, Robbie Burns: 'O wad some Power the giftie gie us, to see oursels as ithers see us!'

References

Ahmed, E. (2001). Shame management: Regulating bullying. In E. Ahmed, N. Harris, J. Braithwaite, & V. Braithwaite (Eds.). *Shame Management Through Reintegration* (211–314). Cambridge, UK: Cambridge University Press.

Ajzen, I. (1988). *Attitudes, Personality and Behavior.* Chicago: Dorsey Press.

Ajzen, I. (1991). The theory of planned behavior. *Organizational Behavior and Human Decision Processes*, 50 (2), 179–211.

Ajzen, I., & Fishbein M. (1980). *Understanding and Predicting Social Behavior.* New Jersey: Prentice Hall.

Allport, G. (1968). *The Person in Psychology.* Boston: Beacon Press.

Appleyard, B. (2011). *The Brain Is Wider Than the Sky: Why Simple Solutions Do Not Work in a Complex World.* London: Orion.

Arseneault, L. (2018). The annual research review: The persistent and pervasive impact of being bullied in childhood and adolescence: Implications for policy and practice. *The Journal of Child Psychology and Psychiatry*, 59 (4), 405–421.

Australian Government Department of Education and Training (2016). *National Safe Schools Framework.* Canberra, ACT: Student Wellbeing Hub.

Australia's Children (2020). Australian Institute of Health and Welfare. Retrieved from https://www.aihw.gov.au/reports/children-youth/australias-children/contents/justice-and-safety/bullying

Bainton, R.H. (1953). *Hunted Heretic: The Life and Death of Michael Servetus* (1511–1553). Boston: Beacon Press.

Ball, H., Arseneault, L., Taylor, A., Maughan, B., Caspi, A., & Moffitt, T. (2008). Genetic and environmental influences on victims, bullies and bully-victims in childhood. *The Journal of Child Psychology and Psychiatry*, 49 (1), 104–112.

Bandura, A. (1999). Moral disengagement in the perpetration of inhumanities. *Personality and Social Psychology Review*, 33, 193–209.

Baron-Cohen, S. (2009). The empathizing-systemizing theory of autism: Implications for education. *Tizard Learning Disability Review*, 14, 4–13.

Bauman, S., Rigby, K., & Hoppa, K. (2008). US teachers' and school counsellors' strategies for handling school bullying incidents. *Educational Psychology*, 28, 837–856.

Beaumeister, R.F. (2008). Free will in scientific psychology. *Perspectives in Scientific Psychology*, 3 (1), 14–18.

Berger, E.M. (1952). The relation between expressed acceptance of self and expressed acceptance of others. *Journal of Abnormal and Social Psychology*, 47, 778–782.

Booth, A.L., Leigh, A., & Varganova, E. (2012). Does ethnic discrimination vary across minority groups? Evidence from a field experiment. *Oxford Bulletin of Economics and Statistics*, 74, 547–573.

Bowlby, J. (1969). *Attachment and Loss* (Vols. 1–2). New York: Basic Books.

Brand, P.J. (2020). *Athens & Sparta: Democracy Vs. Dictatorship*. Retrieved from https://my.uopeople.edu/pluginfile.php/57436/mod_book/chapter/38899/HIST1421.U1.Athens.Sparta.pdf

Bronfenbrenner, U. (2009). *The Ecology of Human Development: Experiments by Nature and Design*. Cambridge, MA: Harvard University Press.

Brown, E.C., Low, S., Smith, B.H., & Haggerty, K.P. (2011). Outcomes from a school-randomized controlled trial of steps to respect: A bullying prevention program. *Psychology Review*, 40 (3), 423–443.

Brown, B., & Merritt, R. (2002). *No Easy Answers: The Truth Behind Death at Columbine*. New York: Lantern Books.

Brown, K.W., Ryan, R.M., & Creswell, J.D. (2007). Mindfulness: Theoretical foundations and evidence for its salutary effects. *Psychological Inquiry*, 18, 211–237.

Bucchianeri, M.M., Gower, A.L., McMorris, B.J., & Eisenberg, M.E. (2016). Youth experiences with multiple types of prejudice-based harassment. *Journal of Adolescence*, 51, 68–75.

Bully Stoppers. Retrieved from https://www.education.vic.gov.au/about/programs/bullystoppers/Pages/default.asp

Burk, F. (1897). Teasing and bullying. *Pedalogical Summary*, 4 (3), 335–371.

Burns, E.A., Fogelgarn, R., & Billet, P. (2020) Teacher-targeted bullying and harassment in Australian schools: A challenge to teacher wellbeing. *British Journal of Sociology of Education*, 41 (4), 523–538.

Butler, B. (2006). Liability for bullying in schools in Australia: Lessons still to be learnt. *Education Law Journal*, 7 (4), 243–254.

Campbell, M.L., Whiteford, C., & Hooijer, J. (2019). Teachers' and parents' understanding of traditional and cyberbullying. *Journal of School Violence*, 18 (3), 388–402.

Carnegie, D. (1936). *How to Win Friends and Influence People*. New York: Simon & Schuster.

Carroll, L. (1965/1982). *The Complete Illustrated Works of Lewis Carroll*. London: Chancellor Press.

Carter, A. (2005). Evolution and the problem of altruism. *Philosophical Studies*, 123, 213–230.

Collie, R.J., Shapka, J.D., Perry, N.E., & Martin, A.J. (2015). Teachers' beliefs about social-emotional learning: Identifying teacher profiles and their relations with job stress and satisfaction. *Learning and Instruction*, 39, 148–157.

Collier, C.W. (1992) Intellectual authority and institutional authority. *Journal of Legal Education*, 42, 155. Retrieved from http://scholarship.law.ufl.edu/facultypub/677

Committee for Children (2012). *Bullying Prevention in Schools Starts with Social-Emotional Learning*. Retrieved from https://www.cfchildren.org/wp-content/uploads/programs/docs/sel-bullying-paper.pdf

Cooper, A., Levin, B., & Campbell, C. (2009). The growing (but still limited) importance of evidence in education policy and practice. *Journal of Educational Change*, 11 (2), 159–171.

Cosma, A., Walsh, S.D., Chester, K.L., Callaghan, M., Molcho, M., Craig, W., & Pickett, W. (2020). Bullying victimization: Time trends and the overlap between

traditional and cyberbullying across countries in Europe and North America. *International Journal of Public Health*, 1, 75–85.
Crane, R., Kuyken, W., Hastings, R., Rothwell, N., & Williams, J. M. G. (2010). Training teachers to deliver mindfulness-based interventions: Learning from the UK experience. *Mindfulness*, 1, 74–86.
Cremin, H., Sellma, S., & McCluskey, G. (2012). Interdisciplinary perspectives on restorative justice: Developing insights for education. *British Journal of Educational Studies*, 60 (4), 421–437.
Cross, D.S., Runions, K.C., Britt, E.F., & Gray, C. (2018). Motivational interviewing as a positive response to high-school bullying. *Psychology in the Schools*, 55 (5), 464–475.
Datta, P., Cornell, D., & Huang, F. (2017). The toxicity of bullying by teachers and other school staff. *School Psychology Review*, 46 (4), 335–348.
David, J. (2020). *Help to Cancel the Cancel Culture*. New York: National Association of Scholars.
Davis, S., & Nixon, C. (2011). What students say about bullying. *Educational Leadership*, 69, 18–23.
Demaray, M.K., Maleck, C.K., Secord, S.M., & Lyell, K.M. (2013). Agreement among students' teachers', and parents' perceptions of victimization by bullying. *Children and Youth Services Review*, 35, 2091–2100.
Dennis, C.J. (1913). *Backblock Ballads and Other Verses*. Melbourne: E. W. Cole.
Dickens, C. (1839/2003). *Oliver Twist*. London: Penguin Books.
Dienstag, J.F. (2006). *Pessimism*. Princeton, NJ: Princeton University Press.
Due, P., Holstein, B.E., Lynch, J., Diderichsen, F., Gabhain, S.N., Scheidt, T., Currie, C., & Health Behaviour in School-Aged Children Bullying Working Group. (2005). Bullying and symptoms among school-aged children: International comparative cross sectional study in 28 countries. *European Journal of Public Health*, 15 (2), 128–132.
Durlak, J.A., Weissberg, R.P., Dymnicki, A.B., Taylor, R.D., & Schellinger, K.B. (2011). The impact of enhancing students' social and emotional learning: A meta-analysis of school-based universal interventions. *Child Development*, 82, 405–432.
Dutton, E., Van der Linden, D., & Lynn, R. (2016). The negative Flynn Effect. A systematic literature review. *Intelligence*, 59, 163–169.
Ecclestone, K., & Hayes, D. (2019). *The Dangerous Rise of Therapeutic Education*, 2nd Edn. London and New York: Routledge.
Egan, S.K., & Perry, D.G. (1998). Does low self-regard invite victimization? *Developmental Psychology*, 34 (2), 299–309.
Ehrenreich, B. (2009). *Smile or Die: How Positive Thinking Fooled America and the World*. London: Grant Book.
Eisner, M. (2001) Long-term historical trends in violent crime. *Crime and Justice*, 30 83–142.
Elgar, F.J., Craig, W., Boyce, W., Morgan, A., & Vella-Zarb, R. (2009). Income inequality and school bullying: Multilevel study of adolescents in 37 countries. *Journal of Adolescent Health*, 45, 151–159.
Ellis, A. (2004). *Rational Emotive Behavior Therapy: It Works For Me—It Can Work For You*. Buffalo,NY: Prometheus Books.
Ellis, A.A., & Shute, R. (2007). Teacher responses to bullying in relation to moral orientation and seriousness of bullying. *British Journal of Educational Psychology*, 77 (3), 649–663.
Espelage, D.L. (2014). Ecological theory: Preventing youth bullying, aggression, and victimization. *Theory Into Practice*, 53 (4), 257–264.
Espelage, D.L., Hong, J.S., Rao, M.A., & Thornberg, R. (2015). Understanding ecological

factors associated with bullying across the elementary to middle school transition in the United States. *Violence and Victims*, 30, 470–487.

Espelage, D.L., Low, S., & Polanin, J. R. (2015). Clinical trial of Second Step middle-school program: Impact on aggression & victimization. *Journal of Applied Developmental Psychology*, 37, 52–63.

Espelage, D.L., Rose, C.A., & Polanin, J.R. (2015). Social-emotional learning program to reduce bullying, fighting, and victimization among middle school students with disabilities. *Remedial and Special Education*, 36, 1–13.

Espelage, D.L., & Swearer, S.M. (Eds.) (2010). A social-ecological model for bullying prevention and intervention: Understanding the impact of adults in the social ecology of youngsters. In S.R. Jimerson, S.M., Swearer & D.L. Espelage (Eds.). *Handbook of Bullying in Schools: An International Perspective* (61–72). New York: Routledge/Taylor & Francis Group.

Ey & Campbell (2020). Do Australian parents of young children understand what bullying means? *Children and Youth Services Review*, 116. Retrieved from https://doi.org/10.1016/j.childyouth.2020.105237

Eysenck, H.J. (1997). Personality and experimental psychology: The unification of psychology and the possibility of a paradigm. *Journal of Personality and Social Psychology*, 73, 1224–1237.

Eysenck, H., & Eysenck, S.B.G. (1975). *Manual of the Eysenck Personality Questionnaire*. Sevenoaks, Kent: Hodder and Stoughton.

Fekkes, M., Pjipers, F.I.M., & Verloove-Vanhorick, S.P. (2005). Bullying: Who does what, when and where? Involvement of children, teachers and parents in bullying behavior. *Health Education Research*, 20 (1), 81–91.

Fénelon, F. (1699/1847). *The Adventures of Telemachus, the Son of Ulysses*. Manchester: Thomas Johnson.

Fetterman, A.K., & Robinson, M.D. (2013). Do you use your head or follow your heart? Self-location predicts personality, emotion, decision making, and performance. *Journal of Personality and Social Psychology*, 105 (2), 316–334.

Filmer, R. (1680). *Patriarcha of the Natural Power of Kings by the Learned Sir Robert Filmer, Baronet*. London: Robert Chiswell.

Flake, E. (2013). If you can't say something nice, say something clever but devastating. *New Yorker*, 14 January.

Fletcher, J.F. (1966). *Situations Ethics: The New Morality*. Philadelphia, PA: Westminster.

Flynn, J.R. (2007). *What is Intelligence?* Cambridge, UK: Cambridge University Press.

Foody, M., & Samara, M. (2018). Considering mindfulness techniques in school-based anti-bullying programmes. *Journal of New Approaches in Educational Research*, 7 (1), 3–9.

Fox, C.L., & Boulton, M.J. (2005). The social skills problems of victims of bullying: Self, peer and teacher perceptions. *British Journal of Educational Psychology*, 75 (Pt 2), 313–328.

Franks, C. (1957). Personality factors and the rate of conditioning. *British Journal of Psychology*, 48, 119–126.

Freud, S. (1901/2018). *The Psychopathology of Everyday Life*. London: Random House.

Fronius, T., Persson, H., Guckenburg, S., Hurley, N., & Petrosino, A. (2016). Restorative justice in U.S. schools: A research review. San Francisco, CA: WestEd. Retrieved from https://www.wested.org/resources/restorative-justice-research-review/

Fry, D.P. (2017). Cross-cultural perspectives on aggression. In P. Sturmey (Ed.). *The Wiley Handbook of Violence and Aggression* (1–12). New York: Wiley.

Garandeau, C.F., & Cillessen, A.H.N. (2006). From indirect aggression to invisible

aggression: A conceptual view on bullying and peer group. *Aggression and Violent Behavior*, 11, 612–625.
Garandeau, C.F., Poskiparta, E., & Salmivalli, C. (2014). A comparison of two approaches tackling acute cases of school bullying in the KiVa anti-bullying program. *Journal of Abnormal Child Psychology*, 42, 981– 991.
Gat, A. (2006). *War in Human Civilization*. New York: Oxford University Press.
Georgiou, S.N., Charalambous, K., & Stavrinides, P. (2020). Mindfulness, impulsiveness and moral disengagement as parameters of bullying and victimization at school. *Aggressive Behavior*, 46 (1), 107–115.
Gladwell, M. (2013). *David and Goliath: Underdogs, Misfits, and the Art of Battling Giants*. New York: Little Brown and Company.
Godfrey, D. (2014). Leadership of schools as research-led organizations in the English educational environment: Cultivating a research engaged school culture. *Educational Management Administration and Leadership*, 44 (2), 301–321.
Goethe, J.W. (1833/1999). *Maxims and Reflections*. London: Penguin Classics.
Golding, W. (1955). *Lord of the Flies: A Novel*, 1st American Edn. New York: Coward-McCann.
Gorsek, A.K., & Cunningham, M.M. (2014). A review of teachers' perceptions and training regarding school bullying. *PURE Insights*, 3. Retrieved from https://digitalcommons.wou.edu/pure/vol3/iss1/6
Graham, S., & Juvonen, J. (2001). An attributional approach to peer victimization. In J. Juvonen & S. Graham (Eds.). *Peer Harassment in School: The Plight of the Vulnerable and Victimized* (49–72). New York: The Guilford Press.
Greco, G., Cataldi, S., & Fischetti, F. (1919). Karate as anti-bullying strategy by improvement resilience and self-efficacy in school-age youth. *Journal of Physical Education and Sport*, 19 (Suppl 5), 1863–1870.
Haeckel, E. (1866). *Generelle Morphologie der Organismen. Allgemeine Grundzüge der organischen Formen-Wissenschaft, mechanisch begründet durch die von Charles Darwin reformierte Descenden- ztheorie. Band 1. Allgemeine Anatomie der Organismen, Band 2. Allgemeine Entwickelungsgeschichte der Organismen*. Berlin: Verlag Georg Reimer.
Haidt, J., & Lukianoff, G. (2018). *The Coddling of the American Mind: How Good Intentions and Bad Ideas Are Setting Up a Generation for Failure*. New York: Penguin.
Hale, R., Fox, C.L., & Murray, M. (2017). As a parent you become a tiger: Parents talking about bullying at school. *Journal of Child Family Studies*, 26 (7), 2000–2015.
Harari, Y.N. (2014). *Sapiens: A Brief History of Humankind*. New York: Harper.
Harrison, T. (2015). Virtuous reality: Moral theory and research into cyberbullying. *Ethics and Information Technology*, 17, 275–283.
Hastorf, A.H., & Cantrill, H. (1954). They saw the game: A case study. *The Journal of Abnormal and Social Psychology*, 49, 1, 129–134.
Heirman, W., & Walruve, M. (2012). Predicting adolescent perpetration of cyberbullying: An application of the Theory of Planned Behaviour. *Psicothema*, 24 (4), 614–620.
Hess, F. (2017). Some advice for champions of social and emotional learning. *Education Week*, 13 December.
Hiduja, S., & Patchin, J.W. (2010) Bullying, cyberbullying, and suicide. *Archives of Suicide Research: Official Journal of the International Academy for Suicide Research*, 14 (3), 206–221.

Hinduja, S., & Patchin, J.W. (2017). Cultivating youth resilience to prevent bullying and cyberbullying victimization. *Child Abuse & Neglect*, 73, 51.

Hirshkorn, M., & Geelan, D. (2008). Bridging the research-practice gap: Research translation and/or research transformation. *Alberta Journal of Educational Research*, 54 (1), 1–13.

Hobbes, T. (1651/2010) *The Leviathan. Revised Edition.* A.P. Martinich & B. Battiste (Eds.). Peterborough: Broadview Press.

Hornby, G. (2015). Bullying: An ecological approach to bullying in schools. *Preventing School Failure*, 60 (3), 1–9.

Hornby, G., Hall, E., & Hall, C. (Eds.) (2003). *Counselling Pupils in Schools: Skills and Strategies for Teachers.* London: Routledge Falmer.

Hughes, T. (1857/1968). *Tom Brown's School Days.* New York: Airmont Publishing Co., Inc.

Humphrey, N. (2013). *Social and Emotional Learning: A Critical Appraisal.* SAGE Publications Ltd.

Humphrey, N., Lendrum, A., & Wigelsworth, M. (2010). *Social and Emotional Aspects of Learning (SEAL) Programme in Secondary Schools.* National Evaluation Research Report, DFE, RRO49. London, England: Department for Education.

Huxley, A. (1946). *The Perennial Philosophy.* London: Chatto and Windus.

Hymel, S., & Bonanno, R.A. (2014). Moral disengagement processes in bullying. *Theory into Practice*, 53 (4), 278–285.

Jansen, P.W., Verlinder, M., Dommisse-van Berkel A., Mieloo, C., Van der Ende, J., Veenstra, R., Verhulst, F.C., & Jansen, W.H. (2012). Prevalence of bullying and victimization among children in early elementary school. Do family and school neighbourhood socioeconomic status matter? *BMC Public Health*, 12, 494–504.

Johansson, S., & Englund, G. (2020). Cyberbullying and its relationship with physical, verbal, and relational bullying: A structural equation modelling approach. *Educational Psychology*, 1–18. Retrieved from https://doi.org/10.1080/01443410.2020.1769033

Jolliffe, D., & Farrington, D. (2006). Examining the relationship between low empathy and bullying. *Aggressive Behavior*, 32, 540–550.

Juhnke, B.A., Juhnke, G.A., Curtis, R.C., Thompson, E.H., Coll, K.M., Fangzhou, Y., Moyer, M.S., & Mullett, A. (2013). Using motivational interviewing with school-age bullies: A new use for a proven, evidence-based intervention. *Journal of School Counseling*, 11 (14), 1–27.

Kant, I. (1783). *Prolegomena zu einer jeden künftigen Metaphysic, die als Wissenschaft wird auftreten können.* Riga: F. J. Hartknoch.

Kelman, H.C. (1961). Processes of opinion change. *Public Opinion Quarterly*, 25, 57–78.

Keltner, D., Ellsworth, P.C., & Edwards, K. (1993). Beyond pessimism – effects of sadness and anger on personal perceptions. *Journal of Personality and Social Psychology*, 64 (5), 740–762.

Kierkegaard, S. (1973). *A Kierkegaard Anthology.* R. Bretall (Ed.). Princeton, NJ: Princeton Paperback Edition.

Kolstrein, A.M., & Jofre, M.I.T. (2012). Bullying: An analysis from the perspective of human rights, target groups and interventions. *The International Journal of Children's Rights*, 21 (2), 1–14.

Koo, H. (2007). A time line of the evolution of school bullying in differing social context. *Asia Pacific Education Review*, 8(1), 107–116.

Lereya, S.T., Samara, M., & Wolke, D. (2013). Parenting behavior and the risk of becoming a victim and a bully/victim: A meta-analysis study. *Child Abuse & Neglect*, 37, 12, 1091–1108.

Lerner, M.J., & Miller, D.T. (1978). Just world research and the attribution process: Looking back and ahead. *Psychological Bulletin*, 85 (5), 1030–1051.

Lewin, K. (1936). *Principles of Topological Psychology*. New York: McGraw-Hill.

Losen, D.J., & Martinez, P. (2020). *Lost Opportunities: How Disparate School Discipline Continues to Drive Differences in the Opportunity to Learn*. Palo Alto, CA/Los Angeles, CA: Learning Policy Institute; Center for Civil Rights Remedies at the Civil Rights Project, UCLA.

Low, S., Cook, C.R., Smolkowski, K., & Buntain-Ricklefs, J. (2015). Promoting social-emotional competence: An evaluation of the elementary version of Second Step. *Journal of School Psychology*, 53, 463–477.

Mahdavi, J., & Smith, P.K. (2002). The operation of a bully court and perceptions of its success: A case study. *School Psychology International*, 23, 327–341.

Maunder, R.E., Harrop, A., & Tattersall, A.J. (2010) Pupil and staff perceptions of bullying in secondary schools: Comparing behavioural definitions and their perceived seriousness. *Educational Research*, 52 (3), 263–282.

Mead, M. (1935/2003). *Sex and Temperament in Three Primitive Societies. New York*: HarperCollins.

Milgram, S. (1965). Some conditions of obedience and disobedience to authority. *Human Relations*, 18(1), 57–76.

Mill, J.S. (1860). *On Liberty*. London: John Parker and Sons.

Molcho, M., Craig, W., Due, P., Pickett W., Harel-Fisch, Y., Mary Overpeck, M., & The HBSC Bullying Writing Group (2009). Cross-national time trends in bullying behaviour, 1994–2006: Findings from Europe and North America. *Journal of Public Health*, 54, 225–234.

Monks P.K., Smith P.K., Naylor, C., Barter, J.L., Ireland, I., & Coyne, I. (2009). Bullying in different contexts: Commonalities, differences and the role of theory. *Aggression and Violent Behavior*, 14, 146–156.

Moore, B., & Woodcock, S. (2017). Resilience to bullying: Towards an alternative to the anti-bullying approach. *Educational Psychology in Practice*, 33 (1), 65–80.

Moreno, M.A., Gower, A.D., & Brittain, H. (2009). Applying natural language processing to evaluate news media coverage of bullying and cyberbullying. *Prevention Science*, 20, 1274–1283.

Morris, D. (1967). *The Naked Ape*. London: Jonathan Cape.

Mynard, H., & Joseph, S. (1997). Bully/victim problems and their association with Eysenck's personality dimensions in 8 to 13 year-olds. *British Journal of Educational Psychology*, 67 (Pt 1), 51–54.

Naylor, P., Cowie, H., Cossin, F., de Bettencourt, R., & Lemme (2006). Teachers' and pupils' definitions of bullying. *British Journal of Educational Psychology*, 76, 553–576.

Nietzsche, F. (1887). *On the Genealogy of Morals - A Polemical Tract*. Translated into English Ian Johnston of Malaspina University-College, Nanaimo, BC.

Ocelli, P. (2019). Op-ed: John Marsden: It's time to be an upstander, not a bystander. *School News Australia*, 6 August.

Olweus, D. (1993). *Bullying at School: What We Know and What We Can Do*. Cambridge, MA: Blackwell.

Olweus, D. (1999). Sweden. In P.K. Smith, Y. Morita, J. Junger-Tas, D. Olweus,

R. Catalano, & P.T. Slee (Eds.). *The Nature of School Bullying: A Cross-National Perspective.* London: Routledge.
O'Meara, A., Davies, J., & Hammond, S. (2011). The psychometric properties and utility of the Short Sadistic Impulse Scale (SSIS). *Psychological Assess*, 23 (2), 523–531.
O'Moore, M., & Kirkham, C. (2001). Self-esteem and its relationship to bullying behaviour. *Aggressive Behavior*, 27 (4), 269–283.
Ortega, R., Elipe, P., Mora-Mercha, J.A., Genta, M.L., Brighi, A., Guarini, A., Smith, P.K., Thompson, F., & Tippett, N. (2012). The emotional impact of bullying and cyberbullying on victims: A European cross-national study. *Aggressive Behavior*, 38 (5), 342–356.
Pabian, S., & Vandebosch, H. (2014). Using the theory of planned behaviour to understand cyberbullying: The importance of beliefs for developing interventions. *European Journal of Developmental Psychology*, 11 (4), 463–477.
Pandya, S.P. (2017). Effect of a spiritual education programme in developing altruism and prosocial behaviour among children. *International Journal of Children's Spirituality*, 22 (3–4), 220–238.
Pandya, S.P. (2020). Building Resilience and Fortitude Among Victims of School Bullying: Lessons from a Customized Yoga Education Program by Older Adult Volunteers. *Contemp School Psychol.* https://doi.org/10.1007/s40688-020-00329-2
Pascal, B., & Trotter, W.F. (1931). *Pascal's Pensées.* London: J.M. Dent & Sons.
Peirce, C.S. (1878/1986). How to make our ideas clear. *Popular Science Monthly*, 12 (January), 286–302.
Pepler, D.J., & Craig, W.M. (1995). A peek behind the fence: Naturalistic observations of aggressive children with remote audiovisual recording. *Developmental Psychology*, 31 (4), 548–553.
Petrie, K. (2014). The relationship between school climate and student bullying. *TEACH Journal of Christian Education*, 8 (1), 26–35. Retrieved from https://research.avondale.edu.au/teach/vol8/iss1/7
Pikas, A. (2002). New developments of the Shared Concern Method. *School Psychology International*, 23, 307–336.
Pinker, S. (2011). *The Better Angels of Our Nature: A History of Violence and Humanity.* New York: Penguin.
Polanin, J.R., Espelage, D.L., & Pigott, T.D. (2012). A meta-analysis of school-based bullying prevention programs' effects on bystander intervention behavior. *School Psychology Review*, 41, 47–65.
Polansky, R. (2011). *Carnage.* France: Wild Bunch.
Polastri, A.R., Cardemil, E.V., & O'Donnell, E.H. (2010). Self-esteem in pure bullies and bully/victims: A longitudinal analysis. *Journal of Interpersonal Violence*, 25 (8), 1489–1502.
Procter, R. (2015). Teachers and school research practices: The gaps between the values and practices of teachers. *Journal of Education for Teaching: International Research and Pedagogy*, 41 (5), 1–14.
Rawls J. (1999). *A Theory of Justice.* Cambridge: Harvard University Press.
Richards, A., Rivers, I., & Akhurst, J. (2008). A positive psychology approach to tackling bullying in secondary schools: A comparative evaluation. *Educational and Child Psychology*, 25 (2), 72–81.
Richardson, G. (2020). *The Australian Newspaper*, August, p. 10.
Rigby, K. (1993). School children's perceptions of their families and parents as a function of peer relations. *Journal of Genetic Psychology*, 154(4), 501–514.

Rigby, K. (1994). Psycho-social functioning in families of Australian adolescent schoolchildren involved in bully/victim problems. *Journal of Family Therapy*, 16 (2), 173–189.

Rigby, K. (1995). The motivation of Australian adolescent schoolchildren to engage in group discussions about bullying. Current problems and resolutions. *Journal of Social Psychology*, 135, 135–136.

Rigby, K. (1997). Reflections on Tom Brown's Schooldays and the problem of bullying today. *Australian Journal of Social Science*, 4, 1, 85–96.

Rigby, K. (1997). Attitudes and beliefs about bullying among Australian school children. *Irish Journal of Psychology*, 18 (2), 202–220.

Rigby, K. (1998). *The Peer Relations Questionnaire: The Technical Manual*. Point Lonsdale, Victoria: The Professional Reading Guide for Educational Administrators.

Rigby, K. (2002). *New Perspectives on Bullying*. London: Jessica Kingsley.

Rigby, K. (2003). Consequences of bullying in schools. *The Canadian Journal of Psychiatry*, 48, 583–590.

Rigby, K. (2006). Implications of bullying for aggression between nations. *Journal of Peace Education*, 3, 175–186.

Rigby, K. (2008). *Children and Bullying. How Parents and Educators Can Reduce Bullying at School*. Boston: Blackwell/Wiley.

Rigby, K. (2011). *The Method of Shared Concern: A Positive Approach to Bullying*. Camberwell, Victoria: ACER.

Rigby, K. (2012a). Bullying in schools: Addressing desires, not only behaviours. *Educational Psychology Review*, 24, 339–348.

Rigby, K (2012b). *Bullying Interventions in Schools: Six Basic Approaches*, American Edn. Boston: Wiley.

Rigby, K. (2013). Bullying in schools and its relation to parenting and family life. *Family Matters*, 91, 61–68.

Rigby, K. (2015). Bullying in Australian schools: Causes, consequences and proposed solutions. In A. Day & E. Fernandez (Eds.). *Preventing Violence in Australia: Policy, Practice and Solutions*. Annandale, NSW: Federation Press.

Rigby, K. (2018). Exploring the gaps between teachers' beliefs about bullying and research-based knowledge. *International Journal of School & Educational Psychology*, 6 (3), 165–175. DOI:10.1080/21683603.2017.1314835.

Rigby, K. (2019). How Australian parents of bullied and non-bullied children see their school responding to bullying. *Educational Review*, 71 (3), 318–333.

Rigby, K. (2020). How do victims of bullying in Australian schools view their perpetrators? As individuals or as groups. Implications for educators *Australian Journal of Education*, 64 (1), 25–39.

Rigby, K. (2020). How teachers deal with cases of bullying? What victims say. *International Journal of Environmental Research and Public Health*, 17(7): 23–38.

Rigby, K., & Bagshaw, D. (2001). What hurts? The reported consequences of negative interactions with peers among Australian school children. *Children Australia*, 26 (4), 36–41.

Rigby, K., & Bagshaw, D. (2003). Prospects of adolescent students collaborating with teachers in addressing issues of bullying and conflict in schools. *Educational Psychology*, 23 (5), 535–546.

Rigby, K., & Barnes, A. (2002). To tell or not to tell: the victimised student's dilemma. *Youth Studies, Australia*, 21(3), 33–36.

Rigby, K., & Bortolozzo, G. (2013). How schoolchildren's acceptance of self and others relate to their attitudes to victims of bullying. *Social Psychology of Education*, 16 (2), 181–197.

Rigby, K., & Griffiths, C. (2011). Addressing cases of bullying through the Method of Shared Concern. *School Psychology International*, 32, 345–357.

Rigby, K., & Griffiths C. (2018). Addressing traditional school-based bullying more effectively. In M. Campbell and S. Bauman (Eds.). *Reducing Cyberbullying in Schools* (17–32). London: Elsevier Press.

Rigby, K., & Johnson, B. (2004). Students as bystanders to sexual coercion. *Youth Studies, Australia*, 23, 11–16.

Rigby, K., & Johnson, B. (2006). Expressed readiness of Australian school children to act as bystanders in support of children who are being bullied. *Educational Psychology* 26, 425–440.

Rigby, K., & Johnson, B. (2006/7). Playground heroes: Who can stop bullying? *Greater Good*, 14–17, Fall/Winter.

Rigby, K., & Johnson, K. (2016). *The Prevalence and Effectiveness of Anti-bullying Strategies Employed in Australian Schools*. Report for the Australian Department of Education. Canberra: ACT.

Rigby, K., Haroun, D., & Ali, E. (2019a). Addressing problems of bullying in schools in the United Arab Emirates. In S. Tucker & D. Trotman (Eds.). *Youth: Global Perspectives, Challenges and Issues of the 21st Century*. New York: Nova Press.

Rigby, K., Haroun, D., & Ali, E. (2019b). Bullying in schools in the United Arab Emirates and the personal safety of students. *Child Indicators Research*, 12 (5), 1663–1675.

Rigby, K., & Rump, E.E. (1979). The generality of attitude to authority. *Human Relations*, 32, 469–487.

Rigby, K., Schofield, P., & Slee, P.T. (1987). The similarity of attitudes to personal and impersonal types of authority among adolescent schoolchildren. *Journal of Adolescence*, 10, 241–253.

Rigby, K., & Slee, P.T. (1991). Bullying among Australian school children: Reported behaviour and attitudes to victims. *Journal of Social Psychology*, 131, 615–622.

Rigby, K., & Slee, P.T. (1993). Children's attitudes towards victims. In D.P. Tattum (Ed.). *Understanding and Managing Bullying*. Melbourne: Heinemann Books.

Rigby, K., & Smith, P.K. (2011). Is school bullying really on the rise? *Social Psychology of Education*, 14 (4), 441–455.

Robinson, G., & Maines, B. (2008). *Bullying: A Complete Guide to the Support Group Method*. London, UK: Sage.

Rokeach, M. (1960). *The Open and Closed Mind*. New York: Basic Books.

Roland, E., & Galloway, G. (2002). Classroom influences on bullying. *Educational Research*, 44 (3), 299–312.

Rosenthal, R. (1985). From unconscious experimenter bias to teacher expectancy effects. In J. Dusek (Ed.). *Teacher Expectancies* (37–65). Hillsdale, NJ: Lawrence Erlbaum Associates, Inc.

Ross, S.W., & Horner, R.H. (2009). Bully prevention in positive behavior support. *Journal of Applied Behavior Analysis*, 42, 747–759.

Roth, G., Kanat-Maymon, Y., & Bibi, U. (2010). Prevention of school bullying: The important role of autonomy-supportive teaching and internalization of pro-social values. *British Journal of Educational Psychology*, 81 (2), 654-666.

Rousseau, J.J. (1772/1998). *The Social Contract*. London: Penguin Classic.

Ryff, C.D., & Keyes, C.L.M. (1995). The structure of psychological wellbeing revisited. *Journal of Personality and Social Psychology*, 69 (4), 719–727.

Salmivalli, C. (2010). Bullying and the peer group: A review. *Aggression and Violent Behavior*, 15, 112–120.

Salmivalli, C. (2014). Participant roles in bullying: How can Peer Bystanders be utilized in interventions? *Theory Into Practice*, 53 (4), 286–292.

Salmivalli, C., Lagerspetz, K., Björkqvist, K., Österman, K., & Kaukiainen, A. (1996). Bullying as a group process: Participant roles and their relations to social status within the group. *Aggressive Behavior*, 22, 1–15.

Seligman, M. (2002). *Authentic Happiness: Using the New Positive Psychology to Realize Your Potential for Lasting Fulfillment*. New York: Free Press.

Shamir, J., & Shamir, M. (1997). Pluralistic ignorance across issues and over time: Information cues and biases. *The Public Opinion Quarterly*, 61 (2), 227–260.

Shariff, S. (2008). *Confronting Cyber-Bullying*. Cambridge: Cambridge University Press.

Shaw, T., Cross, D., Thomas, L.T., & Zubrick, S.R. (2015). Bias in student survey findings from active parental consent procedures. *British Educational Research Journal*, 41, 229–243.

Sheldon, W.H. (1940). *The Varieties of Human Physique (An Introduction to Constitutional Psychology)*. New York: Harper & Brothers.

Shenkin, B.N., & Levine, D.I. (2019). Should the power of the President's Pardon be revised? *Hastings Constitutional Law Quarterly*, 47 (1), 3–18.

Shevlin, A., & Gill, P.R. (2020). Parental attitudes to the Australian anti-bullying "safe schools" program: A critical discourse analysis. *Social Psychology of Education: An International Journal*, 23 (4), 891–915.

Shriver, P., & Weissberg, R.P. (2020). A response to constructive criticism of Social and Emotional Learning. *Kappanonline.org*, 101(7), 52–57.

Singh, N.N., & Singh Joy, S.D. (2021). *Mindfulness-Based Interventions with Children and Adolescents: Research and Practice*. Abingdon, England: Routledge.

Skinner, B.F. (1953). *Science and Human Behavior*. New York: Simon and Schuster.

Slee, P.T., & Rigby, K. (1993). The relationship of Eysenck's personality factors and self-esteem to bully/victim behaviour in Australian school boys. *Personality and Individual Differences*, 14, 371–373.

Smith, B., & Low, S. (2013). The role of social-emotional learning in bullying prevention efforts. *Theory into Practice*, 52 (4), 280–287.

Smith, P.K. (2014). *Understanding School Bullying: Its Nature and Prevention Strategies*. London: Sage.

Smith, P.K., Howard, S., & Thompson, F. (2007). Use of the Support Group Method to tackle bullying, and evaluation from schools and local authorities in England. *Pastoral Care in Education*, 25, 4–13.

Smith, P.K., Mahdavi, J., Carvalho, M., Fisher, S., Russell, S., & Tippett, N. (2008). Cyberbullying: Its nature and impact in secondary school pupils. *Journal of Child Psychology and Psychiatry*, 49, 376–385.

Smith, P.K., Mahdavi, J., Carvalho, M., & Tippett, N. (2006). An investigation into cyberbullying, its forms, awareness and impact, and the relationship between age and gender in cyberbullying. *Journal of Child Psychology and Psychiatry*, 49, 376–385.

Smith, P.K., & Sharp, S. (Eds.) (1994). *School Bullying: Insights and Perspectives*. London: Routledge.

Solberg, M.E., Olweus, D., & Endressen, I.M. (2007). Bullies and victims at school: Are they the same pupils? *British Journal of Educational Psychology*, 77, 441–464.

South Australian Department of Education (2020). *Connected: A Community Approach to Bullying Prevention Within the School Gates and Beyond*. Adelaide: Government of South Australia. Retrieved from https://www.education.sa.gov.au/supporting-students/health-e-safety-and-wellbeing/bullying-prevention-strategydd

Spenser, H. (1874). *Principles of Biology*. New York: Appleton and CoView Metadata.

Starck, J.G., Riddle, T., & Stacey, S. (2020). Teachers are people too: Examining the racial bias of teachers compared to other adults. *Educational Research*, 49 (4), 273–284.

Sutton, J., Swettenham, J., & Smith, P.K. (1999). Bullying and 'theory of mind': A critique of the 'social skills deficit' view of anti-social behaviour. *Social Development*, 8 (1), 117–123.

Swearer, S.M., & Hymel, S. (2015). Understanding the psychology of bullying: Moving towards a socio-ecological diathesis-stress model. *American Psychologist*, 70 (4), 344–355.

Tattum, D., & Tattum, E. (1992). *Social Education and Personal Development*. London: David Fulton.

Teasdale, T.W., & Owen, D.R. (2005). A long-term rise and recent decline in intelligence test performance: The Flynn Effect in reverse. *Personality and Individual Differences*, 39 (4), 837–843.

Thapa, A., Cohen, J., Guffey, S., & Higgins-D'Alessandro, A. (2013). A review of school climate research. *Review of Educational Research*, 83 (3), 357–385.

Thompson, F., & Smith, P.K. (2011). *The Use and Effectiveness of Anti-Bullying Strategies in Schools*. Research Report, DFE-RR098. London: Department for Education.

Thornberg, R., Wänströmb, L., Pozzolic, T., & Sung Hong, J. (2019). Moral disengagement and school bullying perpetration in middle childhood: A short-term longitudinal study in Sweden. *Journal of School Violence*, 18 (4), 585–596.

Thorsborne, M., & Vinegrad, D. (2006). *Restorative Practice and the Management of Bullying: Rethinking Behaviour Management* . Queenscliff, VIC: Inyahead Press.

Toda, Y. (2016). Bullying (Ijime) and related problems in Japan. In P. Smith, K. Kwak, & Y. Toda (Eds.). *School Bullying in Different Cultures: Eastern and Western Perspectives* (73–92). Cambridge: Cambridge University Press.

Ttofi, M.M., & Farrington, D.P. (2011). Effectiveness of school-based programs to reduce bullying: A systematic and meta-analytic review. *Journal of Experimental Criminology*, 7 (1), 27–56.

Twemlow, S.W., Fonag, P., Sacco, F.C., & Brethour, J.R. Jr. (2006). Teachers who bully students: A hidden trauma. *International Journal of Social Psychiatry*, 52 (3), 187–198.

Twemlow, S., Biggs, K.B., Nelson, T., & Twemlow, S.W. (2008). Effects of participation in a martial arts-based anti-bullying program in elementary schools. *Psychology in the Schools*, 45 (10), 947–959.

UNESCO (2018). *School Violence and Bullying: Global Status and Trends, Drivers and Consequences*. Paris: UNESCO.

UNESCO (2019). *Behind the Numbers. Ending School Violence and Bullying*. Paris, France. Retrieved from https://en.unesco.org/themes/school-violence-and-bullying

VanGeel, M., Goemans, A., Toprak, F., & Vedder, P. (2017). Which personality traits are related to traditional bullying and cyberbullying? A study with the Big Five, Dark Triad and sadism. *Personality and Individual Differences*, 106 (1), 231–235.

Veenstra, R., Siegwar, S., Bonne, J.H., DeWinter, A.F., Verhuslt, F.C., & Ormel, J. (2007). The dyadic nature of bullying and victimization: Testing a dual-perspective theory. *Child Development*, 78, 1843–1854.

Veldkamp, S.A.M., Boomsma, D.I., de Zeeuw, E.L., van Beijsterveldt, C.E.M., Bartels, M., Dolan C.V., & van Bergen E. (2019). Genetic and environmental influences on different forms of bullying perpetration, bullying victimization, and their co-occurrence. *Behavior Genetics*, 49, 432–443.

Volk, A.A., Camilleri, J.A., Dane, A.V., & Zopito, A.M. (2012). Is adolescent bullying an evolutionary adaptation? *Aggressive Behavior*, 38, 222–238.

Waasdorp, T.E., & Bradshaw, T.E. (2014). The overlap between cyberbullying and traditional bullying. *Journal of Adolescent Health*, 56, 483–488.

Waasdorp, T.E., Pas, E.T., Zablotsky, B., Bradshaw, C.P. (2017). Ten-year trends in bullying and related attitudes among 4th- to 12th-graders. *Pediatrics* 139 (6) 1–8.

Wachs, S., Bilz, L., Niproschke, S., & Schubarth, W. (2019). Bullying intervention in schools: A multilevel analysis of teachers' success in handling bullying from the students' perspective. *Journal of Early Adolescence*, 39 (5), 642–668.

Webber, M.A. (2017). Bullying: University students bring a moral perspective to school students. *Journal of Education and Learning*, 6 (3), 157–168.

Wei, W., Lu, J.G., Galinsky, A.D., Wu, H., Gosling, S.D., Rentfrow, P.J., Yuan, W., Zhang, Q., Guo, Y., Zhang, M., Gui, W., Potter, J., Wang, J., Li, B., Xiaojie, L., Han, Y.M., Lv, M., Guo, Q., Choe, Y., Lin, W., Yu, K., Bai, Q., Shang, Z., Han, Y., & Wang, L. (2017). Regional ambient temperature is associated with human personality. *Nature Human Behavior*, 1 (12), 890–895.

Weissberg, R.P., Durlak, J.A., Domitrovich, C.E., & Gullotta, T.P. (2015). Social and emotional learning: Past, present, and future. In J.A. Durlak, C.E. Domitrovich, R.P. Weissberg, & T.P. Gullotta (Eds.), *Handbook of social and emotional learning: Research and practice* (3-19). New York, NY: Guilford.

Wilkins, R. (2016). *The Household, Income, and Labour Dynamics in Australia (HILDA) Survey*, Melbourne Institute of Applied Economics and Social Research. Melbourne: The University of Melbourne.

Wilberforce, W. (1797). *A Practical View of the Prevailing Religious System of Professed Christians, in the Middle and Higher Classes in this Country, Contrasted with Real Christianity*. London: T. Caddell.

Williams, K., & Kennedy, J.H. (2012). Bullying behaviors and attachment style. *North American Journal of Psychology*, 14 (2), 321–338.

Wong, S.W., Cheng, H.K., & Ngan, R.M.H. (2010). Program effectiveness of a restorative whole-school approach for tackling school bullying in Hong Kong. *International Journal of Offender Therapy and Comparative Criminology*, 55, 537–553.

Wordsworth, W. (1800). *Lyrical Ballads with Other Poems*, 2nd Edn. London: T.N. Longman and O. Rees.

Wright, R. (1994). *Moral Animal: Evolutionary Psychology and Everyday Life*. New York: Vintage Books.

Wu, G., Feder, A., Cohen, H., Kim, J.K., Calderon, S., Charney, D.S., Mathé, A.A. (2013). HYPERLINK "https://www.ncbi.nlm.nih.gov/pmc/articles/PMC3573269/" Understanding resilience. *Front Behavioral Neuroscience*. (February,15).7: 10. https://doi.org/10.3389/fnbeh.2013.00010

Xiaojing L., Bussey, K., Hay, P., Mond, J., Trompeter, N., Lonergan, A., & Mitchison, D. (2020). Prevalence and correlates of sexual harassment in Australian adolescents. *Journal of School Violence*, 19 (3), 349–361.

Yoneyama, S. (2015). Theorizing school psychology: Insights from Japan. *Confero*, 3 (2), 1–37.

Yoneyama, S., & Rigby, K. (2006). Bully/victim students and classroom climate. *Youth Studies Australia*, 25, 34–41.

Young, S. (1998). The Support Group approach to bullying in schools. *Educational Psychology in Practice*, 14, 32–39.

Zhao, Y. (2018). *What Works May Hurt: Side Effects in Education*. New York, NY: Teachers College Press.

Zimbardo, P.G. (1969). The human choice: Individuation, reason, and order versus deindividuation, impulse, and chaos. *Nebraska Symposium on Motivation*, 17, 237–307.

Index